PANDORA'S JAR

NATALIE HAYNES

PANDORA'S JAR

Women in Greek Myths

PICADOR

First published 2020 by Picador
an imprint of Pan Macmillan
The Smithson, 6 Briset Street, London ECIM 5NR
Associated companies throughout the world
www.panmacmillan.com

ISBN 978-1-5098-7312-8

'Love to Love You Baby', Donna Summer © Giorgio Moroder and Pete Bellotte, Casablanca Records.
'Penthesilea' and 'Greek Myths' by Robert Graves (*Greek Myths*, 2001) is reprinted here by kind
permission of Carcanet Press Limited, Manchester, UK.
'Road to Hell (Reprise)' lyrics written by Anaïs Mitchell, taken from the musical *Hadestown*,
reprinted by kind permission of Treleven Music and Candid Music Publishing Ltd.
'Eurydice' by H. D. (Hilda Doolittle), from *Collected Poems, 1912–1944*, copyright ©1917 by
Hilda Doolittle. Reprinted by permission of New Directions Publishing Corp.
'Eurydice' by Carol Ann Duffy from *The World's Wife*, 1999. Reprinted by permission of Pan Macmillan.
Tales of the Greek Heroes, Roger Lancelyn Green, Penguin, 1958.
'Phèdre' by Ted Hughes reproduced by permission of Faber and Faber Ltd.
'Hold Up', Beyoncé, Words and Music © Beyoncé, Brian Chase, Diplo, Uzoechi Emenike, Emile Haynie,
Ezra Koenig, Kevin McConnell, MeLo-X, Karen O, Doc Pomus, Antonio Randolph, Mort Schuman,
Soulja Boy, Joshua Tillman and Nicholas Zinner. Parkwood, Columbia Records.

Pan Macmillan does not have any control over, or any responsibility for,
any author or third-party websites referred to in or on this book.

9 8 7 6 5 4 3 2 1

A CIP catalogue record for this book is available from the British Library.

Typeset by Palimpsest Book Production Ltd, Falkirk, Stirlingshire
Printed and bound by CPI Group (UK) Ltd, Croydon, CRO 4YY

Visit **www.picador.com** to read more about all our books
and to buy them. You will also find features, author interviews and
news of any author events, and you can sign up for e-newsletters
so that you're always first to hear about our new releases.

For my mum, who has always thought a woman with an axe was more interesting than a princess

Contents

List of Illustrations

Introduction

WHEN HARRY HAMLIN STOOD BEHIND A PILLAR IN THE DARKNESS OF Medusa's lair in the Ray Harryhausen film *Clash of the Titans*, flames flickering off his shield, his face glistening with sweat, my brother and I were transfixed. Perseus holds the shield in front of his eyes to protect himself from Medusa's stony gaze. He watches the reflection of a slithering monster, outlined in front of the fire behind him. This Medusa has a lashing, snakish tail as well as the traditional snakes for hair. She is armed with a bow and arrows, and can knock one of Perseus' comrades off his feet with a single hit. As the man sprawls on the ground, she glides forward into the light. Suddenly her eyes flash bright green. He is turned to stone where he lies.

Medusa fires another arrow, this time taking Perseus' shield out of his hands. Her rattlesnake tail quivers in anticipation of the kill. Perseus tries to catch her reflection in the glinting blade of his sword as she nocks a third arrow. Medusa inches closer as Perseus waits, turning his sword in his hand. The sweat has formed beads across his upper lip. At the crucial moment, he swings his arm and decapitates her. Her body writhes before thick red blood seeps out from her neck. When it reaches his shield, there is a hissing sound as it corrodes the metal.

This film – along with *Jason and the Argonauts* – was a staple of my childhood viewing: it was a rare school holiday when one of them wasn't on TV. It did not occur to me that there was anything unusual about the depiction of Medusa, because she wasn't a character, she

I

was just a monster. Who feels sorry for a creature who has snakes for hair, and turns innocent men to stone?

I would go on to study Greek at school because of these films, and probably also because of the children's versions of Greek myths I had read (a Puffin edition, I think, by Roger Lancelyn Green. My brother tells me we had a Norse one too). It would be years before I came across any other version of Medusa's story, anything that told me how she became a monster, or why. During my degree, I kept coming across details in the work of ancient authors which were quite different from the versions I knew from simplified stories I'd read and watched. Medusa wasn't always a monster, Helen of Troy wasn't always an adulterer, Pandora wasn't ever a villain. Even characters that were outright villainous – Medea, Clytemnestra, Phaedra – were often far more nuanced than they first appeared. In my final year at college, I wrote my dissertation on women who kill children in Greek tragedy.

I have spent the last few years writing novels which tell stories from Greek myth that have largely been forgotten. Female characters were often central figures in ancient versions of these stories. The playwright Euripides wrote eight tragedies about the Trojan War which survive to us today. One of them, *Orestes*, has a male title character. The other seven have women as their titles: *Andromache, Electra, Hecabe, Helen, Iphigenia in Aulis, Iphigenia Among the Taureans* and *The Trojan Women*. When I began hunting out the stories I wanted to tell, I felt exactly like Perseus in the Harryhausen movie: squinting at reflections in the half-light. These women were hiding in plain sight, in the pages of Ovid and Euripides. They were painted on vases which are held in museums all over the world. They were in fragments of lost poems, and broken statues. But they were there.

It was, however, while debating the character of a non-Greek woman that I decided to write this book. I was on Radio 3, discussing the role of Dido, the Phoenician queen who founded the city of

Carthage. To me, Dido was a tragic heroine, self-denying, courageous, heartbroken. To my interviewer, she was a vicious schemer. I was responding to her in Virgil's *Aeneid*, he was responding to her in Marlowe's *Dido, Queen of Carthage*. I'd spent so long thinking about ancient sources I'd forgotten that most people get their classics from much more modern sources (Marlowe is modern to classicists). Dismal though I think the film *Troy* to be, for example, it has probably been seen by more people than have read the *Iliad*.

So I decided I would choose ten women whose stories have been told and retold – in paintings, plays, films, operas, musicals and more – and I would show how differently they were viewed in the ancient world. How major female characters in Ovid would become non-existent Hollywood wives in twenty-first-century cinema. How artists would recreate Helen to reflect the ideals of beauty of their own time, and we would lose track of the clever, funny, sometimes frightening woman that she is in Homer and Euripides. And how some modern writers and artists were finding these women, just like I was, and putting them back at the heart of the story.

Every myth contains multiple timelines within itself: the time in which it is set, the time it is first told, and every retelling afterwards. Myths may be the home of the miraculous, but they are also mirrors of us. Which version of a story we choose to tell, which characters we place in the foreground, which ones we allow to fade into the shadows: these reflect both the teller and the reader, as much as they show the characters of the myth. We have made space in our story-telling to rediscover women who have been lost or forgotten. They are not villains, victims, wives and monsters: they are people.

PANDORA

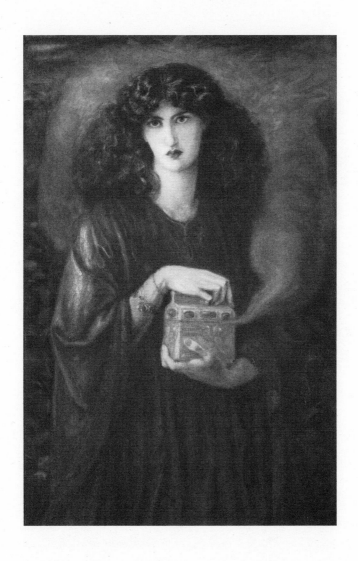

W HEN WE THINK OF PANDORA, WE PROBABLY HAVE A PICTURE in our minds. She holds a box in her hands, or she's sitting beside one. She is opening it either because she is curious to see what's inside, or because she knows what it contains and wants to let it out. Its contents are abstract but terrible: all the evils in the world are now set loose upon us. And, gratifyingly, we know exactly who to blame: the beautiful woman who couldn't leave well alone.

It's obviously a story which finds its echoes with Eve. Do what you like in Eden, Adam is told by God. Eat from any of the trees. Except that one, the tree of knowledge, which is nonetheless placed in easy reach, next to this persuasive talking snake. Eve is then created, but God doesn't tell her what she can and can't eat. She has presumably heard it from Adam, though, because she knows what to say when the snake (whom God has also created) asks her if she can't eat from any of the trees in the garden. Yes, Eve replies, we can. Just not that one or we'll die. The knowledge tree? asks the snake. No, you won't die. You'll just be able to tell good from evil, like God. Eve shares the fruit with Adam, who was with her, as the book of Genesis tells us. And the snake is right: they don't die, though Eve is promised agonizing childbirth as her reward for heeding the snake for whose existence and voice God was entirely responsible.

But Pandora has been particularly ill-served by history, even relative to Eve. Eve did at least listen to the snake and eat the thing she'd been told was dangerous. Pandora did not open a box, either from curiosity or malevolence. Indeed the box doesn't appear in her story until Hesiod's *Works and Days* was translated into Latin by Erasmus, in the sixteenth century, well over two millennia after Hesiod was writing in Greek. Erasmus was looking for a word to convey the Greek *pithos*, meaning 'jar'. As the classical scholar and translator M. L. West describes,[1] Hesiod meant a ceramic storage jar, a metre or so tall. Greek jars are narrow at the base, broadening out to a wide lip. They are not especially stable: look in any museum of classical antiquities and you will see the many cracks and repairs which reveal their intrinsic fragility. Ceramic pots are often beautiful, ornately decorated works of art. But they are not where one would necessarily choose to store a set of evils that will cause mankind untold griefs for millennia to come. Quite aside from anything else – as anyone who has ever swept a kitchen floor will cheerlessly testify – lids aren't always tightly fastened. And we have the advantage of screw-tops, something Pandora assuredly did not.

West conjectures that Erasmus confused the stories of Pandora and Psyche (another character from Greek myth who does carry a box – *puxos*, more usually transliterated as *pyxis* – when she is sent to the Underworld on a quest). It's certainly a plausible theory. So did Erasmus confuse the two women – Pandora and Psyche – or confuse the two similar-sounding words: jar – *pithos*, and box – *puxos* (in Greek; *pyxis* in Latin)? Either way, the loser is Pandora. Because, while it might take effort to open a box, it's much easier to knock a lid off or smash a top-heavy ceramic jar. And yet the linguistically doctored image of Pandora opening a box with malice aforethought is the one which has entered our culture.

Look at artistic representations of her which pre-date the widespread reading of Erasmus (who died in 1536) and she is shown with a jar, even if the painter is seeking to cast her as a villain and the image reflects that. Jean Cousin painted her as Eva Prima Pandora,[2] a blend of Pandora and Eve, around 1550: lying naked, save for a sheet curled between her legs, jar under one hand, human skull under the other. And there are later paintings which also show her with a jar: Henry Howard's *The Opening of Pandora's Vase*[3] in 1834, for example. But the most famous image of her is perhaps from some forty years later, by which time Erasmus' rewrite seems firmly embedded in the collective artistic consciousness.

In 1871, Rossetti completed his portrait of Pandora holding a small golden casket in her hands. The lid of the casket is studded with large jewels, green and purple, which are echoed by the ornate stones in one of the bracelets she wears on her right wrist. The long, slender fingers of her right hand are flexed as she begins to open the box. Her left hand grips the base firmly. The crack opening between the lid and the box itself is just a thin shadow, but already a coil of orange smoke emanates: it is twisting its way behind Pandora's red-brown curls. We don't know what is in the box exactly, but whatever it is, it's sinister. Look at the side of the box more closely, just above Pandora's left thumb, and a Latin inscription makes things appear less promising still: '*Nascitur Ignescitur*'[4] – born in flames. Rossetti made the casket himself, but it has subsequently been lost.

The portrait is well over a metre tall, and its depth of colour is as fiery as the text at its centre: Pandora wears a crimson dress, which drapes over her arms and body from its high round neckline. Her lips are painted in a perfect bow in the same bright red. A tiny shadow under the centre of her mouth creates the impression that her lower lip protrudes towards the viewer. Her huge blue eyes gaze unapologetically at us. The model was Jane Morris, wife of the artist William, with whom Rossetti had been having what we can reasonably conclude was a thrilling affair. Critics asked themselves what William Morris might think of a work showing his wife in such an undeniably erotic light, painted by another man. Fewer people thought to ask how Jane Morris must have felt to see herself illustrating the description of Pandora in Hesiod's *Theogony* as *kalon kakon*[5] – a beautiful evil. And no one asked what Pandora might have thought of the object she was holding so tightly, so dangerously in her beautiful hands.

Perhaps, then, it's time to look at Pandora's story from the beginning, and see how it evolves and how she changes from one writer and artist to the next. As is so often the way with excellent things, we need to go back to the Greeks to see how it began. The earliest source we have is Hesiod, who lived in the late eighth century BCE in Boeotia in central Greece. He tells her story twice, the first time relatively briefly in his poem *Theogony*.

This poem is an origin story which catalogues the genealogy of the gods. First comes Chaos, then Earth, then the Underworld, and perhaps the first character we might recognize: Eros, who softens flesh and overcomes reason. Chaos creates Erebus and Night, Night creates Air and Day, Earth creates Heaven, and so on. Two generations on, we get to Zeus: Heaven (Ouranos) and Earth (Gaia) have multiple children including Kronos and Rhea. Ouranos turns out to be less than ideal parent material, hiding his children away in a cavern and refusing to let them out into the light. To win freedom from their oppression, Kronos eventually castrates his father with a sharp hook given to him by his mother, and throws the disembodied genitals into the sea (which is what creates Aphrodite. This is probably the time to start pondering whether Freud might have something to say about any of this). Kronos and Rhea in turn have multiple children: these pre-Olympian gods are known as Titans. Then Kronos also fails a basic fatherhood test, choosing to swallow each of his offspring whole. Rhea gives birth to Zeus in secret so he won't be eaten, then Zeus forces Kronos to regurgitate his older siblings and takes over the mantle of king of the gods for himself. It scarcely needs saying that family gatherings must have been fraught affairs.

Zeus is often described as clever and strategic, but he is soon thwarted twice by the wily Titan Prometheus. Hesiod is obviously looking for a story that explains why his fellow Greeks sacrifice the bones of an animal to the gods, and keep the choice cuts of meat for themselves. Given that sacrifice should presumably involve the loss of something good, and given that the bones are not the best bit of a dead ox, an explanation is required. So Hesiod tells us that, at a place called Mekone, Prometheus performed some sleight of hand. Given the task of dividing meat into a portion for the gods and one for mortals, he hides the meat beneath the ox's stomach and offers it to Zeus, and arranges the bones for men under a piece of glistening fat. Zeus complains that his portion looks the less appetizing and Prometheus explains that Zeus has first pick, so should choose whichever portion he prefers. The king of the gods makes his choice and only afterwards sees that he has been deceived: mortals get the good stuff and the gods are stuck with a pile of bones.

Prometheus' second piece of trickery is outright theft: he steals fire (which belongs to the gods) and shares it with mortals. He is famously punished for this by being tied to a rock and having his liver pecked out by an eagle. His immortality means that his liver grows back, so the whole grisly business can begin anew each day. Zeus is so incensed by the improvement in mortal lives which fire has brought that he decides to give us an evil (*kakon*)[6] to balance things out. He gets Hephaestus to mould from the earth the likeness of a young woman. The goddess Athene dresses the unnamed maiden in silver clothes and gives her a veil and a golden crown, decorated with images of wild animals. When Hephaestus and Athene have finished their work, they show the *kalon kakon, ant'agathoio*[7] – beautiful evil, the price of good – to the other gods, who realize that mortal men will have no device or remedy against her. From this woman, Hesiod says, comes the whole deadly race of women. Always nice to be wanted.

For a story which is told in so few words, this takes a lot of unpacking. Firstly, why doesn't Hesiod use Pandora's name? Secondly, is Hesiod really saying that women are a separate race from men? In which case, Pandora is very different from Eve: Adam and Eve will be the ancestors of all future men and women alike, but Pandora will be the antecedent of women alone. Thirdly, where's her jar, or box, or whatever? Again, we'll have to wait for Hesiod's second, longer version to find out more. And fourthly, what do we find out about Pandora herself? She's autochthonous, i.e. made of the earth itself. She's designed and created by the gods' master craftsman, Hephaestus, and decorated by the cunning and skilled Athene. We know Pandora is beautiful. But what is she actually like? We get only one phrase which might tell us, before Hesiod gets side-tracked explaining how women will only want you if you aren't poor, and comparing them unfavourably to bees. As Pandora is taken out to be shown to the other gods, who will marvel at how perfectly made she is, she delights in her dress – *kosmo agalomenēn*.[8] It's as though Hesiod has been charmed by this young woman, even as he is describing her as evil and deadly. Just created, and she's taking inno-cent pleasure in having been given a pretty frock.

Hesiod's second, more detailed version of the story is in *Works and Days*. This poem is largely written as a rebuke to his indolent brother, Perses, proving that the poet's passive-aggression isn't limited to women. Siblings are also in his hexametric firing line. Once again, Zeus is angered by Prometheus' theft, exclaiming 'I will give them an evil as the price of fire' – '*anti puros dōsō kakon*'. He goes on to say that Pandora will be an evil 'in which all men will delight, and which they will all embrace.'[9] Again, he orders Hephaestus to do the hard work of creating; Pandora will be made from earth and water and given human voice and strength, but she will have the face and form of an immortal goddess. Athene is charged with teaching her to weave and Aphrodite must give her golden grace, painful desire and limb-gnawing sufferings (these latter two characteristics are presumably the feelings Pandora will provoke in men, but they are integral to her very being).

The gods rush to do Zeus' bidding. Indeed, more gods get involved: the Graces, Persuasion and the Hours all help with golden and floral decorations. The god Hermes gives her a doglike mind (this isn't a compliment: the Greeks didn't love dogs in the way that we do) and a dishonest nature. He is also responsible for both her voice and her name: 'he called the woman Pandora, because all the gods who live on Mount Olympus gave her a gift, a calamity to men.'[10] It is also Hermes, as the messenger of the gods, who takes Pandora away from the immortal realm and delivers her to Epimetheus, brother of Prometheus, as a gift. Prometheus (whose name literally means 'foresight') had warned his brother not to accept any gifts from Zeus. Epimetheus' name means 'hindsight', and perhaps this is why he forgets that a present from Zeus might be something other than a box tied up with ribbon. So Epimetheus receives Pandora and the carefree life of mortals is at an end. Before this point, Hesiod explains, men had lived on the earth free from evils, free from hard work and from disease. But once Pandora takes the huge lid off her jar, that is all over, and mournful cares are now spread among mortals. Only Hope (Elpis)[11] remains inside, retained under the lip of the jar, her unbroken home.

This longer version of Pandora's beginnings answers some questions and raises several more. Pandora is a gift – literally: she is given by Hermes to Epimetheus. She is also all-gifted, insofar as many gods have contributed to her creation, giving her different qualities and skills. This part of her story perhaps reminds us of *Sleeping Beauty*, in which a baby is granted various positive qualities by invited fairies before a malevolent gatecrasher throws a spanner in the works by gifting her the prospect of death by spindle (commuted to an enormously long nap). But Pandora isn't a baby when she receives these gifts, she is a *parthenos*: a maiden, a young woman of marriageable age. So these are not future qualities being bestowed on her, but immediately visible, audible ones: a voice, a dress, skill at weaving. There is a temptation to read her name as meaning 'all-gifted' (*pan* – 'all', *dora* comes from the verb *didomi* – 'I give'). But the verb in Pandora's name is active, not passive: literally she is all-giving rather than all-gifted. As an adjective in Greek, *pandora* is usually used to describe the earth, the all-giving thing which sustains life. There is an Athenian *kylix* (a wine cup) from around 460 BCE, attributed to the Tarquinia Painter, which is now in the British Museum and which appears to depict the scene Hesiod describes. The figures of Athene and Hephaestus stand to either side of a stiff Pandora, still seemingly more clay than woman. She is becoming a *parthenos*, but she is not yet finished, like a doll being dressed up by the skilful hands of the gods. Her name on this pot is given as Anesidora, meaning 'she who sends up gifts', much as the earth sends up the shoots of plants which will feed us and our livestock. So Pandora's intrinsic generosity is erased if we think of her only as gifted.

But is she all-giving of anything we actually want? Or does she just dole out the contents of her jar? Hard work, grievous cares, disease and the like? In which case her name might best be read ironically: thanks for all the trauma you're gifting us. It's curious that Hesiod goes to such lengths to describe the creation of Pandora (right down to the spring flowers put in her hair), but the first we hear about the massive jar she is carrying is when she takes the lid off it after she is sent to Epimetheus. It's hard to imagine she's picked it up somewhere on her way down from Olympus with Hermes. Rather, it seems that Zeus' punishment for men is twofold: the cunning, unavoidable Pandora herself, and the jar of nasties which he sends with her. After all, he is punishing a two-pronged attack on his divine dignity (the trick Prometheus pulled with the sacrificial meat and the theft of fire), so a double revenge seems appropriate. In which case, again, we might begin to wonder why Pandora receives all the blame.

Look at the number of gods and Titans involved in this myth: Prometheus antagonizes Zeus but does give us fire and tries his best to warn Epimetheus about possible retribution. Epimetheus simply ignores or forgets what his brother had warned him about accepting gifts from Zeus, so we can surely lay some of the blame at his door. If he'd been more astute, Pandora would have been sent packing, jar and all, back to Olympus. Or do we give Epimetheus a pass because Zeus is after all the most powerful Olympian god and there isn't much a Titan can do in a battle of wits with him, especially if he's employing all the other gods to help him create and deliver Pandora? But then, why don't we extend the same courtesy to Pandora? She is the mechanism by which Zeus decides to take his revenge, so how much agency does she really have? Stand up to Zeus and your best-case scenario is being struck by lightning and obliterated. Worst-case scenario is having your liver pecked out every day for eternity. It is hard to shake the sense that Hesiod has two pet peeves – conniving women and hapless brothers – and has told us this story in such a way that it contains one of each. But do we really think Pandora should have declined to accompany Hermes, or sat on top of her jar and refused to budge so it couldn't be opened? Does she even know what's inside? Hesiod is keen to tell us of her treacherous, deceitful nature (implanted by Hermes), but we see no indication of that. And, incidentally, Hermes seems to walk away from the whole saga without carrying any blame either.

Hesiod raises one last conundrum when he tells us that Elpis – Hope – remains beneath the lip of the jar. Is this a good thing for mortal men, or a bad one? Do we think Hope is being saved for us inside the jar? Or is it being withheld from us? All the evils which were inside are now out in the world, so would we be in better shape if Hope travelled among them? At least then we might have some positivity to raise our spirits (obviously, this doesn't work if, like John Cleese in *Clockwise*, we 'can take the despair. It's the hope I can't stand'). Is Pandora committing one more act of petulant cruelty by making our lives miserable and then depriving us even of Hope? Or is the jar a safe place, where we know we will always have Hope, as we traverse a world which is now so much more frightening than it was before the jar was opened? Scholars have been divided on their reading of this passage, not least because, although *elpis* is usually translated as 'hope', it doesn't quite mean that. Hope is intrinsically positive in English, but in Greek (and the same with the Latin equivalent, *spes*) it is not. Since it really means the anticipation of something good or bad, a more accurate translation would probably be 'expectation'. Before we can worry about whether it's advantageous to us that it remains in the jar, we first have to decide if it is intrinsically good or bad. This is a genuinely complex linguistic and philosophical puzzle. No wonder it's easier to just blame Pandora.

And plenty of writers have done exactly that. In Roger Lancelyn Green's *Tales of the Greek Heroes*, first published by Puffin in 1958 and many people's first encounter with Pandora, she is roundly stitched up. Not only does she open the casket (which she has been told is full of treasure) while Epimetheus is out, but she 'crept quietly' to do so: she is malevolent and secretive because she knows she is in the wrong. In the most recent Puffin edition, this scene is excerpted inside the front cover for maximum impact. And in Nathaniel Hawthorne's *Tanglewood Tales for Boys and Girls*, which have similarly been the gateway to classics for many children since their publication in 1853, Pandora is even less generously treated. Her story is foreshadowed at the end of the previous chapter, in which she is introduced as 'a sad naughty child' (which coincidentally describes the background of anyone I have ever wanted to know).

Hawthorne's next chapter, 'The Paradise of Children', begins by introducing us to Epimetheus as a child. So that he would not be lonely, 'another child, fatherless and motherless like himself, was sent from a far country, to live with him, and be his playfellow and helpmate. Her name was Pandora. The first thing that Pandora saw, when she entered the cottage where Epimetheus dwelt, was a great box. And almost the first question which she put to him, after crossing the threshold, was this, "Epimetheus, what have you in that box?"'

So far, so bad. Pandora 'was sent', but we aren't told by whom. The passive voice is a tremendous aid in avoiding responsibility (think of all those non-apologies which employ the formulation 'I'm sorry if any feelings were hurt'. So much less effort than actively apologizing for having hurt someone's feelings. 'I'm sorry I hurt you' can be heartfelt and sincere. 'I'm sorry you were hurt' is a reason to boot someone out of your life and never see them again). Zeus, Hephaestus, Athene and Hermes couldn't find a more helpful alibi than Hawthorne here provides for them. Unnamed, unmentioned: their role in Pandora's creation, let alone her arrival at Epimetheus' cottage, is whitewashed from the story. Pandora's interest in the large, mysterious casket is immediate and ongoing: she and Epimetheus fall out over it. She demands to know where it has come from, Epimetheus remembers it was delivered by a man Pandora can identify as Quicksilver (a cute pun, since quicksilver is another name for the metal, mercury, which is in turn the Roman name for Hermes). Hawthorne consistently loads his narrative against her: Epimetheus says things, Pandora – often using the same words – cries pettishly. His irritation is an expression of fatigue, hers of naughtiness. She is to blame for wilfully opening the box, Epimetheus is an accessory at most: 'But – and you may see by this how a wrong act of any one mortal is a calamity to the whole world – by Pandora's lifting the lid of that miserable box, and by the fault of Epimetheus, too, in not preventing her, these Troubles have obtained a foothold among us.' The story is accompanied by not one but two illustrations of Pandora and the box, which is large enough for her to sit on. Again, we are invited to see Pandora's unquenchable curiosity as a sin for which we all must pay.

Both these writers have made choices which reflect the times in which they were working rather than anything we might find in ancient versions of the myth. Myths – Greek ones perhaps especially so – are protean. As mentioned above, they operate in at least two timelines: the one in which they are ostensibly set, and the one in which any particular version is written. The condescending, paternalistic tone in Hawthorne's version of Pandora is far more overt than the irritable misogyny we find in Hesiod. Hesiod may present Pandora as a trick, a construct made by the gods to bring harm to men, but he wants us to know about the reasons Zeus orders her creation, the revenge on Prometheus and the rest. In simplifying the stories for children, Green and Hawthorne both oversimplify, so that Pandora becomes more villainous than even Hesiod intended.

What might have happened if nineteenth- and twentieth-century myth-writers had been more interested in the sources of their stories? If they had looked beyond Hesiod or Erasmus at some of the less well-known versions of Pandora's story? If they had been willing to trawl through fragments of Theognis' *Elegies*, from the sixth century BCE, they might have found a short passage which suggests that Pandora's jar is full of good things rather than bad. When the jar is opened, everything good – Self-control, Trust etc. – flies away, which is why we so rarely find them among mortal men. Only Elpis – Hope – remains, as one good which did not abandon us.[12]

Of course, we might think it unreasonable to expect a children's writer to be hunting through obscure texts like Theognis to present a more complicated story. One of the joys of children's stories is their simplicity. But there is a writer that small children have been reading – in one form or another – for a couple of millennia, a writer who also tells the story of Pandora. It's impossible to say how many people contributed to Aesop's fables: multiple authors wrote the short stories which have been attributed to him. Aesop himself may have been a slave who won his freedom with his wits a hundred years[13] or so after Hesiod was alive, or he may not have existed at all. But what is certainly the case is that his version of the story[14] is closer to Theognis than to Hesiod. Again, the jar is full of useful things. And again they fly away when the lid is taken off. But the guilty party is not Pandora. Rather it is a *lichnos anthropos* – a 'curious or greedy man'. Is it Epimetheus who is responsible this time? The fable doesn't give him a name. But it is certainly a man rather than a woman, and one who is curious rather than evil. In the sixteenth century the Italian engraver Giulio Bonasone seems to have taken Aesop's version as his inspiration. His engraving (now in the Metropolitan Museum in New York)[15] *Epimetheus opening Pandora's Box* is an intriguing piece of work, not least because – in spite of its title – Epimetheus is clearly taking the lid off a huge Grecian jar, its hefty handle turned to face the viewer. None of Hawthorne's infantilization is present here: Epimetheus is a grown man with a full beard. Escaping from this jar are female personifications of various good things: Virtue, Peace, Good Fortune, Health. As is consistently the case in almost every version of the story, Hope is retained.

Visual artists have often been inspired by Pandora, perhaps because she provides them with an opportunity to share the intensity of an affair with their entire social circle (in the case of Rossetti) or the chance to paint an attractive woman mostly or completely naked (in the case of Jean Cousin, Jules Lefebvre, Paul Césaire Gariot, William Etty, John William Waterhouse and many more). Perhaps they didn't consult Hesiod to remind themselves about the silvery robe she delights in. These artists tend to show her in the act of opening either a jar or a box, or being about to do so, or in the immediate aftermath of having done so. Their focus is almost always on the destruction which Pandora has wreaked or will imminently wreak, which is surely a consequence of the mingling of the Pandora and Eve narratives.

The emphasis in Pandora's story for centuries has been her single-handed role in the fall of man. Just as Adam and the snake dodge so much of the blame in Eve's story, so Zeus, Hermes and Epimetheus have been exonerated in almost every later version of Pandora's. The guiding principle when searching for the cause of everything wrong in the world has been, all too often: *cherchez la femme*.

The ancient Greeks also liked to create visual representations of Pandora, but they were much less interested in the opening of the jar, perhaps because the jar simply wasn't that important to them (as we've seen, Hesiod only mentions it in his second version of her story). Or perhaps because competing traditions (as we've seen in Aesop) change the identity of the jar-opener and the contents of the jar. Ancient sculptors and painters instead focus their attention on the moment when the gods all come together to contribute to the creation of all-gifted, all-giving Pandora. This is the scene which appears on some of the finest *kraters* (mixing bowls for the Greeks to add water to their wine) which depict Pandora, such as the one at the British Museum,[16] and one at the Ashmolean[17] in Oxford. Interestingly, the association of Pandora with a box is so complete that the Ashmolean website lists their krater under the heading 'Pandora's Box'. But there is no sign of either the anachronistic box nor even the jar anywhere in the scene, which instead depicts Zeus looking on and Hermes looking back at him, before Epimetheus – armed with a hammer to help sculpt Pandora from the clay – offers a hand to Pandora as she rises out of the ground. Eros hovers above them, presumably to make sure that the couple fall swiftly in love.

It is this scene which was given pride of place on the Parthenon, in Athens. The focal point of this huge temple was its vast sculpture of Athene Parthenos, the patron goddess of the Athenians. The statue stood over ten metres tall, and was made of over a ton of ivory and gold plates (the Greek word for this combination is chryselephantine) attached to a wooden core.[18] This Athene is long gone, but we have writings from ancient authors who had seen both the statue and – crucially for our understanding of how the Greeks themselves viewed Pandora – its sculpted base. This would have been roughly at eye-height for visitors to the *cella* – the inner room of the temple. The base showed the creation of Pandora in sculpted relief. Obviously, it would have been dwarfed by the colossal statue of Athene. But Pandora's inclusion on the focal statue in this sacred building tells us something about how the Athenians thought of her. Athene was crucial to Pandora's creation, after all, giving her a dress and her weaving skills (this is no minor skill in ancient Greece. Rather, weaving was a task which was considered the ideal pursuit for virtuous women. That's why Penelope is weaving and unweaving a shroud for much of the *Odyssey*). Pausanias – the second-century CE travel writer – mentions their connection when he describes the Parthenon for his readers. The statue of Athene stands upright, he says, and there is a Medusa carved from ivory on her breast. On the pedestal is the birth of Pandora who was, as has been sung about by Hesiod and others, the first woman. Before her, Pausanias reiterates, there was no womankind.[19] Again, no mention of any jar or its contents. It seems reasonable to suggest that, for the ancients, Pandora's role as the ancestor of all women was far more important than her disputed role in opening the world to incessant evil. Even if, for Hesiod, these two amount to much the same thing.

The relief from the Parthenon isn't the only missing piece of evidence about Pandora from fifth-century BCE Athens. We have also lost a play by Sophocles called *Pandora,* or *Sphyrokopoi,* which means 'The Hammerers'. We usually think of Sophocles as a tragedian, because his seven surviving plays are tragedies. But in fact he wrote perhaps as many as 150 plays in his lifetime, including satyr-plays, of which *The Hammerers* is one. Satyr-plays were performed after tragedies, and were full of absurdity, silly jokes, and a chorus of satyrs. Sophocles would have produced three tragedies and a satyr-play each time he was entered into the Dionysia, the drama festival in Athens (held in honour of Dionysus, the god of theatre and wine) where his plays were first performed. We don't have a complete set of any of Sophocles' plays: the Theban plays – *Oedipus the King, Oedipus at Colonus* and *Antigone* – are often performed or published together, but they come from three separate trilogies. And we have extensive fragments from only one of his satyr-plays, *The Trackers* (although Tony Harrison filled in the gaps with his brilliant play *The Trackers of Oxyrhyncus*). There is an almost palpable shock in finding Sophocles – the most devastating of poets, in many ways – made jokes. So it is disappointing on at least two counts that we know almost nothing about his version of the Pandora myth. We can guess, from the alternative title, *The Hammerers*, that it focused on Pandora's creation, as the fifth-century BCE Greek sculptors and vase painters did. It seems plausible to assume that the satyrs carried hammers, since these plays usually take their titles from the role played by the chorus of satyrs (half animal, half man, and always with a massive erection. Not all cultural traditions survive intact, but satyr-plays are probably closest to burlesque, if burlesque had more permanently priapic man–horse hybrids singing and dancing in it. Doubtless this niche is being catered for somewhere). The hammers will be employed, as Epimetheus' hammer is about to be used on the *krater* displayed in the Ashmolean, to prepare the clay from which Pandora will be sculpted, or perhaps to free her from the ground (from which she is rising on the Ashmolean pot). If only we had more information about the play, or some fragments of it survived, we might infer more about how fifth-century BCE Athenians saw Pandora and whether they considered her particularly relevant to their city-state, as her inclusion in the Parthenon implies. Sadly, we know nothing definite.

But as informed guesses go, it seems reasonable to suggest that the Athenians included the relief of Pandora in their temple because she was the Ur-woman, the woman from whom all women are descended. The Athenians' attitude to women is hard for us to understand today. The *polis* – the city-state and all the democratic institutions which contributed to it – was a male-only enclave. Only men could vote, or serve on juries, or take part in Athenian civic life at all. Women were more or less cloistered (depending on class, and money) and might go for long periods of time without even speaking to men to whom they were not closely related. The Athenian ideal, espoused in Pericles' funeral oration[20] in 431 BCE, was that women should aspire never to be talked about, either in terms of blame or praise. The greatest virtue, in other words, that an Athenian woman could aspire to was not to be registered, almost not to exist. It is a gratifying quirk of Pericles' character that he could make this speech while living with the most famous (or perhaps notorious) woman in Athens, one mentioned by everyone from comedians to philosophers: Aspasia. Thankfully the hypocrisy of censuring women's behaviour in general while maintaining an entirely different set of standards for the actual women you know has now died out.

Even Greek grammar obliterated women. When Athenian men referred to a group of themselves, they would use the words *hoi Athenaioi* – 'the Athenian men' (the endings of both words are masculine). If a mixed-sex group of Athenians gathered, the phrase used to describe them would be exactly the same – if even one man was present among dozens of women, the word-ending used to describe the group is masculine: *–oi*. For an all-female group of Athenians, the words would be *hai Athenaiai*. I say 'would be' because that phrase is not found anywhere in extant Greek literature:[21] no one ever needs to refer to a group of Athenian women, because they aren't important.

And yet there is Pandora, at eye-height, in the Parthenon, the grandest structure in the grandest city in fifth-century BCE Greece. A temple, and its decorative sculptures of epic battles and religious processions, built for the sole purpose of reflecting and aggrandizing Athenian identity. For all the harsh words about women which we find in the writings of Hesiod or the virtual non-existence required of them in the speech of Pericles (at least as told to us by the historian Thucydides), there is an argument to be made that women were not quite as invisible as we might have thought.

Perhaps it's not surprising that Pandora's role as our ancestor has been largely forgotten today. Instead, her Old Testament semi-equivalent has taken precedence in our collective consciousness. Just as Deucalion (the survivor of the Great Flood in Greek myth) has been largely forgotten while Noah and his ark sail cheerily to salvation, so Pandora has been approximated or replaced by Eve. But why has the box she never carried exerted such a fascination on so many artists and writers? 'Pandora's box' is an idiom, a shorthand in a way that 'Eve's apple' never has been. And no usage of it is ever positive, as in the Aesop version where the box is full of treats which we have inadvertently let slip through our careless hands. At best, we might use it to imply that a set of unforeseen consequences has now come into play. But more usually, when someone opens Pandora's box, it is both negative and somewhat worse than might have been anticipated, or on a much larger and more damaging scale. Like opening a can of worms and finding it to be full of poisonous snakes instead.

It's surely not enough to blame the whole thing on Erasmus. Countless translators have made countless errors in texts through the ages, and most of them have had nothing like the resonance or impact that Erasmus' mix-up of *pithos* and *pyxis* has had. But somehow, he coined an idea which has echoed through the centuries. Everything used to be okay, but then a single, irreversible bad decision was made, and now we all live with the consequences forever. It's reassuring in a way: the problem was caused long before we were born and will persist long after our deaths, so there's nothing we can really do about it. In the immortal words of Valmont in *Dangerous Liaisons*, it's beyond my control. It allows us to be children again: injustice, cruelty and disease are all someone else's fault, so it isn't our problem to try and fix them.

And then there is the question of motive, which is missing entirely from the ancient Greek version of Pandora. Even Hesiod doesn't give us a reason for Pandora opening the jar and letting all the evils out into the world. She just does it. We don't know if it comes from curiosity or malice, we don't even know if Pandora realizes what's inside the jar. We don't know where it came from or how Pandora acquired it. Unlike Eve, who at least gets a line or two of dialogue to explain herself, Pandora is (for all that she has been given a voice by Hermes) mute. Whatever motives we attribute to her are ours, and ours alone.

But once the jar has become a box, and particularly once the box shrinks from a huge *pithos* to become a small, portable *pyxis*, the element of compulsion is undeniable. Is there something in us which is drawn to doing the forbidden? Of course, or the story of Adam and Eve getting themselves booted out of the Garden of Eden wouldn't resonate as it does. They have everything they could possibly want, and all they have to do to continue their paradisal existence is obey a single (arbitrary, snake-undermined) rule. But the lure of the prohibited is undeniable. If a phrase has come out of the Eve story to rival 'Pandora's box', it is perhaps 'forbidden fruit'. It is not that the delicious fruit happens to be forbidden. It is that the fruit is delicious precisely because it is forbidden. The act of prohibition makes the withheld item more alluring than it could ever otherwise have been.

And this is surely even more true when we have been told, and believe, that the prohibition is for our own good. We spend our lives trying – consciously or subconsciously – to protect ourselves from harm. Most of us would never dream of sticking our hands into a flame, because we know it would hurt. But if a waiter wraps a cloth around his hand before placing a dish in front of us and warning us that it is hot, we are almost compelled to touch it. Why? Do we doubt the man? Are we testing whether his judgement of heat tallies with our own? Are we trying to prove to him or to ourselves that our hands are made of sufficiently asbestos-like material for the pain not to hurt? Why wouldn't we simply take his word for it and look after ourselves, the way we do most of the time? Who tests the unknown heat of an object with their skin? It is an undeniably perverse response. Yet, in my heart of hearts, I know I have never in my life wanted to eat anything so much as a sachet of silica gel, on which someone has stamped the words 'Do Not Eat'.

This compulsion is sufficiently widespread to have become a film and television trope in its own right. Perhaps the purest example is a 1986 episode of *The Twilight Zone*, called 'Button, Button', based on a story by Richard Matheson from 1970, and remade in 2009 as a feature film, *The Box*. Norma and Arthur live in an apartment and are beset by money worries. One day, a mysterious box is delivered with a button on top, and a note saying that a Mr Steward will visit them. Steward arrives when Arthur is absent (are we meant to think of him as Epimetheus, carelessly ignoring the warning of the note?) and tells Norma the deal. If she and Arthur press the button, they'll receive $200,000. But – and it wouldn't be *The Twilight Zone* without a catch – someone they don't know will die. The couple discuss the proposition: is every life as important as every other? It could be someone who is already dying of cancer, it could be a peasant whose life is wretched. Or, Arthur says, it could be an innocent child. And almost as difficult for them to comprehend as the ethics are the physics of the deal. They open the box, and discover no mechanism within. No one would know if they had pressed the button or not. Arthur throws the box out, but Norma retrieves it. Eventually, the temptation is too great for her, and she presses the button. Like Hawthorne's version of Epimetheus, her husband doesn't stop her, but is upset just the same. The next day, Steward arrives with a briefcase containing the promised money. He removes the box and explains that it will be reprogrammed and offered to someone they don't know. The sting in the tail is never spelled out more explicitly than that, but we are presumably meant to infer that Norma's life now depends on the choice made by the next recipient of the box. An ungenerous person might wonder if Arthur has done quite well out of this exchange, since he will presumably get to keep the cash and might lose a wife who has already provoked in him a visibly angry response. Maybe he won't even miss her.

Like so many *Twilight Zone* episodes, the story interrogates the darker side of human nature: what would you do if you were desperate? Or not even desperate, but just poor and getting poorer? How much do you value the lives of people you don't know? We might think we would respond differently to the offer, but we all ignore the traumas of strangers every time we watch the news. How else could we survive? We can't care as much about every single person alive as we do for our loved ones. And there is an ethical difference – isn't there? – between ignoring a stranger who needs help, or money, or a kidney, and actively killing them. Neglect isn't the same as animus. But to the person on the receiving end of no help (no medicine, no food, no kidney), the death they face is awfully similar to the one they would face if you deliberately assassinated them.

The portability of a box with unknown contents somehow adds to its desirability. The great *pithos* which Pandora has in Hesiod's poem is infinitely less compelling than the jewelled casket she is holding in Rossetti's painting. The need to open it, to find out what's inside, only increases as the size of the box decreases. There is no sense of jeopardy in the BBC's 1984 adaptation of John Masefield's novel *The Box of Delights*, when the mysterious old Punch-and-Judy man, Cole Hawlings, opens the box for Kay Harker. The programme's title implies that the box is – incredibly unusually for any version of the container-of-a-mysterious-unknown trope – a good thing, and that its contents are nothing to be feared. There are plenty of other things to be scared of in this world: the deeply sinister Abner Brown, his clergymen-henchmen who seem to turn into wolves or foxes, the crazed Arnold of Todi who first created the box hundreds of years earlier. But the box itself is not something we have to fear; only its temporary loss will cause us to worry later on. Instead, it is a passport to wonder: the first thing Kay sees emerge from the box of delights is a phoenix, which he knows doesn't exist. He can travel through both time and space using the box, and into adventures that are improbable but wonderful. In the final moments of the final episode, we discover that the whole fantastical story has been a dream as Kay travels home for the Christmas holidays. His sleeping imagination has morphed the people on his train into villains all intent on acquiring the magic box. Perhaps this reveals an important truth about how we view an unknown quantity, like the contents of a mystery box: the compulsion to know what it is isn't remotely diminished by the rarity of it turning out to be something we want.

This is never truer than in the astonishing 1955 noir movie, *Kiss Me Deadly*, starring Ralph Meeker. The film has a terrific premise: detective Mike Hammer is driving along a quiet road when he picks up Christina, a desperate hitchhiker on the run from a lunatic asylum. They are soon being chased and find themselves in terrible danger: she doesn't survive the journey and Hammer is nearly killed. He pursues the mystery of where Christina came from and why she was being chased. The twisting plot is everything we love about noir: every suspect seems to end up dead, every lead becomes a dead-end.

Finally, Mike finds the secret Christina was trying to tell him about. It is a Russian doll of a Pandora's box – a box within a box within a locker in a private country club. When Hammer touches the box, he can feel it pulsing with an inner heat. This is an unexpected development in a noir film: we're expecting it to contain diamonds, or stacks of dollar bills, or ideally a Maltese Falcon. Suddenly, the film seems to be entering the world of the supernatural, which sits oddly against the noir tone. But we soon discover that the box contains far more earthly terrors: it is full of highly explosive radioactive material (a reflection of the time in which the film was made). The box would have exploded sooner or later anyway, but it's hard to avoid the conclusion that Hammer would have been less at risk if he'd resisted the temptation to find and then open the elusive box.

The strange, compelling and unpredictable nature of Pandora's box has inspired musicians as well as artists and film-makers. *Love to Love You Baby*, Donna Summer's 1975 album, contains easily the best song with the title 'Pandora's Box'. 'Promises are made to be broken,' sings Summer. 'That's all I ever learned from loving you/ And when you opened up your love to me/ You opened up Pandora's box.' Orchestral Manoeuvres in the Dark released a different song with the same title in 1991, with a music video full of clips of Louise Brooks in the 1929 silent film *Pandora's Box*. Pandora isn't mentioned by name in the song (though it does reference a 'dangerous creation', which could easily be read as Hesiodic by the enthusiastic classicist). In the same year, Aerosmith also released a compilation album, *Pandora's Box*, whose title track dates back to 1974. One interview suggests a theme of women's liberation inspired the lyrics, but, to the untrained ear, it sounds a lot like Steven Tyler has the hots for a woman named Pandora, whose box is euphemistic rather than metaphorical. Though perhaps I am being unfair, and there simply isn't anything which rhymes with 'proud', other than 'well-endowed'.

Even when it isn't explicitly named as an instance of Pandora's box, we know the trope when we hear or see it. In 1994, cinema-goers flocked to Quentin Tarantino's cult hit *Pulp Fiction*. It grossed more than $200 million, which is unusual for a film which also won the Palme d'Or at Cannes. The film has many iconic moments, not least of which is the briefcase which acts as a MacGuffin: we never know why the characters want it, but our desire to know what it contains is only heightened by other people's responses to it. It is valued so highly by characters we believe in that we in turn believe it must be valuable. Yet we never find out why. We only know, as with *Kiss Me Deadly*, that when the box is opened, it contains something which emits light. Fans have speculated on what this might be, but the film never tells us and nor has its writer-director. In 1995, Samuel L. Jackson told *Playboy* magazine that he had asked Tarantino what the case might contain, only to receive the reply: 'Whatever you want it to be.'[22]

And that, surely, is the real secret hidden inside Pandora's jar. It's also an excellent description of Pandora herself. Earlier in this chapter, I quoted the oxymoronic description of her in Hesiod's *Theogony*: *kalon kakon*[23] – 'a beautiful evil' – which Zeus gives to mortals as a penalty for the fire that Prometheus had stolen for us. The phrase is usually translated that way round (a 'pretty bane' is how she is described in the Oxford World's Classics edition). But both words are adjectives, and both can have a moral or physical meaning: *kalos* can be fine, beautiful, pretty, and also morally good, noble or virtuous. *Kakos*, equally, can be bad or evil, and also inept, ugly, unfortunate. We could translate the phrase the other way around: rather than being a beautiful evil, Pandora could be an ugly good. We never do translate it like this, though, because there is so much other evidence piled up in favour of the traditional version: all the gods provide Pandora with lovely qualities, so she must be beautiful. And anyway, Zeus demands her creation as *ant' agathoio* – in return for the good thing (fire). The word *agathos* really is unambiguous: it always means something desirable or good. But the word *anti* is a bit more fluid. It can mean opposite, before, in return for, for the sake of. Translators have always assumed that Pandora is beautiful but evil because Zeus demands payback for the fire mortals have illicitly gained. But *kakon* doesn't have to have a moral dimension at all: we could translate it with equal accuracy to mean a loss, a misfortune, an injury. Something bad for us, but not something ill-intentioned in its own right. Zeus may wish us ill, in other words, but that doesn't mean Pandora herself is evil, any more than the lightning which Zeus hurls at those of us who displease him is evil. Lightning is neutral, neither good nor bad, however much we fear it. Perhaps we can accept that Pandora is the same, unless we choose to see her otherwise.

JOCASTA

In the fourth century bce, the comic poet Antiphanes made a pointed remark about the relative difficulty of writing comedy over tragedy.[1] Comedians, he has a character explain, have to invent their plots. Whereas a tragedian just has to mention Oedipus and the audience knows everything else: that his father was Laius, his mother was Jocasta, who his daughters were, what he would do, what he had done.

Was Antiphanes correct, and is he still? Does everyone today know who Oedipus was? And what more do we know about him, beyond the barest branches of his (admittedly complex) family tree? Equally relevant, what do we know about his mother, Jocasta, who shares his downfall? And how does her character shift in the different versions of the stories told about the royal house of Thebes, one of the best-known of all Greek myths? Its modern notoriety is at least in part thanks to Freud, who, in his famed Oedipus complex, posited that all boys go through a phase of wanting to kill their fathers and have sex with their mothers.

Only seven Sophocles plays have survived to the present day, the most famous of which was and remains *Oedipus the King*. Its title in Greek is *Oedipus Tyrannos*, and, for reasons which defy common sense, it is routinely referred to today as *Oedipus Rex*, in spite of the fact that no one involved in it is Roman (the word *rex* is the Latin for 'king') and it makes any normal person think of dinosaurs, which do not feature. About a century after it was first produced, Aristotle would discuss it favourably in his *Poetics*, implying that it was still regularly performed and would be well known to his audience. He thought it the perfect tragedy.

Astonishingly, given its enduring popularity, *Oedipus Tyrannos* only came second in the competition when it was first staged (perhaps in 429 BCE). Sophocles was beaten by Philocles, the nephew of Aeschylus. Ancient and modern scholars have used this fact to prove the terrible stupidity of judges when it comes to making the right choice in creative contests. A generous person might wonder whether perhaps Philocles was not too bad a playwright, if he could produce something which beat *Oedipus*. But certainly his contemporaries were having none of it: the comedian, Aristophanes, referred to Philocles' work leaving a bad taste in the mouth.[2]

The story of Oedipus has an archetypal, almost elemental quality. But what actually happens in that story is very much less certain than we might think. Let's start with Sophocles, since his is the version most likely to be known today, and look at the plot in some detail. The story of Oedipus covers perhaps twenty years and multiple distinct locations (Corinth, Delphi, a crossroads outside Delphi, Mount Cithaeron and Thebes). But the action takes place in a single day and at a single location, outside the gates of the royal house of Thebes (a city-state in Boeotia, in central Greece). Cramming so much backstory into one place and time is – quite aside from the beauty of the verse and the mesmerizing momentum of the plot – an absolutely breathtaking achievement. Particularly when you consider that *Oedipus Tyrannos* is only 1,530 lines long: you could easily see it twice in the time it takes to watch *Hamlet* or *King Lear*.

The play begins with Oedipus, king of Thebes, offering to do whatever it takes to release his fellow citizens from the plague that besets the city. A priest tells him that they need his help: after all, many years earlier, Oedipus freed the city from the Sphinx, so he is known to be good at solving problems. Oedipus is way ahead of them: he has already sent his wife's brother, Creon, to Delphi to ask the Oracle for advice. He's barely finished explaining this when Creon appears onstage with the news that Thebes is polluted with the plague because it is harbouring the murderer of the previous ruler, King Laius. Oedipus asks where Laius died. On his way to Delphi, is the answer. Set upon by thieves and killed. Why didn't you hunt down his killers at the time? asks Oedipus. The Sphinx told us to leave it, his brother-in-law replies. Right, says Oedipus, I'll solve the crime, even though I wasn't here then.

Tiresias, the blind seer, enters and tells Oedipus to leave well alone, implying that he – Oedipus – is himself the man he seeks, the killer of Laius. Oedipus is livid: are you conspiring with Creon, he asks, so he can be king? Remember how I solved the Sphinx's riddle? Do you really want to try and overthrow me? Tiresias warns him that he will regret his words and leaves, muttering the terrible truth about Oedipus' parentage. Oedipus and Creon then also argue, the latter being understandably peeved to find that he has been accused of treason. It was your idea to ask Tiresias for help, Oedipus replies. And now he says I'm the killer. Which I'm not, because I wasn't even here then, so you must be conspiring with one another. No, Creon replies. I don't want to be king. I have plenty of power as your brother-in-law, thanks.

And then, at last, almost halfway through the play, Jocasta enters. She intervenes between her husband – Oedipus – and her brother – Creon, telling Oedipus that he is wrong to suspect Creon. Fine, says Oedipus. He'll probably destroy me, but by all means let him go. Why are you so angry? Jocasta asks. Tiresias says I killed your first husband, Laius, Oedipus says. What do prophets know? she replies. An oracle told Laius he'd be killed by his own son and he wasn't. He was killed by strangers, by bandits, at a place where three roads meet. And his son, our son, was exposed to death years earlier on the mountain when he was three days old.

Wait, Oedipus says. Did you say a place where three roads meet? What did he look like, Laius? He looked a bit like you, says Jocasta. Was he definitely attacked by bandits? Oedipus asks. Did someone say there was a survivor? Send for him. Jocasta wonders what he is frightened of. Well, Oedipus replies, you know I grew up in Corinth. A drunk man at a banquet once told me I was adopted. So I went to Delphi and asked the Oracle, and she told me that I would kill my father and have sex with my mother, and I'd produce incestuous offspring. To avoid this dreadful fate, I decided never to return to Corinth. And, on my way out of Delphi, I met a rude old man at a place where three roads meet and we argued and I killed him (he started it, by the way). I killed his men, too. And now I am afraid that it was Laius and he and I were related and I've done something terrible. But this witness we've sent for apparently said they were attacked by a group of men, in which case, that wasn't me and it's okay.

I remember the witness coming back to Thebes, Jocasta says. He definitely said 'bandits', not one bandit, don't worry. And anyway, prophecies don't mean anything[3] – my son was killed as a baby before he could kill Laius, remember? That's true, Oedipus says. But send for the man anyway. Jocasta leaves the stage, and when she returns, she prays to Apollo. It's a bracing change of attitude, since – only moments ago – she was saying oracles were meaningless.

Suddenly a messenger arrives from Corinth to tell Oedipus that Polybus, the king of Corinth and the man Oedipus believes to be his father, is dead. Jocasta and Oedipus are delighted: if Polybus is dead, then Oedipus didn't kill him. I said not to worry, says Jocasta. Everything's down to chance. You didn't kill your father and you won't marry your mother. Loads of men dream of sleeping with their mothers – it means nothing.[4] And at least you definitely didn't kill your father.

But then the messenger reveals that Oedipus was indeed adopted. He had no need to avoid Corinth after all. The messenger gave

Oedipus to Polybus and Merope when he – Oedipus – was just a baby, with his feet pinned together, hence his name: Oedipus, in Greek, means 'swollen foot'. Where did you get me? asks Oedipus, horrified. From a Theban shepherd, comes the answer. This turns out to be the very man who witnessed and survived the attack on Laius. Jocasta suddenly understands the truth, and begs Oedipus to stop pursuing the mystery of who killed Laius, and of who he is. He refuses to listen and she runs into the palace, saying the only name she has for him is 'wretched'.[5]

The shepherd finally arrives and reluctantly confirms the messenger's story. Oedipus then sees what Jocasta has already guessed: they are not only wife and husband, but mother and son. He goes into the palace, but of course we cannot follow him. We must wait until a palace servant rushes out to say that the queen is dead by her own hand. In one of the most memorable sequences in all of theatre, he then tells us that Oedipus found his wife, hanged, took the brooch pins from her dress and put out his own eyes. Now he has truly seen who he is, he cannot bear to see anything else: blindness is the only possible response. At his own request, he is banished from the city (and his children) by Creon, who assumes the throne.

The play moves with an astonishing momentum. The revelations come raining down on Oedipus so quickly that we barely have time to catch our breath. In one short day, he goes from king, husband, father and son, to widower, murderer, ruin, exile. An equally devastating fall from grace happens to Jocasta, and yet we almost forget about her. But her fate is at least as terrible as that of her son, perhaps more so, because she had less information than he did to begin with, so she has had no time to psychologically prepare herself for anything. When she tells Oedipus about the prophecy Laius received[6] all those years ago, her words are quite plain: the god said that Laius would be killed by their son. As far as she knows, as she explains, her husband was killed by thieves and her son wasn't among them, because he died at three days old, his feet pinned together, slung onto an untrodden place on the mountain. She describes the loss of her baby so bluntly and briskly that it is easy to imagine that it's not much more than a plot point, that it wasn't an especially harrowing ordeal. Child abandonment wasn't uncommon in the ancient world, and child mortality was enormously high: at the time Sophocles wrote these scenes, perhaps as many as a third of infants didn't survive to adulthood. But which of us would mourn a child less because other people's children died too? Jocasta must have been – by temporal necessity in this version of the myth – a very young bride to Laius, because she was still capable of having four children with Oedipus. If she was sixteen when Oedipus was born, and he was sixteen when he arrived in Thebes having bested the Sphinx, she would be thirty-two when they wed, which seems to fit the timeline reasonably well. So by the time she and Oedipus married, she had spent half her life living with the knowledge that she had had a healthy child and he was taken, maimed and left to die. There can be few tortures more cruel.

And once Laius had insisted that her child be killed, she would have known there was no chance of having another (in some versions of the myth, which we'll look at in more detail below, Laius only impregnates her because he gets hopelessly drunk and is overwhelmed by lust. Did she know throughout her pregnancy that the baby would be killed? Or would Laius have let her keep it if she had given birth to a girl? The prophecy is specific about it being his son[7] who would kill him). There are years of grief behind this short speech of Jocasta's. No wonder she tells Oedipus not to listen to prophecies: what good have they ever done her? And after all her pain, Laius was killed by bandits, as any unfortunate traveller might be.

But let's think about what she knows of the oracles involved in this story, compared with what Oedipus knows. She has been told one thing, which is that Laius would be killed by his – their – son. She thinks this is impossible because her son has died, but even if by some miracle it had happened, that is all the information she ever had, and it has long since ceased to be important. Oedipus, meanwhile, has far more to work with. Firstly, there's the drunk at the banquet who tells him he's adopted. He questions his parents, but they deny it. Still, he's uncertain, so he goes to Delphi to consult the Oracle. Apollo doesn't answer the question about adoption, but does tell him something far more terrible: that he is destined to kill his father and marry his mother. One might legitimately suggest that, if it has been predicted that you will kill your father and marry your mother, and if you had (separately) been told you were adopted, it might be a good idea to avoid killing any men of an age to be your father and marrying any women who could conceivably be your mother. That he doesn't, and that we don't feel compelled to shout this out during productions of *Oedipus Tyrannos*, is testimony to Sophocles' skill and the sheer, relentless pace of a play that allows Oedipus to pelt towards the realization of his crimes while somehow also dangling the truth just out of reach for what feels like forever. Nonetheless, he entered into their marriage knowing far more than Jocasta possibly could about its potential horror. So at some level, conscious or subconscious, he is surely less shocked than she must be by their horrific crime, since she only knows about its possibility on the same day that she finds out its truth.

And when that day of reckoning finally comes, Oedipus' celebrated cleverness is at the very core of the play. The chorus beg him to help lift the plague, to help solve the crime of who killed Laius, because he is famously clever. Both the priest at the beginning of the play and Oedipus himself mention his brilliance in solving the riddle of the Sphinx. And yet it is Jocasta, long before Oedipus, who realizes the truth of who they both are: wife and husband, mother and son.

She is the cleverest person in the room and we barely notice it because we're too busy concentrating on Oedipus. She has time to withdraw into the palace, make the decision to take her own life and carry that out, all before he works out what she realizes immediately.

And when Jocasta hangs herself, she is making an explicit statement. In Greek myth, hanging is usually the method of suicide employed by virginal girls (it is the method Antigone, the daughter of Jocasta and Oedipus, will employ in Sophocles' *Antigone*, for example). So when Jocasta hangs herself, she is not only ending what she perceives to be a cursed life and marriage. She is also wishing herself back to the time before Oedipus was conceived, to when she had never been married, never had a child, never had sex.

Why has it been so easy for audiences to overlook the terrible fate which befalls Jocasta? We're encouraged, certainly, to focus on Oedipus: he has more than five times as many lines as any other character in the play. And the character who has the second-largest number of lines isn't Jocasta, it's Creon. In this 1,530-line play, Jocasta has just over 120 lines: not even a tenth of the whole. So perhaps it's inevitable that we respond more to Oedipus' predicament. Also, he is still alive at the end of the play. His face (or theatrical mask, as it would have been in fifth-century BCE Athens) is a ruin of blackened sockets and pain. Jocasta's hanging takes place offstage, so we aren't made to confront the horror of what has happened to her in quite the same way.

This strange fate of Jocasta's – to be overlooked, even as she is demolished by the same destiny that overtakes her son – is one which seems to follow her through history. But it didn't begin like that. In her earliest incarnation, we meet her when she is already dead. In Book Eleven of Homer's *Odyssey*, Odysseus visits the Underworld.

He needs to consult the now-dead Tiresias about his best route home, and while he's there he sees a parade of the famous dead. Among them is *kalēn Epikastēn*, beautiful Epicaste, the mother of Oedipus.[8] She committed a grave act in ignorance, Homer tells us. She married her son. The whole story takes Homer ten short lines to explain: Oedipus killed his father and married her. The gods immediately made these things known to men. Oedipus lived in Thebes among the Cadmeans, suffering greatly at the hands of the gods. She went down to Hades, having fastened a noose to the lofty roof, over-whelmed by grief, leaving many sorrows behind for him.

The differences between this earliest extant version of the myth and the Sophocles version are important. Firstly, Jocasta has a different name: Epicaste isn't a variant spelling. It's definitely the same woman, though, as we can see from the description of what happened to her. But then the story deviates from the version we know: the gods make things known *aphar* – 'immediately'.[9] In Sophocles' version of the myth, Oedipus and Jocasta have four children before their incest is revealed. The Oracle had told Oedipus he would produce incestuous offspring when he went to consult Apollo at Delphi all those years earlier. But this is obviously not part of the story Homer is telling: here, the revelation takes place as soon as Oedipus and Epicaste are married. There is also no mention of Oedipus being blinded, or banished: he remains living among the Cadmeans (a poetic word for Thebans: Thebes was founded by Cadmus). Epicaste hangs herself, as in Sophocles, and Oedipus is left with a raft of sorrows. Brief as it is, the story is told from both perspectives in roughly equal amounts; it starts and ends with Epicaste.

The issue of whether Oedipus and Jocasta / Epicaste have children has provoked debate for millennia. Pausanias, in his *Description of Greece*, doesn't believe that Oedipus and Jocasta had children together, quoting the above passage from Homer to back up his argument.[10] Rather, he says, the children's mother was a woman named Eurygeneia, the daughter of Hyperphas. This is made quite clear, Pausanias adds, by the author of the *Oedipodeia*. Sadly, for those of us who would like to know more about this version of events, the *Oedipodeia* – an epic poem about Oedipus written around the same time as the *Iliad* and the *Odyssey* were composed – does not survive. But still, we can glean from Pausanias (who, living in the second century CE, could presumably lay his hands on a copy) that Oedipus and Jocasta marry, have their incestuous relationship revealed immediately, or near enough, and then Oedipus goes on to remarry and father children with a second wife.

If the story shifts as it does between Homer and Sophocles, what are the elements that remain intact in both? Son kills father, mother and son marry, the true nature of their relationship becomes known, mother hangs herself. But even those stark details don't hold up in every version of the myth. When Euripides takes on the story of Jocasta in his *Phoinissai* – *The Phoenician Women* – in 409 BCE, he presents us with yet another variant. The play is set some time after the revelation that Jocasta and Oedipus are mother and son, and it begins with a long speech by Jocasta. So right from the outset, we can see a crucial difference between Euripides' version and the over-lapping versions of the story in Sophocles and Homer: in Euripides, Jocasta doesn't die when the truth about her marriage is revealed. She doesn't hang herself, she continues to live in the royal palace of Thebes. Her sons, Polynices and Eteocles, are heirs to the throne. Their response to Oedipus' disgrace and self-blinding was to lock him away in the palace as a prisoner and hope everyone would forget about him. Their mother, on the other hand, has remained a valued member of the royal household. *The Phoenician Women* was produced about twenty years after *Oedipus Tyrannos* was performed at the Dionysia, and Jocasta's opening monologue therefore serves a dual function. It sets the scene for the play we're about to watch. But it also jolts us into acknowledging that the story we're watching now isn't quite what we thought it was (Euripides makes a habit of this, as we'll see later, with *Medea*).

Jocasta begins by telling us the backstory so we know where we are now. She starts with Laius. He and Jocasta were childless, she explains, so he went to consult the Oracle at Delphi. Apollo was quite certain and specific about Laius' prospects of fatherhood. Have a child, and he'll kill you, and your whole house will run with blood.[11] Pretty unequivocal advice, we might think. But Laius disregarded it when he was drunk. Realizing his error, he arranged for the child to be exposed on the mountains, but servants of Polybus (the king of Corinth) found the baby and gave him to their queen, who tricked the king into believing the child was hers.

It's interesting just how much more focus there is on the feelings of women in this speech than in any earlier version we have. Euripides was an astonishing writer of women. He wrote more and better female roles than almost any other male playwright who has ever lived. Which is all the more remarkable when we remember that the actors playing female roles in the Athenian theatres would have been young men, and the audience may very well have been all-male too, at least at the Dionysia when these plays were first performed. It's not just that women in Euripides' plays have agency and make decisions which advance the plot (although they do), it's also that he writes them with a rare insight into areas which simply don't feature in men's lives in the same way. The Oedipus story which Sophocles gives us can be read almost as a parable for male anxiety (this, surely, is part of what made it so fascinating to Freud, who liked to theorize about men because he found women such a puzzle). Laius is terrified of being overpowered by his son (the fear of literal or metaphorical castration at the hands of sons is a theme throughout Greek myth, as we saw in the last chapter, with Ouranos, Kronos and Zeus).

Polybus is terrified of not having a male heir and so is willing to take an abandoned child and call it his own. The secrecy which he and Merope maintain over this adoption is part of the problem: if they had been honest with Oedipus about his origins, he might never have left Corinth to consult the Oracle, and then fulfilled his awful destiny. Oedipus' paranoia and swiftness to anger are revealed early in the play: Creon and Tiresias aren't conspiring against him, as he initially believes, but his fear that they seek to undermine him is genuine and crippling. We can easily believe this man was provoked to a lethal fury by Laius' obnoxious driving when they met at the crossroads (*Oedipus Tyrannos* must be the earliest example of a tragedy caused by road rage).

At every stage in his Sophoclean story, the destiny Oedipus tries to avoid is brought closer by the actions of men, well-meaning or otherwise: Laius who fathers him and can't kill him; the shepherd who won't kill him; the Corinthian messenger who saves him; the drunk man who tells Oedipus he's adopted; Polybus who lies about the adoption; Laius again, who antagonizes him and assaults him; Tiresias who always knew the truth but refused to divulge it. And underpinning the whole thing, an anxiety which was prevalent throughout the ancient world, as we can see from the laws which restrict women's behaviour and movement: who is the father of this child? No one ever really knows except the mother.

And no one thinks to ask the mother how she feels, until Euripides comes along and gives Jocasta the opening monologue of *The Phoenician Women*. And the rawness of her pain is almost tangible even years after the events. Laius fathered her son while drunk, and when he realized he'd ignored Apollo's advice, he pierced the baby's ankles with a metal pin and handed him over to servants to abandon him on the mountain. This is all the information we need to make sense of the story (it's pretty much what we get in Sophocles). But Euripides gives Jocasta more to say. The shepherds don't give her child to Polybus, the king. Rather, she says, they take the baby to the queen (Euripides doesn't name Merope, but let's call her that) and she passes the baby off as her own. Just this small detail gives us a huge insight into Merope's life. She and her husband have clearly been trying and failing to conceive: she wants a baby, and for that baby to be thought of as her own child. She and Polybus presumably have sex – because he believes Oedipus is their son – but are not sufficiently close for him to be surprised when she claims to have given birth with no warning. Not only is there a physical gap between them (most people would notice if a woman who had never looked nine months pregnant suddenly produced a child, particularly if they were married to that woman), there is also an emotional gap: Merope and Polybus both wanted a child, it seems, but she can only have one if she lies to him. Presumably, unlike in Sophocles' version, he didn't want to adopt.

And look at the language Jocasta uses to describe what happened: She nursed the child my labour pains produced.[12] The physicality of the two women – of Jocasta's body being wrenched in pain, of Merope's body producing milk for a child she hadn't given birth to – is devastating. Jocasta's terrible loss, the agony of being deprived of her newborn son, is not forgotten, even decades later. Because how could it have been? And how can we blame Merope for anything when her body was crying out for the child she unexpectedly acquired? Do the Corinthian servants know of her desperation? Is that why they bring the child to her rather than Polybus?

Jocasta hurries through the description of Oedipus killing Laius. Why drag it out, she asks. *Pais patera kainei*: 'son killed father'.[13] And then she goes on to explain that Creon, her brother, had been so keen to get rid of the Sphinx (who was outside Thebes making a nuisance of herself) that he had offered Jocasta in marriage to whoever solved the Sphinx's riddle. It's all very well making this kind of blanket offer, but you certainly open yourself up to the risk of having to marry your sister off to a much younger (and, as it transpires, related) man. Creon is another name in the list of men who – for good reasons and bad – have caused Jocasta and Oedipus untold grief.

But there are two more names to add to the list in this Euripidean version of Jocasta's story: the sons she bore to Oedipus, Polynices and Eteocles. As soon as they are old enough, the shame they feel for their father's crimes means they decide to lock Oedipus away, a prisoner in his own palace. He is so incensed by this that he issues the unholiest of curses upon them, praying that they should turn on one another. To try and avoid this curse (these sons have apparently learned nothing from their father's attempts to evade his destiny), the two young men decide that Polynices should go into voluntary exile for one year while Eteocles has the throne. At the end of a year, they will swap.

They don't, of course. Eteocles refuses to give up the throne, and Polynices declares war on his city (this is also the plot of Aeschylus' play *Seven Against Thebes*. Thebes has seven gates to defend, so seven heroes march against it). Jocasta has stepped in to try and resolve the impasse, persuading her sons to meet and talk before all-out war destroys the city. She concludes her opening speech by begging Zeus to intervene and make peace between the two men.

But Zeus doesn't hear her prayer and discussions between Polynices and Eteocles break down. Jocasta finally gives way to despair, saying: I have given birth to so many sorrows.[14] The double meaning is evident. Jocasta takes her daughter Antigone with her to try to reason with her warring sons. But they are too late. The two men kill one another in single combat and Jocasta takes the sword which lies on the ground between them and drives it through her own throat.

Euripides' version of Jocasta has a great deal more to say than Sophocles' (and no one speaks in Homer's version). She also has a lot more to do. Because she doesn't die at the point when her maternal relationship with Oedipus becomes known, and because Oedipus stays in Thebes but behind closed doors, Jocasta acquires a political role. She negotiates with her sons like a high-level diplomat. Her role as their mother is not the only card she plays (she pleads with Eteocles to think what will happen to the young women of Thebes, for example, if the city loses the war he and Polynices are determined to have). And when she cannot save her boys, she takes her own life in a masculine way: she dies on the battlefield, using a sword picked up from between the bodies of her sons to end her life. This Jocasta is a very different woman from the one we thought we knew.

And it isn't only Euripides who presents Jocasta in this light. He and Sophocles would almost certainly have known a work by the lyric poet Stesichorus which focused on a different part of the Theban story. This poem sadly doesn't survive. Or at least it didn't, until an incredible (and relatively recent) stroke of luck. At the turn of the twentieth century, Egyptologists across Europe were pursuing their mania for collecting relics and removing them from Egypt. Howard Carter may be the best-known in the UK, but in France, Pierre Jouguet and Gustave Lefebvre were accruing their discoveries at a new institute for Egyptology at the University of Lille. One of the objects they acquired was a mummy, packed into its case with cartonnage – strips of papyrus – to keep it from being damaged. Quite understandably, all interest was focused on the mummy, none at all on the packing material. So it wasn't until 1974 that the scraps of papyrus were investigated, and read. They were covered in Greek writing, which included some poetry. And among the poems were 120 lines which scholars have identified as being a dramatization of the Theban story by Stesichorus of Himera, a lyric poet who lived about 150 years before Sophocles wrote *Oedipus Tyrannos*.[15] More excitingly still, they are lines which appear to be the voice of Jocasta. It seems tremendously appropriate that she was hiding in plain sight for over seventy years before anyone noticed.

This Jocasta is – as we will surely recognize from Euripides – hoping that prophecies which have been issued will not come true. But the plot seems far closer to Euripides than Sophocles: Jocasta is alive after her marriage has been uncovered as incestuous, and her sons are at war with one another for the throne of Thebes. She prays that, if the prophecies which have been spoken must come true, she will die before her sons fulfil their dark destiny. She even proposes a diplomatic solution to the problem of Eteocles and Polynices. One should keep the throne, she suggests, and the other should take ownership of all Oedipus' gold and possessions and go off into exile as a rich man.[16]

There are two things to note about this: the first is that in every version of her story, Jocasta becomes a more complex, more rounded character with every word she says. In *Oedipus Tyrannos*, we get a fairly slender portrait of a woman whose life is entirely dictated by the decisions of men. In *The Phoenician Women*, we finally hear her talk about what that means and how it feels. And here, in the earlier fragment of the Lille Stesichorus, we have a strong political leader, negotiating with warring parties who happen to be her sons. This version of her (along with Euripides' many echoes of it) informs the similar version of Jocasta we find in Statius' *Thebaid*, an epic Latin poem – based on several Greek models – which was written in the late first century CE.

The second thing we might notice is how irrelevant Oedipus seems in consequence. The character who owned the stage in Sophocles is simply not important in this earlier speech by Stesichorus. In Oedipus' absence, his wealth and throne are being divided between his sons in the hope of preventing a war. Jocasta seems not to consider his feelings or opinions: her regal power, and the political and military emergency, means she doesn't have to. This is perhaps also why Oedipus doesn't appear in *The Phoenician Women* until 200 lines before the end. When women take up space, there is less available for men. But it means we get a whole story instead of half of one. It scarcely needs saying that our understanding of the story of Oedipus is enriched when we know the story of Jocasta, and vice versa.

But Jocasta can be hard to find. Her invisibility is only heightened by the absence of her in the visual arts, where we might expect to find vase paintings or sculptures of one of myth's most notorious mothers. In fact, no certain image of Jocasta survives from the ancient world at all. There is only one vase which scholars have even sought to associate with a scene in *Oedipus Tyrannos*. The play was so celebrated in the fifth and fourth centuries BCE that it seems impossible that vase painters wouldn't have wanted to reproduce scenes from it. And yet we don't have any cup or vase which presents us with an unambiguous image from Sophocles' masterpiece. The most common representation of Oedipus (and one which has proven inspirational to painters throughout history) is from his life before the events of the play, when he is answering the riddle of the Sphinx. A beautiful cup in the Vatican Museums from around 470 BCE shows this scene:[17] Oedipus sits pensively, chin resting on his hand, legs crossed, pointed hat shielding his busy brain from the sun. In front of him, on a small pedestal, sits the Sphinx, tail winding out behind her, wings poised. She looks down at Oedipus, awaiting his answer. In some versions of the myth, when she does eventually receive his response, she throws herself off a cliff. Oedipus, we might note, is a dangerous man to play games with.

So if we have no unambiguous images of Jocasta, what of an ambiguous one? There are fragments of a large *krater* in the Archaeological Museum in Syracuse, Sicily.[18] They show a grave, dark-haired, bearded man and a woman standing behind him, holding her robe up to her face. She has a deeply serious expression. They must be the parents of the two small children with dark curls and long robes who stand beside them – one in front of their father, one next to their mother. The adults seem to be receiving news from a white-haired man to our left, and whatever the news is, it apparently isn't good. Behind the robed woman is a column and, behind that, a second woman stands, facing the opposite way. Her hand is held up to her cheek, fingers splayed: is she eavesdropping on the main scene?

Expert pot-readers have suggested that this scene is from Sophocles' play: that it represents the moment when the Corinthian messenger reveals that Oedipus was adopted and Jocasta realizes the terrible truth, a truth that her husband will soon work out. Her robe lifted to cover her face gives us a visual jolt, reminding us of the fabric she will tie round her neck. The pins which hold the drapes of her dress in place are the ones Oedipus will use to put out his eyes. The two children are Antigone and Ismene, the couple's daughters, who aren't present in the messenger scene in Sophocles, but appear at the end of the play to bid their father farewell. Perhaps the vase painter has included that element from the later scene for additional pathos.

But none of this ingenious reading tells us who the other woman, the listening one, might be. There are no other female characters in Sophocles' play, besides Jocasta and the children. And are the children definitely girls? The pot has been assumed to be Oedipus and Jocasta because their two daughters are the girls we are mostly likely to remember when we think of young sisters in Greek myth. The rest of the scene – older man, younger man and woman, other woman nearby – is pretty non-specific. But if the girls are actually boys, as Professor Edith Hall has proposed,[19] the scene could be from another play entirely. Have we assumed the children are girls because we expect girls to have long hair and long dresses? That sounds plausible enough until Hall points out the similarity with a vase painting of a scene from Euripides' *Alcestis*.[20] Alcestis has a son and a daughter, and the son appears to be wearing a long robe, just like the children on the Syracuse pot. So perhaps the couple on this pot are Oedipus and Jocasta, but they may well not be.

Jocasta has been similarly ill-served by later artists. Again, Oedipus is often shown solving the riddle of the Sphinx (which is itself an unusual image: how often does one see a painting which can best be described as 'Man Thinks of Answer to Random Question'?) but rarely with his wife. There are two interesting nineteenth-century French paintings of her, one by Alexandre Cabanel and one by Édouard Toudouze. Cabanel's *Oedipus Separating from Jocasta* (1843)[21] shows Oedipus embracing one of his daughters, presumably Antigone. The other daughter, Ismene, is catching the body of her mother as she loses consciousness. An old woman behind her – swaddled in a green robe, her face a mask of horror – helps Ismene support Jocasta's weight. Jocasta is falling backwards from her husband: only the very tips of the fingers of her left hand graze Oedipus' hand as she slips away.

Twenty-eight years later, Édouard Toudouze[22] painted a version of the scene we have looked at in Euripides' *The Phoenician Women*. Oedipus sits holding the white hand of his wife, who is draped in black, dead at his feet. His old battle-helmet is on the step next to him, decorated with a sphinx, commemorating his great victory over the monster. A flame-haired Antigone comforts her father, looking down at her poor mother. Antigone's two brothers, Polynices and Eteocles, are laid out behind her, united in death as they could not be in life. Every other character, dead or alive, is obscured by the presence of Oedipus. Even their names are lost: the painting is called *Farewell of Oedipus to the Corpses of his Wife and Sons*.

Does this give us a hint at the answer of where Jocasta disappears to? The fixation on Oedipus sucks all the light and air out of the rest of the Theban cycle. This is exemplified by Freud's response to Sophocles: it's Oedipus who gets the complex. The other characters in Oedipus' immediate family never seem as fully formed because in practically every version of the myth they and their stories are different, and perhaps, as a modern audience, we simply prefer the certainty of Oedipus: always killing his father and marrying his mother, no matter what else happens. In some versions of the Theban saga, Polynices is the aggressor and Eteocles the victim; but sometimes it's the other way round. In Sophocles' version of *Antigone*, she is the older sister, engaged to her cousin Haemon, but forced to suicide by the cruel regime of her uncle, Creon. In the fragments we have of Euripides' version of *Antigone*, however, she survives the wrath of her uncle, and lives to marry Haemon; they go on to have a son. In Euripides' *The Phoenician Women*, things are different again: Haemon doesn't survive to marry her. And when the French playwright, Jean Anouilh, took on Antigone's story in 1944, he reversed the birth order of Ismene and Antigone: appropriate, if excessive, religious fervour in an older sibling in fifth-century BCE Athens becomes the behaviour of a rebellious younger sibling during the Second World War. As we change, so these characters have also changed as if to match us.

We can find out more about Jocasta, unpeel the layers to discover what they might reveal, but we have to look hard to do it. In the work of poets and playwrights, she shifts so we can never quite get a fix on her, this woman who marries her son and either does or doesn't take her own life, does or doesn't bear four more children, does or doesn't become a diplomatic political power in her own right, does or doesn't take her life when her sons destroy one another. And in the visual arts she disappears from view almost entirely. I suspect we don't see her reflected back at us from paintings because she has committed the ultimate sin against art: she is an older woman. And while painters never tire of showing us women and girls in their twenties or teens, they tend to be far less keen to show us a woman in her forties or fifties.

There is an additional danger to Jocasta, perhaps, which is that she is a woman who has power that we don't quite understand. Again, this is partly because it shifts and she changes along with it. In *The Phoenician Women*, she is an important regal figure, but in her earlier life, which she tells us of at the start of that play – robbed of her baby, married off at her brother's whim to whoever solved the riddle of the Sphinx – she was little more than a chattel. And how is it that she and Oedipus marry, in spite of the warning he has had about a sexual relationship with his mother? Can we conclude that she is fiercely attractive to him? This idea provoked sniggers even in the ancient world: in Aristophanes' comic play *The Frogs*, he has the tragedian Aeschylus say that Oedipus was the unluckiest man who ever lived:[23] abandoned in the cold, two swollen feet, and then he marries a woman old enough to be his mother. The very idea.

Perhaps Oedipus isn't attracted to Jocasta, but just wants to marry into the kingdom of Thebes (although he is already son and heir to the king of Corinth, so he is hardly lacking in status before he meets Jocasta). But in most versions of their story, they go on to have four children: this is no marriage of convenience, but one of love, and perhaps even lust. We know the alternative – a sexless, distant marriage – is perfectly possible (Merope's husband Polybus not even realizing that she had adopted a son rather than given birth to one). But Oedipus and Jocasta do not have that, so she is that rarest and most dangerous of things: a woman who doesn't become invisible to men even as she ages. How do we cope with a woman like that? All too often, the answer has been to ignore her.

And that is the core of Jocasta, although some writers and artists have chosen not to see her. She is a woman of sexual potency who transforms from total passivity at the hands of Laius in her youth to something far more complicated, far harder to categorize, as she ages. No wonder it took the genius of Euripides to put words into her mouth.

HELEN

HELEN OF TROY, HELEN OF SPARTA. NO MATTER WHICH CITY WE attach her to, she is both a threat and a promise: Helen of Joy, Helen of Slaughter, as Priam calls her, in Simon Armitage's *The Last Days of Troy*. She is the face that 'launch'd a thousand ships / And burnt the topless towers of Ilium', as Marlowe has Dr Faustus describe her. 'Sweet Helen,' he continues, 'make me immortal with a kiss.' This version of Helen makes no reply to Faustus. In fact, she says nothing at all. A beautiful woman whom men find all the more alluring because she is essentially mute? I know, I always think the shock will kill me too.

Marlowe didn't coin the idea of a thousand ships: the phrase appears in Aeschylus' *Agamemnon*, and in Euripides' plays several times.[1] Andromache, for example, in his play of the same name, describes Greece as *chilionaus*, 'having a thousand ships'. The number became integral to Helen's myth (although Homer's *Iliad* actually lists rather more than a thousand ships: almost 1,200 in fact). Helen's name has even been used as a tongue-in-cheek unit of measurement: if one Helen is so beautiful that she launches a thousand ships, then a millihelen is the unit of beauty required to launch a single ship. Isaac Asimov claimed to have coined the term.[2]

But all those ships, all that destruction, all for the sake of one woman? Was Helen intrinsically ruinous? Or is it possible that she has provided a convenient cover story? That's certainly what Euripides allows her to argue in *The Trojan Women*: the defence of Helen is almost as old as the accusations against her. But if we are truly to understand Helen, perhaps we should begin at the beginning. Which in this instance – somewhat surprisingly – is an egg.

Almost everything about Helen is contested, beginning with her parentage. She is brought up as the daughter of Tyndareus, king of Sparta, and his wife, Leda. But most sources, at least from Homer onwards, call her the daughter of Zeus.[3] In Euripides' play *Helen*, she describes Tyndareus as her father, but explains there's a story that Zeus took the form of a swan fleeing from an eagle, and used this deceit to get into Leda's bed. It raises a number of questions, even for those of us accustomed to the quirks of Greek myth. Leda is more susceptible to a seductive swan than a seductive man? That is a niche porn category. Or perhaps it isn't: the image of Leda and her swan/swain has been enormously popular in visual arts throughout history. Tintoretto, Leonardo da Vinci and Michelangelo all painted versions of this story, although only copies of the latter two survive. Tintoretto's swan looks particularly pleased with himself as Leda tries vainly to conceal her birdmance from a maid. She places a hand on the swan's wing, as though she might be able to pass the rest of him off as some sort of elaborate cushion. Leonardo's Leda looks down at the four babies (one of whom is Helen) that have emerged from a pair of cracked eggshells at her feet, and her expression seems to convey that she now rather regrets the whole feathery affair. Only Michelangelo gives the scene an intimacy which seems to have an actual sexual charge: the swan's neck emerges from between Leda's embracing thighs and they gaze at one another lovingly, mouth to beak.

A beautiful fresco of the same scene was uncovered in Pompeii in 2018, on the Via del Vesuvio. The story was so popular among the Romans, in fact, that they used it to decorate mass-produced lamps. The Pompeian fresco shows a decidedly sneaky-looking swan nestled in beside a rather worried Leda, her brown eyes wide. His webbed foot is balanced on her naked left thigh, and archaeologists believe the image would have decorated a bedroom wall. Well, if not there, then where?

Even Helen doesn't seem fully convinced by the story of her birth, however. He tricked my mother Leda into bed, she says, if that story is true.[4] But then her next words make the whole thing seem unimportant: 'I'm called Helen.' Egg, swan, believe what you like about her parents: she's Helen, and you all know who that is. In one version of the story, however, Leda plays a different role. In the lost epic poem, the *Cypria*, we're told by Pseudo-Apollodorus (an Athenian scholar writing about the poem in the second century BCE) that Helen was the daughter of Zeus and the goddess Nemesis.[5] Nemesis changed into a goose to escape the prospect of imminent, unwanted sex with Zeus. In response to this, Zeus became a swan and had sex with her anyway. Nemesis ditched the egg containing the embryonic Helen and a shepherd found it and gave it to Leda, who kept it in a box until it hatched. When Helen appeared, Leda raised her as her daughter. In Euripides' play, Helen says she has always been considered a *teras* – which can be translated as freak, portent, or monster.[6]

Whichever version of the myth we prefer, Zeus appears to have fathered Helen in swan form, and Helen seems to have been born from an egg. She is then raised in Sparta by its king and queen, Tyndareus and Leda. She is one of several siblings, perhaps all born from eggs (as the Leonardo painting shows). Her most notorious sister was Clytemnestra (the two sisters would marry two brothers: Menelaus and Agamemnon). And their most famous brothers were Castor and Polydeuces, whose exact parentage is as contested as Helen's. They are either both sons of Tyndareus, both sons of Zeus, or one of them was a son of Zeus (Polydeuces, known later as Pollux). They're often referred to in Greek texts as the Dioscouri, sons of Zeus.

If Helen's birth is a little peculiar, it is her childhood – when she is kidnapped – that is more upsetting for a modern audience. Theseus

– best-known for his labyrinthine minotaur-slaying – is no longer a young hero, but a man of around fifty years of age when Helen is a child.[7] After the deaths of their respective wives, Theseus and his friend Pirithoos decide they would both like to marry daughters of Zeus. Pirithoos wants to try abducting Persephone from Hades, which we might best characterize as a needlessly risky endeavour. Theseus decides that he would like to make Helen his wife. She is seven years old at the time Theseus abducts her. Even ancient authors – whose ideas of sexual propriety do not always coincide with our own – are squeamish about this. Plutarch[8] tells us that most earlier writers tell the story this way: Theseus and Pirithoos snatched Helen away from the temple of Artemis in Sparta (there is an additional pathos in this detail: Helen was dancing in honour of Artemis, the virgin goddess, when she was abducted). Once they had made their escape, they drew lots to decide who should get Helen as a wife. Theseus won the draw, and they put Helen in the safekeeping of another friend near Athens, with instructions to keep the whole affair secret.

Helen's brothers, the Dioscuri, then demanded Helen's return. The people of Athens could not return her because they didn't know where she had been hidden, so Helen's brothers declared war on Athens. Fighting was fierce, but the brothers and their army were victorious. They then took Helen back to Sparta, and also enslaved Theseus' mother, Aithra, whom he had left as a companion for her. The women in Theseus' life rarely prosper: his lovers, most famously Ariadne, are abandoned, his wife Phaedra takes her own life, his mother is enslaved in retribution for his actions.

A Greek historian, Diodorus Siculus, writing in the first century BCE, tells us Helen was ten years old at the time of this abduction,[9] but she surpassed all in beauty. Adding three years to Helen's age makes the story no more palatable, at least to us. The notion of a child being more beautiful than all other women or girls, and this being a valid reason to kidnap her, is a deeply unsavoury one. Not least because, in some versions of this story, Helen has given birth to Theseus' daughter[10] before she can be reclaimed and taken home. But the ancient historians who relate this story seem to find it pretty unpleasant too, hence their rather ham-fisted attempts to make it less so (explaining her great beauty in spite of her extreme youth, for example).

So, even as a child, Helen apparently caused a war. But most of us would feel that this was an unfair characterization of the events described above. Surely we would all stop short of blaming a child for her own abduction? In fact, it is the behaviour of Theseus and Pirithoos – determined to take wives with little thought for the consequences – and the response of Castor and Polydeuces that causes blood to be shed. Helen is nothing but a beautiful pawn.

So what of the second war fought over Helen? The Trojan War is one of literature's greatest stories, an epic saga which has shaped storytelling in the western world for more than two and half thousand years. Two of our very earliest texts tell the story of this conflict, one way or another: Homer's *Iliad* is set in the final, tenth year of the war, his *Odyssey* in its aftermath. And who do the Greeks and Trojans alike blame for the catastrophic loss of life on all sides? Helen, of course. In Euripides' *The Trojan Women*, Hecabe, the queen of Troy, finally meets Menelaus, Helen's Greek husband who waged a ten-year war for her return. Her first words to this man who has cost her everything – her husband, her sons, her city – are brutal: I praise you, Menelaus, if you'll kill your wife. Avoid seeing her, or she'll fill you with longing. She captures the eyes of men, destroys their cities, burns down their houses, she has such magical power. I know her, and you know her, and so does everyone who has suffered.[11]

It is a bracing introduction to the woman who is about to arrive onstage. Before we look at Helen's response, let's go back to the very beginning of the war. In fact, let's go back earlier still, to see how justified Hecabe's fury might be. What did persuade all those Greeks to set sail for Troy and fight for the return of the wife of a man many of them would never even have met? And how did Helen end up married to Menelaus in the first place?

Ostensibly, Helen's stepfather, Tyndareus, has a minor role in her story. But if we are to give any single mortal the blame for setting the Trojan War in motion, we might legitimately say it was him. Faced with a flotilla of suitors for his beautiful stepdaughter, he was nervous of choosing one over the others. Kings from all over Greece – either in person or by messenger, depending on the version of the story we read – made their offers for Helen when she reached marriageable age. The offers were all accompanied by gifts, which must have dulled the pain of betrothal admin a little. But Tyndareus could see the risks involved: whomever he chose as the lucky bride-groom, he would be making very many more enemies than friends. And given the power disparities between the suitors – some able to command large armies, others less so – how to pick one without several other mighty candidates either declaring war or abducting Helen? As we have seen, this wasn't an idle concern: heroes like Theseus and Pirithoos might well have decided that they were en-titled to the most beautiful woman in the world.

So Tyndareus came up with a plan. In order to be considered as Helen's potential husband, the suitors had to pledge an oath (in person, if they had turned up in Sparta to make their case. At home, taken on trust, if they were conducting the whole thing remotely). This story wasn't mentioned by Homer in either the *Iliad* or the *Odyssey*, but it was almost certainly related by Stesichorus in the mid-sixth century BCE, and later writers like Pseudo-Apollodorus also refer to it, with varying numbers and names of suitors.[12] Each man had to swear that, if he was unlucky in his bid for Helen, he none-theless agreed that he would fight for her safe return to her husband, whoever he was, if she was taken away by another man.

The simplicity of the plan was impressive. All those rival claims, all the potential jealousies cancelled out at a stroke: the price for having a chance to marry Helen was defending the man who did marry Helen. Pseudo-Apollodorus also tells us that Odysseus came up with the idea for this oath, and it has the ring of an Odyssean scheme: simple, brilliant, but with a sting in the tail. Once all had agreed to it, either Tyndareus chose Menelaus or, as Euripides and other writers[13] have it, Helen chose her own bridegroom. And if every suitor was less than delighted, then at least they could be content that a war of the kind begun by Theseus with the Dioscuri had been averted: no Greek hero would be so foolish as to take on the collective might of every other Greek leader. The only thing which didn't seem to have occurred to anyone, not even the sharp-witted Odysseus, was that Helen might be taken from her home by a man who hadn't sworn the oath. One who wasn't even a Greek.

Paris, or Alexandros (to give him the name some Greek writers prefer), was a Trojan prince. The son of Priam and Hecabe, the king and queen of Troy, he seduced or abducted Helen from her home in Sparta, again depending on the version of the myth you prefer. In the *Iliad*, Homer has Helen berate herself for eloping with Paris,[14] saying she should have drowned in the sea before she had come with him to Troy. She wishes that Paris had been a better man, but it is herself she wishes dead. She blames them both for Troy's predicament, but she names herself first: 'because of me and Alexandros . . .' And this version of the story – handsome prince meets beautiful queen, who abandons her husband to run away with him – provides the ammunition Hecabe needs for her vitriolic assessment of Helen's character in *The Trojan Women*. Indeed, it has provided countless writers with the opportunity to blame Helen for the war: she is the face that launched a thousand ships, after all. Paris' lovely face doesn't warrant a mention, apparently.

But when Euripides has Helen arrive onstage, immediately after Hecabe has demanded that Menelaus kill her, he presents things rather differently. His Helen is nowhere near as accepting of either sole or major responsibility for the war. She is on trial for her life, albeit somewhat after the fact; the whole Greek army has already decided that she deserves to die: 'They gave you to me to kill,' Menelaus tells her.[15] So Helen makes what we recognize as the speech for the defence that she didn't receive, as her death sentence was decided in her absence. It is a dazzling piece of writing: a legal defence, given in verse, which makes the audience wonder if Euripides should have turned his hand to the law during the theatrical off-season.

Helen begins by saying that, because Menelaus regards her as an enemy, he doubtless won't answer no matter how well she speaks.[16] So she will reply to the charges she suspects her husband will level at her, and offer a few counter charges in return. She goes immediately on the offensive. Firstly, she says, Hecabe is to blame for the war because she's the one who gave birth to Paris. Priam had a prophetic dream about his son when Paris was born, and still he wouldn't kill him. As we've already seen with Oedipus, this may sound unreasonable to us, but the world of Bronze Age myth is full of children being killed by their parents for various reasons. Even in the fifth century BCE, when Euripides' play was being performed, the exposure of unwanted children was commonplace. Although to modern ears, the argument 'You ignored a prophecy about your child and didn't kill him' might not cut too much ice, it is reasonable to suspect that Euripides' audience might have been more ambivalent. And indeed the question is concrete and mathematical for Hecabe: if she and Priam had killed Paris as a baby, their many other sons might not have died in the war Paris started. It's not just a question of preferring the life of her child over the lives of the rest of the Trojan citizens. It's about choosing one child's life (lost now, anyway, at the end of the war) over many of her other children's lives. In the scene Euripides placed just before this one, Hecabe had watched as her grandson, Astyanax (the son of her son Hector, and his wife, Andromache), was taken away to be killed by the Greeks because they didn't want him to grow up to avenge his late father, the greatest of all the Trojan warriors. The ramifications of Hecabe's choice are painfully real and recent, both for her and for the audience watching the play.

Helen then turns to the divine cause of the Trojan War, which again puts responsibility with Paris and with the goddess, Aphrodite, who assists him. She describes the judgement of Paris, in which he is asked to choose which goddess – Aphrodite, Athene or Hera – is prettiest and should therefore be the recipient of a golden apple inscribed 'To the Most Beautiful' (this cause of the war is barely mentioned by Homer and even then it isn't until the final book of the *Iliad*).[17] Helen mentions that the goddesses all tried to bribe him to get the result each desired: Athene offered him the power to destroy the Greeks in war, Hera offered him a kingdom encompassing Asia and Europe. But Aphrodite, Helen says, praising my appearance, offered me to him if he said she was most beautiful. In other words, Paris was responsible for choosing as he did, the goddesses were responsible for bribing him, and Aphrodite was the one who offered Helen to Paris with no thought for anyone else (the gods are often portrayed as thoughtless brats in Euripides' plays). Helen is collateral damage. In fact, she goes further, suggesting that, if Paris had preferred one of the other goddesses, Menelaus might well have found himself conquered by a barbarian army or ruled by a barbarian king, namely Paris. Greece got lucky, Helen says. I was destroyed. Sold for my beauty. I'm reproached by you; you should put a crown on my head.[18]

Now, Helen continues, it is time to consider the main charge. At this point, it seems only fair to say that no version of Menelaus in any telling of their story conveys the intellectual capacity to argue with a woman of such considerable cleverness. Maybe Odysseus could have taken her on, but not Menelaus. Euripides loved to write clever women, he does it over and over again: it is one of a thousand wonderful things about him.

So, why did Helen sneak off from her marital home with Paris? Again, she cites Aphrodite as the cause: Paris was accompanied by not a minor god, she says. The Greeks often employed litotes – deliberate understatement – in their legal speeches. And Helen uses it perfectly here: Aphrodite is one of the most powerful gods there is, so describing her as 'not minor' reminds us just how fearsome she is. And Menelaus doesn't dodge blame either. *O kakiste*, Helen says – you're the absolute worst. You left him – Paris – in your Spartan home while you went off to Crete.[19] This is another point which would have resonated with the play's fifth-century BCE audience. Athenian wives (certainly the wives of wealthy Athenians) would never have been left alone in their homes with a strange man. Athenian laws revealed an almost neurotic fear that another man might somehow impregnate your wife. Although Helen's point might not carry much weight with a modern audience, it certainly would have done with Euripides' audience. A respectable male citizen would not leave his wife alone in the company of any man who wasn't either her brother or her father.

Finally, Helen addresses her own weakness in falling for Paris. What led me to betray my fatherland for a stranger? she asks. Well, even Zeus can't resist Aphrodite: he holds power over the other gods, but he's a slave to her. So you should make allowances for me.[20] And this is certainly the impression we get of Aphrodite from most sources: she is irresistible to gods, let alone mortals (or demi-gods).

One last charge to answer, Helen says: why didn't I come back to you, Menelaus, after Paris died? Well, I tried. I was caught *pollakis* – 'many times' – trying to escape Troy and return to you. I was taken *bia* – 'by force' – as a wife by Deiphobos. The use of *bia* is unequivocal: Helen has been in a forced marriage since the death of Paris. She describes herself in this last relationship one more time: *pikrōs edouleus* – 'bitterly enslaved'.

Isn't our view of Helen changed by this extraordinary speech? The woman who is mute in Marlowe's *Dr Faustus* is as clever and articulate as she is beautiful in Euripides' *The Trojan Women*. The catalogue of wrongs done to her is remarkable. Perhaps we don't agree with her interpretation of every event (Hecabe certainly doesn't: she responds to Helen's defence, since she is clearly better-equipped than Menelaus for a battle of wits). But Helen's arguments are compelling: Aphrodite really is that powerful, Menelaus really did abandon her with Paris. Hecabe doesn't answer Helen's point about her repeated attempts to escape, she instead asks why Helen didn't kill herself as she should have (she doesn't suggest that Paris might have done the same, for shame at having brought war upon his home and family. Or indeed that she and Priam might have done so, having failed to act on the prophecy which had warned them that Paris would destroy their city if he was allowed to live). The final straw for Hecabe is that Helen has appeared – in the aftermath of the fall of Troy when everyone else is wearing rags – perfectly dressed.[21]

At the end of this extraordinary debate, Menelaus declares himself in agreement with Hecabe. And yet, rather than kill Helen, he orders his men to put her on his ship bound for Sparta. Euripides' audience (who would surely have known her role in the *Odyssey*, which we'll come to shortly) knows what Hecabe immediately realizes: there is no way Menelaus will kill Helen once they get home.

There is an interesting question raised by Helen's speech which she doesn't ask. Why was Paris chosen to judge between the goddesses? And did no one care about the catastrophic consequences of his choice? Paris was simply given the job of deciding which goddess should take home the coveted trophy: a golden apple, with the words *tē kallistē* – 'for the most beautiful' – engraved on it. The apple was dropped among the goddesses at the wedding of Thetis, a sea-nymph, who would go on to be the mother of Achilles. They squabbled over who it was for, but they never asked who dropped it. If they had, they might have discovered it was Eris, the goddess of strife and discord. In other words, the whole point of the apple was to cause trouble, and it does.

So how does Paris find himself in the invidious position of being the judge? It's inconceivable that he could pick one goddess over the other two and not acquire a pair of seriously powerful enemies. Who would agree to perform such an unenviable task? The answer is that Zeus decides Paris should do the choosing (no fool he: Zeus would have been choosing between his wife and sister, Hera, his daughter Athene, and the goddess who can cause him so much trouble, Aphrodite. No wonder he directs Hermes to put some hapless mortal on the case instead). And from the moment Paris makes his choice, Troy is in jeopardy. Throughout Greek myth, Hera is especially unforgiving of any slight (as women seduced by Zeus usually discover to their cost).

Which brings us back to the original question: why do the gods give the decision to Paris, in particular? The answer is that they want Troy to have powerful enemies or (if Helen was correct in her prediction of what would have happened to Menelaus and the Greeks had Paris chosen Hera or Athene as the recipient of the apple) to become a powerful threat to the Greeks. The gods have deliberately, intentionally stirred up trouble between the Greeks and the Trojans, and they have used Paris and Helen to do so.

If we keep following the causation of the war back, step by step, we eventually find ourselves here: the war is caused by Paris taking Helen from Menelaus, but Helen is promised to Paris by Aphrodite in exchange for the golden apple, and the apple is put in among the goddesses by Eris, and she gets it from where? We're told in the lost epic poem *Cypria* that Themis (the goddess of Order) and Zeus planned the Trojan War between them. One ancient commentator on the *Iliad* tells us why that might have been: the earth was groaning beneath the weight of so many people. Zeus had instigated an earlier war (the Theban wars, which, as we saw, blighted the life of Jocasta). In the ensuing years, the number of mortals continued to rocket.

Another war was needed. It is a powerful metaphor, and interesting that the notion of the earth being too full of too many people is not one which arrived among us when the global population hit the billions. Rather, it began when the earth held only tens of millions.[22]

But let us return to Helen. Are we really going to blame her, and Paris, if the gods had decided to start a war? Helen herself asked the question of Menelaus: what was she supposed to do when Aphrodite had decided that she and Paris would be together? But the backstory of the war suggests something bigger than divine vanity was at stake anyway. Even if Helen and Paris had resisted the power of Aphrodite (which Zeus himself can't manage), then war would still have come between east and west, Greece and Troy, because the gods had already decided that it was necessary.

And this idea, that the war was fought irrespective of Helen, is one which ancient writers played around with. Not least, Euripides. In his play *Helen*, he presents a very different version of Helen's story from the one we see in *The Trojan Women*. *Helen* was first performed in 412 BCE,[23] three years after *The Trojan Women*, which had asked so many unsettling questions about the nature of war and the devastation it wreaks on the lives of victims and victors alike. Euripides' plays come from a time when Athens was almost always at war: the Peloponnesian War, against their one-time ally, Sparta, began in 431 BCE and continued until 404 BCE. By the time *The Trojan Women* was written, Euripides and his audience would have heard plenty of speeches in the Assembly, in favour of and against the war. If Euripides was trying to advocate military caution with his plays (which are an incredibly subtle, sophisticated critique against war, rather than overt propaganda), it didn't work. In 415 BCE, Athens embarked on a ruinous additional campaign against the Sicilians, which wiped out the best part of a generation of men by the time the campaign ended in 413 BCE. Athens would fight on against Sparta for another nine years, but after such major losses, the war was unwinnable.

So perhaps when he was writing *Helen*, for performance in 412 BCE, Euripides wanted a break from thinking about war. Or perhaps he wanted to ask the most difficult question of all: what if the war you're fighting is for an unjust or specious cause? Because that is the premise of this play, which is set in Egypt. It opens with Helen telling the audience where she is: the very first word of the play is 'Nile'. Helen explains her origins (born from an egg), and goes on to recap the story of the judgement of Paris. But with a crucial distinction: Hera was so annoyed at being deprived of victory over Athena and Aphrodite that she interfered with Paris' reward. Instead of taking Helen back to Troy, Paris actually took an *eidolon*[24] – a breathing simulacrum of her, made out of air. Helen goes on to make the case we saw in that *Iliad* scholar's comment: then Zeus' plans added to my troubles, she says. He wanted a war between the Greeks and the wretched Trojans to reduce the weighty mass of people on Mother Earth. The woman 'set out as a prize for the Trojans to defend and the Greeks to win had my name, but she was not me.'[25] But Zeus didn't forget about Helen. She was concealed in a cloud and taken by Hermes to Egypt, to live out the war in the palace of Proteus. Proteus, Helen adds, was the most restrained of men, so she has been faithful to Menelaus. It is a fantastic touch by Euripides: Helen has been denounced as a whore, is deemed responsible for countless deaths, and yet here she is, blamelessly living in Egypt, untouched for the past ten years. And none of that will count for anything: when the Greek hero and survivor of the Trojan War, Teucer, arrives onstage a few moments later, he will say that 'the daughter of Zeus is hated by the whole of Greece.'[26]

Euripides was a tremendous innovator and invigorator of Greek myth, but he didn't invent this alternative version of the Helen story. There are fragments of earlier, Archaic writers, including the elusive Stesichorus, who tell a similar story,[27] that it is an *eidolon*, an image of Helen, that goes to Troy while the real woman waits out the war somewhere else, usually Egypt. We read of Stesichorus' lost version in Plato's *Republic*, where we're told that men fight over phantom pleasures and pains 'just like Stesichorus says the *eidolon* of Helen was fought over at Troy, by those ignorant of the truth'.[28] If this was a good enough example for Plato to use (admittedly in a pretty high-end conversation), then it can't have been little-known, or known only by those who'd seen Euripides' play. It's specifically the version told by Stesichorus which is mentioned. So way back in the late seventh or early sixth century BCE, an alternative narrative, exculpating Helen, existed. And it was still reasonably well known in the fourth century BCE by Plato and those for whom he was writing. How could a person be both here and in Troy? Menelaus asks Helen, when Euripides reunites husband and wife in his play. A name can be in lots of places at once, she replies. A person can't.[29]

This version of Helen's story is almost entirely forgotten now: even the Euripides play isn't often performed, although Frank McGuinness' excellent adaptation was staged at the Globe Theatre in London in 2009. It has been entirely supplanted by the version we know best, where she sails with Paris to Troy, followed by her husband Menelaus and the massed armies of the Greeks. We have seen from Hecabe's response to Helen in *The Trojan Women* that Helen wasn't a popular visitor to Troy. Just as Helen is hated by the Greeks for causing the war, she is hated by the Trojans for bringing the Greek forces to Trojan shores. And yet, the relationship between Helen and the family of Paris is more complicated than Hecabe's murderous wrath first suggests. Hector, Paris' brother, goes looking for him in Book Six of the *Iliad* to urge him to stop skulking behind the city walls and come and fight a war which he did, after all, begin. We find a rather whiny Paris, but the relationship between Hector and Helen seems respectful and affectionate. The rage that Hecabe has for Helen after Troy has been destroyed is not shared by her son who is going out and fighting to try and prevent this outcome. Of course, we might assume that Hecabe's views on Helen are calcified by the loss of her beloved Hector in single combat with the greatest of the Greek warriors, Achilles.

This battle animates the final part of the *Iliad*: Hector kills Achilles' closest friend Patroclus and strips his armour from him, Achilles is moved to unquenchable fury, the two men fight and Achilles kills Hector. He then desecrates Hector's body, tying the great warrior behind his chariot by the feet and dragging him around the walls of Troy. Even in the violence of war, desecrating a corpse is a shocking thing for any man to do. Ensuring that the fallen have proper burial – irrespective of how they died – is a religious duty (as Antigone argues about her fallen brothers in the Theban wars: it doesn't matter that one brother fought to defend Thebes and one was attacking it. She has a religious and familial obligation to bury them both as her brothers, whether they are traitors or heroes). Achilles takes the body of Hector back to his camp and leaves it unburied. After several days, Priam, Hector's father and the king of Troy, sneaks into the Greek camp to try and ransom back his dead son. It is a moment of almost unbearable pathos: an old man on his knees, begging his son's killer to return the body for burial. Achilles allows the Trojan king to buy back Hector's body and leave the Greek camp unmolested. The Trojans are finally able to bury their greatest defender, and the *Iliad* concludes with Hector's belated funeral. The poem is bookended by its two greatest warriors, one Greek, one Trojan: the first line of the first book is, 'Sing, goddess, of the wrath of Achilles', and the final line of the final book is, 'Thus they held the funeral of Hector, tamer of horses'.[30]

Funerals are women's work in the world of Bronze Age myth: it is women who tear their garments and rend their skin, women who wash corpses and lay bodies out for burial. As we might expect, therefore, it is Andromache, the wife of Hector, who speaks first at his funeral, lamenting his loss for herself and for their baby son, Astyanax. Hecabe, Hector's mother, speaks next. But then, astonishingly, it is not one of Hector's sisters who speaks third, but his sister-in-law, Helen.[31] Andromache and Hecabe both speak about Hector's prowess in battle: this is the funeral of a prince of Troy and a warrior, after all. But Helen doesn't mention this side of Hector at all. Instead, she speaks movingly about his kindness. She describes the twenty years since she abandoned Sparta (we must presume that she and Paris spent ten years together en route to and then in Troy before the Greeks turned up to fight for her return, if Homer's chronology is to make sense), and they don't sound pleasant. She talks of the harsh words she has received from Paris' brothers, sisters, sisters-in-law and mother (although Priam was always kind to her, she says). But Hector never spoke to her with anything but kindness. And if others were unkind in his hearing, he asked them to stop. Helen weeps for herself and for Hector, the only man who was a friend to her.

Now, of course, we might choose to read this as entirely in keeping with the Helen we saw Hecabe raging about in *The Trojan Women*. Typical self-absorbed Helen, only valuing Hector for the qualities he displayed towards her, grieving for herself now he's dead because of a war she started, sad that she has lost one of the many men besotted with her (at least his poor old father is still fulfilling that role). But this sells the speech rather short. Greek lamentations often commemorate the dead by focusing on how the living will struggle to cope without them: Helen isn't being especially solipsistic in this context. Everyone can talk about the military might of a man who died in battle after ten long years of keeping an army at bay. So why shouldn't someone speak of his kindness, his generosity? We're reminded by Helen that Hector was a human being behind the walls of his city as much as he was a warrior before them. It is a perfect way to bring the poem towards its end, with only Priam left to speak over the body of his dead son.

And Homer shows us one further, perhaps more unexpected development of Helen's character in the *Odyssey*. Telemachus, Odysseus' son, visits Sparta to try and find out what might have happened to his errant father (Odysseus takes ten years to get home to Ithaca from Troy: an assortment of women, nymphs, monsters, cannibals, cows, weather and a brief visit to the Underworld reduces his average speed considerably from that of the outbound journey). Telemachus is welcomed into their home by Menelaus and Helen. The former has clearly become no less hospitable since Paris came to visit and ran off with his wife, although his guard, Eteoneus, is suspicious of a young man arriving at the palace unannounced. He goes inside to tell Menelaus, who promptly shouts at him for not being more welcoming. Menelaus does stick around to have dinner with his guest this time, though, so perhaps he has learned something.

They all sit and eat and talk about the war, and about Odysseus' heroics in particular. But as they talk of warriors who died in battle, Menelaus becomes emotional and weeps. Helen decides she will mix something into the wine they're drinking: drugs which she has received from Polydamna, a friend in Egypt.[32] These drugs are potent mood-changers: the Greek word is *nepenthes* – banishing pain or sorrow. Homer tells us that, if someone consumed them, even if they then saw their parent or sibling die, or even if they saw their child being killed, they wouldn't weep. Without saying anything to anyone, Helen mixes the drugs into the wine and tells a slave to pour it out. No wonder Menelaus didn't kill her when they got back to Sparta. Is it because he was dazzled by her beauty or dazed by her narcotics?

Stories of impossibly beautiful women who find countless men vying for their affections are common in folklore and myth. There are a few counter-examples of ruinously beautiful men pursued by women and men: Dorian Gray, Valmont. Joseph, who tempts Zuleikha (or the wife of Potiphar, depending on which religious text you prefer), is another: in one story in the Sefer ha-Yashar or Book of Jasher,[33] Zuleikha is so besotted with Joseph that it damages her health. Other women mock her for her infatuation, so she invites Joseph to walk through the room as they peel oranges with knives. His beauty is so compelling that the women cut their hands open as they try to peel the fruit. They don't even notice until Zuleikha makes them look down to see they are covered in blood. And she has to see this beauty every day, she reminds them.

But the ability to start a war, to destroy an army rather than a handful of individuals, is a rarer quality. It demands a kind of other-worldliness which Helen perhaps refers to when she calls herself a freak or monster in her eponymous play by Euripides. It is incredibly difficult to find a story of a man who is so beautiful he can provoke the sort of desire that might cause a war. Armenian folklore tells the story of Ara the Beautiful,[34] a mythical king of Armenia in the eighth century BCE (so four hundred years or so after Helen made her journey to Troy, or possibly Egypt). Semiramis, the queen of Assyria, falls in love with Ara. Her soldiers invade Armenia, with strict orders to capture Ara alive. But he is killed in the battle and Semiramis places him in a room in her palace to be licked back to life by the gods. In some versions of the story, the gods oblige her. In others, Ara is lost for good. But the story doesn't seem to have captured the imagination of poets, composers, artists and playwrights in the way that Helen's has done. Perhaps this simply reflects a cultural readiness to accept the destructive nature of female beauty, whereas we tend not to think about male beauty in that way. Though in Roman Britain, there is also Tacitus' story of Cartimandua, queen of the Brigantes. She divorced her husband Venutius and married an armour-bearer named Vellocatus. Venutius takes this rejection as we all might, and declares war on his ex-wife and her new husband.[35] He is eventually victorious, and our evidence for Cartimandua ends there. But how much of this skirmish is down to politics and how much is down to passion is hard to say: it's certainly unusual for a woman to ditch a king for a lowly armour-bearer. Tacitus exhibits little generosity in his writings about her, but that isn't unusual for Tacitus (who is rarely generous, particularly on the subject of women in any kind of political context).

Helen has inspired some outlandish retellings of her story, from a silver-painted Elizabeth Taylor in Richard Burton's film of *Doctor Faustus* to *The Simpsons*, who magnificently portray her with a quasi-Grecian version of Marge's hairdo and a cigarette in a holder, as though she were an ageing Holly Golightly. Even Agatha Christie wrote a story, 'The Face of Helen', which was published in the *Mysterious Mr Quin* collection. Like most of these stories, it is rather peculiar. Quin and his friend Satterthwaite are at the opera when they see a girl beneath them, sitting in the stalls, who has pure gold hair. 'A Greek head,' is how Satterthwaite describes her. 'Pure Greek.'[36] They are impressed with her hair but they can't see her face. Satterthwaite is sure it 'won't match. That would be a chance in a thousand.' When they finally see her from the front, the men are astonished. She is an example of sheer beauty, and Satterthwaite immediately quotes Marlowe's line about launching a thousand ships, before comparing the woman to 'The Helens, the Cleopatras, the Mary Stuarts.'

Gillian West, Christie's modern-day Helen, turns out to be a beautiful but prosaic woman, a talented but not great singer, and the object of affection of two men. She becomes engaged to Charlie, and therefore rejects Philip, who appears to take things on the chin while plotting a sinister revenge. He makes Gillian an engagement gift of a wireless and a complicated glass vase with a delicate sphere seemingly balancing upon it. His somewhat convoluted plan is that she will listen to the opera on the wireless, a high note will crack the glass sphere, and a poisonous gas will be released into her sitting room and finish her off. Sadly for Philip, Satterthwaite puts the pieces of the puzzle together (Philip's glassblowing skills, his career in chemical weapons during the war) and saves Gillian in the nick of time. A stray cat which dashes into the flat is not so lucky, but provides a convenient posthumous proof of Satterthwaite's thesis. On discovering his failure, Philip throws himself in the Thames, provoking London's least-concerned policeman to remark that he heard a splash and supposes it must be suicide, before moving on to something more important (gathering stray cats before any more are poisoned, perhaps). 'It's not always their fault,' the incurious policeman remarks to Satterthwaite, before not jumping into the water to try and save Philip. 'But some women cause a lot of trouble.' Satterthwaite agrees and wonders if Helen of Troy was also 'a nice, ordinary woman, blessed or cursed with a wonderful face.'

Christie's version of the Helen story is obviously a sympathetic portrayal of a beautiful woman whose other qualities don't rival her beauty. We have no sense of Gillian as a person, really: when she reveals to Satterthwaite that she has become engaged to Charlie, we get no idea why she might prefer Charlie to Philip, or what she might be looking for in a fiancé. We don't even get a sense of why she is happy to trust Satterthwaite – a man she has just met – with these relatively intimate details of her life. After making her acquaintance at the opera, Satterthwaite then simply bumps into her and Charlie at Kew Gardens. As is often the way with coincidence, it is narratively unsatisfying: not only do we not know enough about Gillian to say why she picked Charlie over Philip, we don't even know whether she prefers cacti or shrubs.

The passion of Helen is entirely missing from Gillian, a woman who inspires passion with her beauty but doesn't particularly seem to experience it herself. We can't imagine this woman abandoning her husband and child for a handsome stranger, or beguiling the king of the city she elopes to, or articulating her innocence, or doing anything very much, except being extremely pretty and being rescued by a man from the murderous scheme of another man.

The original series of *Star Trek*, always keen to borrow from the Greeks and Romans, reworks Helen into the infinitely more exotic-sounding Elaan of Troyius. In this episode from 1968, the crew of the USS *Enterprise* are on a diplomatic mission. Two planets, Elas and Troyius, are at war. The ruling councils of these planets have decided that a marriage between Elaan and the Troyian ruler might secure a long-awaited peace. Captain Kirk and his men have the job of escorting the reluctant and scornful Elaan to Troyius while the Troyian ambassador tries to teach her the customs of her new planet. The exoticization of Elaan (played by France Nuyen) sits uncomfortably with us now, fifty years later: we are invited to view this woman as a beautiful but uncivilized barbarian, quick to resort to violence and then tears.

It's still a fascinating twist on the Helen story: Elaan's imminent marriage is expected to stop a war, rather than start one, so a complete reversal of the story of Helen and Paris that we find in the *Iliad*. Here, the diplomatic weight behind a marriage between two warring cultures has turned it into something potentially positive, and everyone is trying to make sure the wedding goes ahead. Everyone except the bride herself.

Her reluctance to marry – her conviction that a Troyian husband is beneath her – is also an interesting variation on the story. We get this same sense in Ovid's letter from Helen to Paris in his *Heroides*. This collection of poems written from mythical figures (mostly women) to their absent lovers is a wonderful, surprising take on Greek myth. The Helen letter is a response to a letter she has received from Paris. He has tried to impress her with his wealth and prospects. But she is far more pragmatic, unable to ignore the loss in status and reputation that will accompany her if she leaves her home for her Trojan lover. For Ovid's audience, Paris – the Trojan – is a barbarian, a man from the exotic east. Helen is a Greek, which is less respectable in first-century BCE Rome than being a Roman, but definitely better than being a barbarian.

For *Star Trek*'s audience, Elaan is not only the barbarian (the *Enterprise* and her crew are the civilizing force in this and almost all *Star Trek* episodes). She is also the warrior. We don't meet her Troyian husband-to-be, but his ambassador is somewhat snooty and effete. He is certainly no match for Elaan when she loses patience and stabs him: only the swift attention of the medical team of the *Enterprise* saves his life. It is – no huge surprise – Captain Kirk who ends up having to be a civilizing influence on Elaan. Well, civilizing in some ways: again, fifty years after its initial broadcast, we flinch to see him hit her after she has hit him.

The elements of the story which more closely retell the Helen myth are equally interesting. Elaan's beauty and charisma are so remarkable that, when she is beamed on board the *Enterprise*, the crew spontaneously go down on bended knee to her. Even Mr Spock, who is famously, half-Vulcanly unemotional, is compelled to kneel before her, albeit with one eyebrow raised. In the time-honoured tradition of a romantic comedy, Elaan and Kirk argue, hate each other and then fall in love. We might wonder if this is to be another twist on the story we think we know: perhaps this is the forbidden relationship that Helen/Elaan should not be having, while her absent Troyian groom is not Paris, the adulterer, but rather a virtual Menelaus – the man who has claim to her, but foolishly leaves her alone in the company of one of history's (or, rather, the future's) great womanizers.

Sabotage, Klingon attacks and a last-minute fix of the warp drive by the tireless Scotty accompany the *Enterprise* as she makes her way to Troyius. By the time they reach their destination, we are genuinely worried for Captain Kirk: he has witnessed Elaan's tears, which, we are told, means he will be enslaved for life. Dr McCoy heroically works to create an antidote to this biochemical reaction, but the episode ends with Kirk not needing it after all: he is sitting on the bridge of his ship, perfectly content. How? Well, as Spock points out, Kirk's great love is the *Enterprise*, which infected him long before Elaan did. It is another nice twist on the Helen myth: after her relationship with Paris ends, she goes back to her first husband, Menelaus. In *Star Trek*, Elaan has no first husband. Rather, it is Kirk who returns to his first love. And so the story of Helen, Paris and Menelaus is cleverly broken up and reformed to lose a war and gain a spaceship.

Strange variants on the Helen story are not a preserve of science fiction, incidentally. Even *Star Trek* might stop short of the Helens we see in the work of an obscure ancient author, Ptolemaeus Chennos or Ptolemy the Quail. This Ptolemy lived in Alexandria, in Egypt, at the beginning of the second century CE. He composed a *Strange History* – a set of peculiar stories based on Greek myths. For him, there are many Helens,[37] which he has presumably collected from other mythographers: there is Helen, the daughter of Leda, who gave Paris (Alexandros) a daughter, and had an uncanny knack of imitating voices (this unlikely nugget is also in Homer).[38] But then, after the Trojan War, there are multiple Helens: one, a daughter of Clytemnestra, who is killed by Orestes, one who worked with Aphrodite, one who raised Romulus and Remus. He mentions a woman who ate three kid goats a day who is also called Helen (though presumably she may have been too busy digesting goat to answer to her name). And then there is the daughter of Musaeus, a poet who wrote about the Trojan War in the eighth century BCE, before Homer. This Helen owned a *diglosson arnion* – 'a bilingual sheep'.[39] It's impossible to see how this Helen isn't the most famous woman in the ancient world, when one comes across a bilingual sheep so rarely. Ptolemy also mentions a Helen who was loved by the poet Stesichorus,

Helen of Himera. This is a particularly cute point because one story which the ancients told about Stesichorus was that he lost his sight after writing ungenerously about Helen of Troy. His vision was only restored when he composed a more generous account of her. Let that be a lesson to us all.

Perhaps the most extraordinary Helen is one who doesn't survive, however. There is a lost tragedy by Sophocles, called *The Demand for Helen's Return*.[40] Only a few tiny fragments exist today, so we can get little sense of the plot overall. But the Helen they depict is a remarkable variation on the version we have seen in Homer and Euripides. This Helen is so tormented by her wrongdoing that she is considering suicide by drinking poison: bull's blood. A second fragment describes her driving writing implements – pencils – into her cheek. None of the Helens we have met – from the child bride in the story of Theseus to the adulterous woman in Homer, from the powerful orator in Euripides to the self-possessed wife in Ovid – none of these women is as pitiable as this Sophoclean creation: a woman so damaged by a lifetime of being defined by her beauty that she finally seeks to obliterate it by self-harm. And not just self-harm, but the most horrific, visible kind: she specifically disfigures her face which so many men have sought to possess. That she uses the precise tool which poets and scribes have used to create her myth, to tell her story kindly and unkindly, fairly or unfairly, is especially poignant. The greatest beauty the world had ever known, trying to take away the cause for all those words written about her, using the object which wrote them. Perhaps this is an image – however distressing – we need to keep in our minds when we think about Helen. That whether or not we consider her responsible for a war (or two wars) matters less than what she believes.

So many artists have tried to capture Helen: she invariably reflects the ideals of beauty in whichever age they create her, from *Star Trek*'s

Elaan (with her black ringlets and purple, sparkly leotard) to Rossetti's Helen of Troy (a wide-eyed blonde, modelled on Annie Miller,[41] whose hands clutch at her necklace but whose face seems almost empty of expression). And so we are left – as Ptolemy's curious list suggests – with an array of Helens, none of whom seems quite real, and all of whom seem to represent the desires of their creators. Look at the certainty with which Achilles is drawn – his speed, his anger, his love for Patroclus, his commitment to honour and immortality through fame: he is defined by what he wants, and strives for, and loses. And then think of Helen, and how much harder she is to pin down: her confused parentage, her contested childhood, her multiple marriages. One of our earliest narrative traditions states that the most notorious fact about her – that she eloped with Paris – is actually a lie: the real Helen is elsewhere, while a war is fought over an unreal creature, an image. In fact, the more we try to understand her, the more she seems to elude us: Helen of Troy, Helen of Sparta, Helen of joy, Helen of slaughter.

MEDUSA

H<small>E WHO FIGHTS MONSTERS, NIETZSCHE TELLS US, SHOULD TAKE</small> care that he himself does not become a monster.[1] But what happens when we look at this advice from the other direction? Is this how monsters are created: are all monsters heroes who went astray? Not in Greek myth, certainly. Some monsters are born that way and others, especially female monsters, are turned monstrous after a bruising encounter with a god. In the case of Medusa, she can cite both kinds of genealogy, depending on who tells her story.

Most ancient authors follow Hesiod's lead and describe three Gorgons: Sthenno, Euryale and Medusa.[2] They are the daughters of a sea god, Phorcys (a son of Gaia), and his sister Cēto, who produce a tremendous array of sea-monster offspring, including Echidna (a fearsome sea-snake), and sometimes also Scylla, who chomps her way through several of Odysseus' crew. Hesiod notes an unusual aspect of Medusa's condition: her two sisters are immortal and ageless, but she herself is mortal – which Hesiod considers a wretched fate.[3] He doesn't emphasize that Medusa must therefore also be prone to ageing, but the correlation is surely implied. Nor does he explain how she has turned out to be mortal when her parents are gods and her siblings are immortal. He simply states that it is the case. To grow old and die might be considered miserable enough, if all your relatives are going to live, ageless, forever. But for Medusa, being mortal will result in a premature and grisly fate.

And she has a pretty unhappy existence even before we consider the end of it. It's not always clear that Medusa is a monster from the outset, though perhaps one could argue that the offspring of a sea-god and a sea-monster was always likely to have monstrous leanings. Several ancient authors, from Hesiod to Ovid, suggest something different though: Medusa began her life as a beautiful woman. Things only change after the sea god Poseidon seduces Medusa 'in the soft, damp meadow', as Hesiod puts it.⁴ This phrase has precisely the same double meaning in Greek as it does in English: Hesiod might mean that the god and the Gorgon had sex in an actual damp meadow, or the damp meadow might be a euphemism for Medusa's vagina (you will have to insert your own joke about being turned to stone here, as I am far too mature). The gods are usually capable of seducing whoever they choose (with a few exceptions), and it seems likely then that at this stage in her life, at least, Medusa is beautiful. Certainly, she is in the lyric poet Pindar's twelfth Pythian Ode. He describes her as *euparaou* – 'with beauteous cheeks'.⁵

This sexual encounter with Poseidon is a recurring feature of Medusa's story, but the mood and location of their encounter vary, as do the consequences (we'll come to her offspring later on). What is presented by Hesiod as consensual and idyllic is given a far darker spin by Ovid. In his *Metamorphoses*, Medusa is *clarissima forma* – 'most beautiful in her appearance'. She has multiple suitors attempting to woo her: this is not the snaky monster we have come to expect. This glorious woman has no feature more eye-catching than her gorgeous hair (I discovered this, says Ovid's narrator, from someone who said he'd seen it). But then Medusa is raped by Poseidon in a temple of Athene.⁶ Ovid uses a brutal word – *vitiasse*⁷– which means to injure, defile or damage. Athene shields her eyes to avoid the sight of her temple being profaned. As we might expect from a goddess who so rarely favours women and so often favours men, Athene takes her revenge on the wrong person. Rather than punish Poseidon (which may be beyond her: he is at least as powerful as she is), she instead punishes Medusa, turning the Gorgon's hair into snakes. It is the perfect illustration of Athene's clever cruelty that she destroys the feature of which Medusa must have been most proud. For modern readers, this disfiguration might bring to mind the French women whose heads were shaved after the Second World War because they were perceived to have collaborated with the Nazis. The punishment for having been considered beautiful by the enemy is to be turned into something less beautiful, as viciously as possible.

There is an interesting feminist reading of this part of Medusa's story, which suggests that we might see Athene's transformation of Medusa as an act of sisterly solidarity. In this interpretation, Athene saves Medusa from further sexual assault by making her undesirable to male gods who can and do force themselves on her. Medusa is also armed against attackers, because she has the power to turn them to stone. But it isn't at all clear from Ovid's telling of the story that Medusa's petrifying appearance is a gift from Athene, or indeed that it post-dates her snaky conversion. The only metamorphosis that Ovid mentions is the changing of her hair into snakes. It is perfectly possible that Medusa was always able to turn living creatures to stone: her immortal sisters seem unaffected by this, so perhaps Poseidon is similarly impervious. There is a second, greater difficulty with this interpretation: anyone who spends time with Athene in almost any story told about her will struggle to see her as a cheerleader for other women. Her most enduring fondness is not for a woman at all, but for Odysseus. And he is hardly the hero you would wish your sister to marry, unless your sister had bullied you relentlessly as a child.

In this metamorphosis, the focus of Ovid's attention – and ours – is on the head of the Gorgon. There is no description of her body being transformed into a monstrous shape. Even before Medusa is decapitated by Perseus, we are drawn to her head, rather than the whole of her. Unless, of course, her head is the whole of her.

The earliest visual representations of Gorgons are highly stylized images, which we'll look at shortly. Earlier still, we find *gorgoneia*: monstrous heads, which probably reflect the fears of the societies that created them. They are perhaps also connected to Humbaba, a divine monster of earlier Mesopotamian myth, who first terrorizes and then is beheaded by Gilgamesh.[8] The *gorgoneia* are incredibly strange: huge mouths full of teeth, protruding tongues and tusks, often beards. They can be found carved onto the pediments of temples, decorating armour or sometimes on one side of a coin. In the *Iliad*, Homer says that Athene has a terrible Gorgon head on her aegis, or breastplate, to unnerve her enemies.[9] Agamemnon also has a grim-faced Gorgon head on his shield,[10] so mortal and goddess alike use the Gorgon head to provoke fear. And it clearly works: Homer also mentions a Gorgon head in the *Odyssey*. And this one is not a decoration on a shield, but is an actual creature which apparently lives (or maybe 'dwells' would be the more appropriate verb) in the Underworld, doing the bidding of Persephone.[11] After a trip down to Hades to commune with the dead, Odysseus makes a hasty retreat in the fear that Persephone might send this head after him. Odysseus is made of stern stuff – he has made the journey to the Underworld, for a start – yet he is scared of even the possibility of seeing this disembodied head. But then, who wouldn't be scared of a hovering Gorgon head? Its reputation is clearly formidable and far-reaching. Visitors to the Archaeological Museum in Olympia can see a wonderful example of a *gorgoneion*, which dates to the first half of the sixth century BCE. This shield decoration is a circle surrounded by three large wings. In the centre is a hideous face: bulbous nose above distended mouth, its thick tongue outstretched. A garland of twisting snakes surrounds her.

There have been many attempts to derive a definitive meaning from these Gorgon heads, or more accurately, Gorgon faces or masks. Archaeologists, anthropologists and psychologists have sought to connect them to various natural phenomena: storms, for example. Gorgons are renowned for the strident noise they make, as Pindar confirms when he explains that Athene created many-voiced flutes to try and imitate the *eriklanktan goön*[12] – 'deafening wail' – that emanates from the mouth of Euryale, one of Medusa's sisters. So the connection with thunder and storm clouds is a tempting one. More convincingly, the Gorgon is thought to be a representation of the animals we might fear, particularly if we slept outdoors: perhaps her snakish hair stands in for snakes (which are often poisonous in Greek myth) or even a lion's mane. The snakes that surround the Olympia shield decoration are certainly reminiscent of a mane. And the sound of a lion's roar in the darkness or an unseen snake's hiss would be the stuff of nightmares for many of us. Is a Gorgon head a way of making our nebulous nightmares less terrifying, by carving them into solid objects we can touch or hold, made of metal and stone? And is it then something we can use to assist us?

The frightening appearance of the *gorgoneion* is precisely what makes it so powerful as a decorative design. It acts as an apotropaic device: something which wards off danger, particularly the supernatural kind. What better thing to have on your shield than something which scares you, so will definitely terrorize your enemies? And what better way to master your own fears than by taking them and turning them away from you to face whoever you are about to fight? In Homer's description of the Gorgon, she is accompanied by Terror and Fear.[13] These personifications are clearly who you need on your side in a battle. If they are to be found on either side of your *gorgoneion*, so much the better for you, and so much the worse for your enemies.

If the Gorgons start out as heads (as they seem to be in Homer, and in some early artworks), when do they acquire bodies, and how? And, perhaps most importantly, why? It seems to be the case that the *gorgoneia* appeared in all kinds of locations, which suggests a folklore origin: round monster heads which serve multiple possible functions, from scaring your enemy to facing your fears. And the Greeks – storytellers always – wanted to explain these strange creatures, so they added them into their stories, which is why Hesiod and Pindar tell us about three Gorgons, and give them names, and describe their appearances and their capacity to make a cacophonous racket. The decorative heads have become characters. But then these authors and their audiences needed an explanation for all the disembodied Gorgon heads they could see around them, if the Gorgons now had bodies and backstories. Something was required which explained the separation of Gorgon head from body, and so we come to Perseus, who decapitates Medusa for reasons we'll go on to explore. Medusa and her sister Gorgons seem to exist, and certainly *gorgoneia* exist, before the hero who conquers them. In other words, Perseus was most likely added to Medusa's story to explain her existence and our interest in her separated head, rather than Medusa appearing in Perseus' story to give him a monster to fight.

Unsurprisingly, Gorgons acquire monstrous bodies to go with their terrifying faces. Their name means terrible or fierce, and ancient authors were happy to oblige. They are described in this way in *Prometheus Bound*, a fifth-century BCE tragedy which is often attributed to Aeschylus, though its specific date and author have been much debated. Here, the Gorgons are *drakontomalloi* – 'snake-haired' – and *katapteroi* – 'winged'.[14] They are also *brotostugeis* – 'hated by mortals', or 'mortal-hating' (the word can be active or passive). This description is borne out by contemporary vase paintings: there is a fifth-century BCE Athenian amphora in the State Collection of Antiquities in Munich which depicts just such a Gorgon:[15] she has wings as well as arms, snakes around her brow and long ringlets spanning across her neck and shoulders. Her mouth is wide and open, as with the *gorgoneia*. Her tongue hangs out and she has large tusks on either side of it, pointing both up and down. Her wings suggest she is flying, her legs that she is running. She is caught mid-stride, her feet encased in tight boots. Her spotted skirt is knee-length and her calves are bare and finely muscled. Her arms are in a runner's pose, one reaching up in front of her, one reaching down behind her: she is moving at speed. Both her wrists are adorned with bangles. She may be a monster, but she still has a taste for jewellery. She looks athletic and powerful, both human and inhuman.

And yet this mighty creature will be decapitated by Perseus, although he will need the assistance of several gods to succeed. This is something he is fortunately well-placed to receive, since he is the son of Zeus. And Zeus impregnates Danae, Perseus' mother, in an even more inventive way than he manages with Leda. Danae's father Acrisius receives word from an oracle that if his daughter gives birth to a son, that son will kill his grandfather. Acrisius is not one for risk-taking, so he locks Danae away in an underground room, perhaps made of stone. Zeus is undeterred by this seeming impenetrability and converts himself into a shower of gold, so he can rain down on Danae through gaps in the roof. No mention is made of any unusual sleeping position Danae might have adopted to break up the boredom of being locked underground, but suffice it to say that, however gravity and golden rain coincide, she becomes pregnant. The resulting child is Perseus, whom Ovid calls *aurigenae*[16] – 'born from gold'. When Acrisius discovers his daughter has borne a son in spite of his best efforts, he reacts with his customary proportionality and puts them both in a wooden chest which he floats out to sea. Zeus ensures the chest remains seaworthy and lands safely. The two are found by a fisherman who takes them to his brother, a king named Polydectes.

Polydectes promptly falls for Danae and, wishing to pursue his goal uninterrupted,[17] he sends Perseus off on a quest for the head of Medusa. In Pseudo-Apollodorus' version of the story, we can immediately see the advantage Perseus has by being the son of Zeus:[18] Athene and Hermes accompany him on his quest, which makes things quite a bit less complicated than they might otherwise have been. They guide him to the Graiai, the three sisters who have between them only one eye, which they share (and one tooth, according to

Pseudo-Apollodorus, which is also shared). Perseus swipes both eye and tooth and refuses to return them until the Graiai reveal the whereabouts of the nymphs who can loan him winged sandals (these are usually worn by Hermes) and a *kibisis* – or 'rucksack', which seems to be the closest translation.

The text of the Pseudo-Apollodorus manuscript is corrupted here, but Hesiod's *Shield of Heracles* offers further information. He describes Perseus fleeing after decapitating Medusa. Perseus is flying (thanks to the winged sandals) at the speed of thought.[19] He also has a black-sheathed sword held across both shoulders with a bronze belt. The Gorgon's head is carried on his back in his silver *kibisis*. But this is no ordinary rucksack, it is one designed to carry a powerfully destructive item: the head of the Gorgon. It is, Hesiod tells us, *thauma idesthai* – 'a wonder to behold'.[20] It is silver, with gleaming gold tassels. It must be strong to contain something as heavy as a head and its snakes, and it must be of a thick fabric to contain Medusa's lithifying gaze. Is the bag made from actual silver and decorated with actual gold? It would be formidably heavy, but then Perseus is gold-born and his sandals are used to carrying Hermes and whatever he is ferrying around, so he's surely built for the load. Perseus has also been able to borrow the cap of Hades (one hesitates to compare nymphs to Wombles in virtually any regard, but they certainly seem to make good use of the things that they find). The cap holds the grim darkness of night, Hesiod says:[21] in other words, it makes the wearer invisible.

It is interesting to note just how much assistance Perseus requires to help him decapitate Medusa. Two Olympian gods help him to reach the Graiai, who help him to find the nymphs, who equip him with winged shoes, a fancy backpack and a hat which bestows invisibility. And yet, most of this equipment is for his getaway, when he needs to escape from Medusa's sisters. Medusa herself doesn't put up a fight, because Perseus decapitates her when she is asleep. According to

Pseudo-Apollodorus, Perseus goes for Medusa's head purely because she is the only mortal one of the three Gorgons (who are here described with their customary snakes, as well as having large tusks like pigs, bronze hands and gold wings). Perseus finds them when they are all asleep and once again receives the assistance of a god. Athene guides his sword hand towards Medusa's sleeping neck; Perseus looks away into his shield's reflection as he beheads her.

It is not, as described by Pseudo-Apollodorus, a very heroic act. And the killing looks especially brutal when it is shown in Greek vase painting. There is a red-figure *pelike* – jar – in the Metropolitan Museum in New York,[22] which stands almost half a metre high and was painted by an artist named Polygnotos. It dates to around the middle of the fifth century BCE and shows Perseus attacking Medusa. His gaze is averted from her; he looks behind him at Athene, who stands calmly to our left. She holds her spear, her expression is placid. Perseus is sporting the winged sandals and a winged cap. Medusa is asleep, her wings are stretched out behind her. Her face is drawn with just a few simple lines – one for each eyebrow, one for each closed eye, two for her nose and mouth. She reminds me a little of Paul Klee's line drawing *Forgetful Angel*. Medusa is – unusually, at this point in her story – shown as a beautiful woman, rather than an even partial monster: there are no snakes here. She wears a dress with a pattern of squares down the front and zig-zags along the seams. Her lovely face is resting on one of her hands, her ringlets are squashed against her chin. And Perseus is slicing through the back of her neck with a curved blade.

This pot is frankly extraordinary. It might be the most sympathetic depiction of Medusa in any medium. It reveals what so much of the myth obscures: stripped of the monster/hero dynamic, all we see is a man beheading a woman.

The immediate aftermath of the decapitation can be seen on a small *hydria* – water jar – in the British Museum, attributed to the

Pan Painter.[23] Athene, Perseus and Medusa are again all present, and this scene is filled with movement. To the left, Perseus is creeping away from the body of Medusa. His right leg is stretched out in front of him; his left leg is poised to follow it, heel already lifted from the ground. He is wearing calf-length boots which flare away from his ankles like wings, and the winged helmet. In his left hand is the curved blade of his *harpe* – a sickle-shaped sword. His right arm is outstretched, palm upwards: is it for balance? Or is he triumphant? On the right-hand side, Athene is hastening after Perseus. Her sheer dress has a polka-dot pattern, we can see her left leg through the fabric as she runs. She is holding her skirt up in her left hand, for ease of movement, and she carries her spear on her right shoulder.

Perseus is looking behind him, but not at Athene. Instead he looks down, at the body of Medusa which fills the centre of the scene. Over Perseus' left shoulder hangs the *kibisis*, into which Medusa's head has been roughly stuffed. We can still see her eyes over the top of it, but they are closed. Her hair is also visible, in neat waves pinned under a hairband. Again, this is not the face of a monster, it is the head of a woman. Her body is remarkable: she half-lies, half-kneels on her right hip, legs curving behind her at the knee. She's wearing a short chiton – dress – with little sleeves which drape from her shoulders. Her arms are stretched out, her fingers are long and elegant, pressing lightly into the ground, still supporting her weight. Her pale wings flutter behind her. Blood flows from her neck down the front of her dress.

Both these vase paintings show a deeply ambivalent response to the beheading of Medusa. It is a necessary part of Perseus' heroic narrative, and he is an indisputable hero, a son of Zeus no less. His heroic status is not being questioned: both vases show him wearing divine possessions or gifts, and with Athene assisting him. But the winged shoes, cap and special knapsack seem to reveal a second level of ambivalence: Perseus is a hero favoured by the gods, but he is also an insufficient hero, one who needs copious divine assistance to complete his quest He is not being presented as a giant-slayer, a monster-killer. The ingenuity we might see in an image of Odysseus blinding the Cyclops or the strength of Heracles killing the Hydra is missing.

Our best-known version of Medusa and Perseus – despite the hard work of museum curators around the world – is probably in *Clash of the Titans* (made in 1981 and shown by law every Bank Holiday Monday since). Harry Hamlin's Perseus uses his shield as a protective mirror when he takes on a fully conscious Medusa who could petrify him at any moment: her reflection doesn't have the same fatal power as her undiluted gaze. This creates a dramatic tension in the movie which is undeniably absent from the Pseudo-Apollodorus story, and from the pots which show the Gorgon asleep or already beheaded. Perseus is hunting a monster which is hunting him right back. He is armed with a sword, she with a lethal stare.

He also has a more heroic reason to get Medusa's head in the first place. For our ancient sources, Perseus was simply doing the bidding of Polydectes (who wanted Perseus out of the way so he could more easily seduce Danae, Perseus' mother). But our modern taste for hero narratives requires something a bit juicier than this. So the Perseus of *Clash of the Titans* needs to acquire the head of a Gorgon to save the life of the beautiful Andromeda, who has been tied to a rock and menaced by a kraken (an especially frightening sea-monster, not least because it has swum a long way south – and back in time a couple of millennia – from thirteenth-century Norse myth. It is hard to escape the conclusion that the *Clash of the Titans* kraken is so named purely for the delight of audiences in hearing Laurence Olivier – who plays Zeus – say, 'Release the kraken'. For the record, I consider this a perfectly legitimate reason to ignore any amount of mythological chronology and geography). The sea-monster in the Medusa story is mentioned in our Greek sources, though, even if it's not a kraken. And even if turning the monster to stone with Medusa's head is an afterthought once Perseus has acquired it, rather than his reason for beheading her in the first place.

In his description of this scene, Pseudo-Apollodorus rather pleasingly refers to Andromeda as *boran thalassiō kētei*[24] – 'food for a sea-monster'. The word *kētos* (meaning 'sea-monster') is particularly resonant in this story, because ancient Greek sea-monsters share this name with Cēto (in Greek, she is spelled Kēto), the mother of the Gorgons, and indeed also the Graiai. As, in fact, do modern-day whales and dolphins, whose infraorder is Cetacea, from the same root.

We're accustomed to reading Greek myths to examine the fractured relationships between parents and children, but we often overlook this one, and the way a daughter is used to kill a representation or even manifestation of her mother. Perhaps the monster element is what puts us off. Yet surely the way Medusa is weaponized post-mortem against (at the very least) an echo of her mother – a sea-monster in her mother's image and sharing her name – has its parallels with Oedipus killing his father, Laius. Oedipus is alive while Medusa is dead, but both are the unwitting assassins of their parents. If killing a man seems somehow less forgivable than killing a sea-monster, we might do well to remember one story about Laius (for example, in Euripides' lost play *Chrysippos*)[25] that tells of him kidnapping a young man and raping him. Ashamed at what has been done to him, the young man, Chrysippos, kills himself with a sword. There is more than one kind of monster.

Clash of the Titans also shifts the chronology of one of this story's other mythic creatures: Pegasus. In the film, Pegasus is presented as a magical horse belonging to Zeus and loaned to Perseus to assist him in his quest, along with Bubo, an enchanting clockwork owl.

For the Greeks, this might have been a perplexing development, because Pegasus is born (fully formed, alongside his brother Chrysaor, a giant) from Medusa's severed neck. Both flying horse and giant are the offspring of Poseidon and Medusa, according to Pseudo-Apollodorus.[26] Medusa's spilled blood is also fecund: Ovid tells us that, as Perseus carries her head away over Libya, her blood drips onto the desert sands.[27] These drops of blood turn into various snakes, in what we might describe as a rare act of herpetohaematogenesis: the creation of snakes from blood. Libya, Ovid drily explains, is infested with snakes.

It scarcely needs saying that by separating Medusa from her family – her Gorgon sisters, her sea-monster parents, her equine and gigantic sons – we make her seem more disposable. A family of monsters may not seem like much of a family (although these things are all relative, I suppose, if you'll forgive the pun), but they are part of who she is. Modern versions of the Medusa story have tended to focus on Perseus; she is a relatively minor monster in Rick Riordan's bestselling novel *Percy Jackson and the Lightning Thief*, for example, although at least she was played by Uma Thurman in the 2010 film adaptation. Because of this shift in focus, we have lost sight of who Medusa is and what she means to those closest to her.

She is not a monster to her sisters. Pseudo-Apollodorus tells us that Sthenno and Euryale chase Perseus after he decapitates Medusa. He only escapes them because he is wearing the helmet of Hades, which makes him invisible. But it is important for us to note – given the solitary, hermit-like creature that tends to be portrayed in modern interpretations of her – that Medusa does not go unmissed or un-lamented.

The lament (or *oulion thrēnon* – 'deadly dirge', as Pindar would have it)[28] is another largely forgotten aspect of the Gorgons. Those huge mouths and lolling tongues which we see in so many examples of Gorgons and of *gorgoneia* are not just distended for the visual effect of a monstrously large, animalistic mouth. They also convey the capacity to make noise, and discordant noise at that. Both Medusa's sisters pursue Perseus, according to Pindar, before Athene rescues him. As mentioned above, Pindar also tells us Athene creates the flute (an instrument closer to pan pipes than a modern flute) to imitate the sound made by the swift jaws of Euryale. And later authors echo this: Gorgons make a grim noise. And if history has taught us anything, it is that women making a noise – whether speaking or shouting – tend to be viewed as intrinsically disruptive. Men are treated differently: the Greek hero Diomedes, for example, who fights against the Trojans in Homer's *Iliad*. Like most Homeric heroes, he is usually described with one of several stock epithets. One of these phrases is '*boēn agathos* Diomedes'[29] – which is usually translated as 'Diomedes of the loud war cry', although literally it means 'Diomedes, good at shouting', which is somewhat less poetic. However we choose to translate the phrase, it is clearly not a criticism. A war cry is an impressive part of Diomedes' heroic character, just as speed is a crucial element in the skills of 'swift-footed Achilles'. But the noise made by the Gorgons is always described negatively as deadly, baleful, a dirge. Is that because it's discordant? Or is it because they are female and they're making a loud noise? Diomedes' cry is surely also baleful and deadly to any hapless Trojan who might be facing him. But his shout is seen as something positive and martial, whereas the Gorgons' cry is something strange and terrible.

It is interesting to compare the relative fortunes of Medusa and another mortal who undergoes a divinely wrought transformation: Midas. Midas was king of Phrygia (now Turkey) and, like Medusa, he can claim divine parentage: in one tradition, his mother is the goddess Cybele. One day, Midas showed kindness to the satyr Silenus, who was a close friend of the god Dionysus. In return for this kindness, Dionysus granted Midas a wish, and was saddened when Midas chose to have everything he touched turn to gold. As Ovid tells the story, in Book Eleven of the *Metamorphoses*,[30] Midas is at first delighted by his new power: he changes a twig, then a stone, a clod of earth, an ear of corn and an apple into gold. So far, so good. Things go wrong when he tries to eat and the bread, meat and wine he attempts to consume are converted into gold too. Midas begs Dionysus to remove his new power: like so many wishers in so many stories, he has realized that what seemed like a good idea at the time is a far from uncomplicated blessing. Dionysus is uncharacteristically forgiving, and tells Midas to bathe in a river at its source. The king obeys the god, and plunges his body into the river. The gold flows from him into the waters. Even though this happened long ago, Ovid reminds his readers, when the river floods now, tiny bits of gold still appear in the nearby fields. Nathaniel Hawthorne, when he tells the story of Midas, adds in the tear-jerking element of a daughter whom Midas turns to gold with his embrace. But for Ovid, it is simple survival rather than paternal guilt (or rather, gilt) which makes Midas seek to return Dionysus' gift.

Midas doesn't have his gliding power for very long, admittedly. But he does have to make the journey to the River Pactolus near the city of Sardis with it. And a well-informed and amoral adventurer might fancy some of Midas' power for himself. It is clearly the case that owning one of his hands (or any body part, since wine turns to molten gold in his throat, as far as Ovid is concerned)[31] would be less perilous than having the power yourself, so long as you had something like a *kibisis* or other divine object to contain it. Actually, a golden glove would presumably do it: even Midas can't turn something to gold if it is gold already. And yet, it doesn't seem to occur to any impecunious hero to kill Midas on his way to the river, or even to lop off a finger or a toe. The divine assistance required to achieve this minor amputation would surely be less than Perseus needs to behead Medusa. And the quest for a golden body part isn't unknown in Greek myth: ask Jason, who set sail in the *Argo* to acquire a golden fleece (although this had already been removed from its original ovine owner). But Midas remains unmolested while Medusa is decapitated, even though he has displeased a god with his poor decision-making just as Medusa displeased Athene by being raped. Midas' body remains whole, even if he later displeases a second god, Apollo, prompting the punishment of having his ears changed into those of an ass. At least he gets to keep them. Indeed, they might even improve his hearing. And certainly they would prove more efficient at shooing flies. Meanwhile, Medusa is objectified to such an extent that her head becomes nothing more than a tool. These two children of gods are treated in remarkably different ways.

The crucial difference is one of perspective. We are encouraged to imagine Midas' story from his point of view. What must it be like, we imagine, as we follow his experiences in the *Metamorphoses*, to have everything we touch turn to gold? How would it feel to crack our teeth on golden bread? How would it taste to have liquid gold in our throats? We imagine the experience from the inside out. But with Medusa, we're encouraged to see her from the outside: how do we attack her? How do we avoid her gaze? How can we use her decapitated head? We never stop to ask ourselves what it must be like to be her, possessed of a deadly gaze just as Midas is possessed of a deadly touch. And yet, just as Midas discovers with his temporary power, it must be incredibly isolating. Medusa cannot look at a friend, a person, even an animal without killing them. This perhaps explains why she lives in a cave, as a surviving fragment of an Aeschylus play, *The Phorcides*, tells us.[32] Her sisters are either immune to her gaze or they are protected from it by the gloom of the cave, because they all live together without any risk of petrification. Yet her power is sufficient even after death to stop a sea-monster in its tracks, and to turn Atlas – a giant – into a mountain (Perseus petrifies him in a fit of pique, after Atlas refuses to welcome him into his home, having been given a dire warning from an oracle that a son of Jupiter would cause him harm. Oracles are often full of trickery, but in this instance, it has a point). So any visual contact with anything mortal – no matter how vast or powerful – is out of bounds to Medusa, unless she is prepared to destroy it. Her world must be one of darkness and statues.

The objectification of Medusa is nowhere more obvious than when we consider what happens to her head after her death. Perseus uses her to assist him against giants, monsters and assorted human irritants: her lethal gaze creates far more carnage after her death than it ever did before. Perseus apparently doesn't share Medusa's desire to minimize the harm she causes. Once he has seen off the sea-monster and rescued Andromeda, he stops for a rest on the shore. He washes his hands (cleanliness is next to demi-godliness), but pauses before putting Medusa's head down on the *dura harena* – 'hard sand',[33] in case he damages it. He makes a small cushion for it, out of leaves. It is a horrible moment in the story: the concern Perseus takes to avoid harming Medusa's head – which has proved so useful to him – could not be more different from the way he treated her when she was alive. She is more valuable to him as a weapon than she was as a living creature.

But what happens to Medusa after she has been used to kill everyone Perseus has taken exception to? She becomes what her artistic antecedents always were: a *gorgoneion*. Not only because she is now just a head, but because her head is given by Perseus to Athene. We can see the exact moment this happens on a vase held in the Museum of Fine Arts in Boston and attributed to the Tarporley Painter,[34] which was made in southern Italy in the early fourth century BCE. On the left-hand side of the scene is Perseus, still sporting his winged boots and fancy hat. He has just handed Medusa's head to

Athene; she holds it in her right hand. On the right, Hermes leans on a tree trunk, his legs idly crossed. But we shouldn't be deceived by his casual body language: all three figures are looking down at the ground as Athene holds the head up. They clearly believe Medusa's gaze would turn them to stone, gods or not. Athene holds a spear in her left hand which is so long that its tip extends beyond the parameters of the painting. Propped against her right hip is her round shield. Because it is at an angle, it catches the reflection of Medusa's head. The artist had obviously studied reflections, because he has painted her head upside down in the shield face, as it would be. Pseudo-Apollodorus tells us that Athene fastened the Gorgon head to the centre of her shield,[35] in which case this reflection is showing us exactly what's to come.

This story, then, takes us all the way back to where we began – in literary terms – with the earliest representation of a Gorgon in Homer's *Iliad*. There, Athene wore the Gorgon head on her aegis (although Medusa is not specifically named by Homer, and nor does he mention Perseus in relation to beheading a Gorgon). But is it really possible that the whole Perseus saga was created to explain why Gorgons are so often shown as only heads, *gorgoneia*? Why not? Greek storytellers created a monster. As so often with female deities, she becomes tripled, acquires two sisters (there are three Seasons, three Furies, three Graiai, three Graces . . .). Then they needed an explanation for why she was so often depicted as just a head. So the decapitation story develops.

If Ray Harryhausen's animated Medusa is the (relatively) modern incarnation that most of us knew best growing up, that may have changed in recent years, thanks to a pair of memes. One well-known image of Medusa and Perseus is the statue carved by Antonio Canova at the end of 1800, called *Perseus Triumphant*. It is held in the Vatican, at the Pio Clementino Museum.[36] There is also a copy at the Metropolitan Museum in New York.[37] Perseus is depicted as a formidably handsome hero. He is naked, his weight is on his left leg, his right leg trails slightly behind him, like a dancer. He holds a short sword in his right hand: near the tip, it has an extra curved blade arcing upwards. He wears the winged cap we've come to expect and has ornately worked sandals on his feet. His cloak is hanging off his left arm, and with his left hand he is grasping the hair of Medusa, which is a combination of snakes and curls. Her mouth is slightly open and we can just make out her tongue behind a neat row of teeth: a nod to those early Gorgons with their huge mouths and lolling tongues, perhaps. Perseus looks coolly proud of his trophy.

The statue is part of a long tradition showing Perseus in this way. Benvenuto Cellini's extraordinary bronze *Perseus with the Head of Medusa* – which was made around 1550 and now stands in the Piazza della Signoria in Florence – is a much gorier affair than the Canova marble. This Perseus – all mottled green muscles – holds aloft a head of Medusa whose eyes and mouth are slightly open, as though she has just exhaled her final breath. The mass of snakes and curls mingle with a mass of dripping flesh beneath her sliced neck. Perseus stands on top of Medusa's headless corpse in a repulsively triumphalist posture. His winged feet trample her ruined torso, her right arm hangs limp over the statue's plinth, her left hand grasps at her foot, the sole of which faces us as we look at the statue head-on. There is something disturbingly intimate about seeing the bare feet of her corpse. This image was notoriously reworked to feature the two contenders for the 2016 US presidential election, in what was first an ugly cartoon and later a hugely successful meme: you could buy the image printed onto T-shirts and tote bags. To some people, a woman with power and a voice is always a monster. And for some of these people, death and disfigurement are an appropriate response to such women.

The second Medusa meme appeared two years later, and its origins are somewhat more complicated. Ostensibly, it is a photograph of a statue made in 2008 by the Argentine-Italian artist Luciano Garbati. But it is extremely difficult to find any trace of the statue prior to the existence of the meme, which appeared at around the same time as Professor Christine Blasey Ford's testimony of sexual assault to the US Senate Judiciary Committee. The image is striking and extremely sharable: a statue of Medusa stands alone in front of a completely black background. She is naked, just like Perseus in the Canova and Cellini images, and is lithe, young, strong. Her hair is a mass of snakes, but they are beautiful, not grotesque: they look more like curling dreadlocks. Her expression is calm, her eyes gaze out at us unapologetically. Her arms are by her side and she holds a sword in her left hand. In her right hand is the decapitated head of Perseus, which she holds by the hair. It is an exact reversal of the Canova image. Some versions of the meme came with an accompanying text. 'Be thankful we only want equality', it reads, next to Medusa's head. Below Perseus' decapitated neck, it continues, 'and not payback.'[38]

It was the perfect illustration of what many women felt and continue to feel about the violence they experience at the hands of some men. Not only do these women face it in their daily lives, but they see it all around them presented as a norm, everywhere from newspaper headlines to the walls of art galleries and museums. Thousands of people walk past the Cellini statue in Florence every day; thousands more see the Canova in New York and in Rome. Medusa may have snakes for hair, but she still has the face and body of a woman. The Canova sanitizes this with its gleaming white marble. The name of the statue may be *Perseus Triumphant*, but it is only a triumphant image if you associate yourself with Perseus. The Cellini shows Perseus defiling Medusa's body so brutally that it must come from anger or contempt, or a combination of the two. It is no

less shocking than when Achilles does the same to Hector in Books
Twenty-Two and Twenty-Three of the *Iliad*: dragging his corpse
around the walls of Troy, refusing to bury him or to allow anyone
else to do so for days, until the gods finally intervene in Book Twenty-
Four. And yet Cellini's Perseus gazes down at the ground, even as
he holds Medusa's head aloft and in front of him: there is no possibility he might accidentally catch her petrifying eyes. He is still afraid
of her, even after he has beheaded her and trodden her down. If
you're looking for a better metaphor for virulent misogyny, I'm afraid
I don't have one.

We are so accustomed to seeing this image that we barely notice
the cruelty which underpins the story: it's just a hero and his trophy.
We walk past it in the same way we might half-heartedly notice a
statue of St George and a dragon: it's only a dragon, who cares? But
Medusa isn't a monster like a dragon. She's a woman who was raped
and then punished for it with snakish hair. Her lethal stare is a local-
ized peril: avoid her and you would never be in danger, because she
keeps herself far away from mortals. She is damaged first by a god,
then by a goddess. And finally Perseus comes looking for her to kill
her and mutilate her, to satisfy the whim of another man. No matter
who she encounters – besides her sisters – they only want to injure
her.

The shock of seeing Garbati's reversal of this, of Perseus' head
in Medusa's hand, is incredible. It jolts the viewer into acknowledging
a double standard: it is so rare in art to see men objectified, even
rarer for the objectifier to be a woman. It reminded me of a scene
in season three of the Netflix show *Orange is the New Black*,[39] where
two of the female inmates plan and then prepare to rape a male
prison guard who has raped one of them. The scene is toe-curling
and shocking in equal measure. Is the show really going to allow two
characters we have come to like, or even love, to behave in such a
horrific way: raping an unconscious man with a broom handle? In

the end, they can't go through with their revenge attack. It is an enormous relief for characters and viewers alike. And yet, we have seen the scenes of male-on-female rape. Be thankful they just want equality, and not payback.

Long before the Garbati meme, however, there was a gender-reversal of Perseus decapitating Medusa. The tale of Judith and Holofernes dates back to perhaps the second century BCE and can be found in the Book of Judith, which appears in some versions of the Old Testament. The Assyrian general, Holofernes, is blockading the town of Betulia.[40] Deprived of food and water, the Betulians hold out for as long as they can, but, after several weeks, they are reduced to near-surrender. Judith befriends Holofernes by walking to his tent and introducing herself as a widow: she is so beautiful, his soldiers allow her to enter. Holofernes invites her to stay for dinner, during which he gets drunk. Once he is unconscious, Judith prays for her god to assist her, and beheads him. She takes his head back to Betulia and the Assyrians – deprived of this necessary part of their general – withdraw.

The parallels between this story and that of Medusa and Perseus are as revealing as the differences. Firstly, Judith has to go and find Holofernes. Her quest is somewhat shorter than Perseus', but she still needs to seek out her target. Second, she needs to take advantage of his feeling of security in his own space: this is not a battlefield killing. Next, Holofernes, like Medusa, is unconscious when he is killed. His superior power might otherwise have produced a different outcome. And Judith, like Perseus, is reliant on assistance from a god to help her commit the actual beheading.

But the differences are also crucial: Holofernes is the aggressor in this story (well, unless you can find an account by an Assyrian). He has cut off a whole town from food and fresh water. And when Judith finally kills him, it is in desperation, just a few days before her town would be forced to surrender. Of course, we might feel that

Perseus is similarly forced into his quest, but being asked to fetch an unlikely object for a king is considerably less of a moral duty than trying to save men, women and children from thirst and starvation (even if that king is a villain trying to marry your mother). Judith hopes that by committing her murder, she will save a town full of people; Perseus kills Medusa and then goes on to commit hundreds more murders: in Pindar's tenth Pythian Ode,[41] he turns an entire island populace to stone, while Ovid has him petrify two hundred people during a fight at his own wedding.[42] That's certainly one way to make sure you have enough cake to go around.

A few metres away from Cellini's *Perseus with the Head of Medusa* in Florence is a copy of a bronze sculpture by Donatello, of Judith and Holofernes. The original was cast in around 1460, and stands in the nearby Palazzo Vecchio. Judith has a remarkable set to her jaw as she raises her sword. Her chin juts forward as she steels herself for the task ahead. Both characters are clad in respectable drapery and the bronze of Holofernes' bare chest has been rendered without much muscular detail: there is none of the athleticism of the naked Perseus in Cellini's image. Similarly with Artemisia Gentileschi's *Judith Beheading Holofernes*, which was painted in 1611–12 and can be found in the Museo Nazionale di Capodimonte, in Naples. Here, Judith and her maid approach the task of beheading this enemy general with all the weary efficiency of two women doing the laundry. Nothing about this killing is presented as erotic. Judith is a widow, she lives a life of complete chastity after the death of her husband.[43]

Conversely, there is, it seems, always a sexual element to the beheading of Medusa. Freud saw it as a castration myth, because his need to make everything about the male experience apparently precluded him from noticing that it is Medusa who gets beheaded and that she might therefore be a more relevant archetype for women than men. A Freudian slip, perhaps. If you were looking for a gendered psychological interpretation of the Medusa story, surely it would make more sense to suggest that it represents an abiding fear of the power of the female gaze.

Sexually charged representations of Medusa continue to the present day: look at the women who have played or been photographed as her: Uma Thurman in the *Percy Jackson* film; Rihanna (as styled by Damien Hirst) as a naked Medusa, hair full of snakes, and a pair of snake-eyed contact lenses to boot, on the cover of *GQ* magazine.[44] These beautiful women are playing with the duality of Medusa (or one duality, at least). She is a monster, but also a deeply desirable woman. Indeed, we're hard-pushed to find an asexual depiction of Medusa in contemporary culture, although *The Lego Movie* manages it beautifully, if briefly.[45] Her Lego snake hair is particularly good.

Even when Medusa is not viewed as a monster by an ancient author, her desirability is apparently intrinsic to her story. The second-century CE geographer Pausanias offers an account of her in which he promises to miss out all the fantastical elements and stick to the rational parts of her story.[46] For Pausanias, Medusa is a warrior queen who ruled the Libyans who lived near Lake Triton, and hunted and led them into battle. One day, Medusa is encamped with her army and Perseus (leader of the opposing army) assassinates her in the night. Wondering at her beauty even in death, Pausanias continues, Perseus cut off her head so he could take it and show it to the Greeks. The story may have been stripped of the fantastical, but its sexualised fear and objectification of women have survived just fine.

Let's conclude by going back to one of the earliest depictions of Medusa, which shows her alongside her offspring, the winged horse Pegasus and the giant Chrysaor, who – most versions of the myth tell us – sprang fully formed from her severed neck. And yet this sculpture – originally on the pediment of the temple of Artemis on

Corcyra (modern-day Corfu) and now displayed in Corfu's Archaeological Museum – shows Medusa with her head very much still attached.

The Archaic temple and its pediment sculptures date back to the early sixth century BCE. We see Medusa at her most strange and monstrous: bulbous tongue out, snakes slithering out of her hair. She also wears a pair of snakes as a tight belt around her short dress: their bodies are twisted together and their heads face one another across her mid-torso. Her head and body are facing straight out at the viewer, but her highly muscled legs are sprinting sideways, as if she is fleeing her killer. She is flanked by both of her children, although they are less intact than she is (the sculpture is made of porous limestone). Behind Pegasus and Chrysaor, on each side of Medusa is a large cat, a lion or a panther, tying Medusa to the goddess Artemis in her role as mistress of wild animals – *potnia therōn*. This is a pleasing echo of Medusa's face in those early *gorgoneia*, if we interpret them as apotropaic devices to help rid us of our fears of wild animals: Artemis controls wild creatures, and here is Medusa in pride of place on Artemis' temple, surrounded by snakes and big cats. Already our fear of the unknown wild seems a little more manageable.

No wonder Medusa's name means 'ruler' or 'guardian'.[47] She is dual in her nature, both a monster and a protector (as I write this, a small terracotta *gorgoneion* looks up at me from my desk. I have always preferred to see her as a protection rather than a threat). Indeed, Medusa is made up of dualities. She is beautiful and hideous, one of a trinity and yet alone. She is the mother of two mythological creatures, but also the slayer of one. She is most powerful after death, a death which occurs only because she was temporarily powerless in sleep. She gives birth in the act of dying.

One final illustration of her dual nature: once the god Asclepius has learned the healing arts, he is capable of saving the dying and bringing the dead back to life. This, Pseudo-Apollodorus tells us (long after he has finished with the story of Perseus), is because the goddess Athene gave Asclepius two drops of the Gorgon's blood.[48] The blood from the left-hand side of her body is deadly, but the blood from the right-hand side of her body is *sōtērian* – salvation. Medusa is – and always has been – the monster who would save us.

THE AMAZONS

Amazons were 'a bunch of golden-shielded, silver-axed, man-loving, boy-killing women.'[1] The fifth-century BCE historian Hellanikos of Lesbos presumably doesn't intend this list as a compliment, but it certainly makes me want to join them. It's not the only description of these warrior women that might leave the reader wondering just how much disapproval is vying with desire. If Hellanikos is aiming only to tell us of Amazonian martial prowess and barbarian habits, he surely wouldn't need to mention the man-loving element, unless loving men is itself a sign of an unnatural, barbarian woman (which it may well be). The boy-killing, incidentally, is his explanation for how the tribe of Amazons remains all-female: they must get rid of any male children one way or another. But, as mentioned above, many ancient societies had no problem with killing or exposing what they perceived as weak baby boys (and any kind of baby girls), so his disapproval is perhaps not quite as pointed as ours would hopefully be, on the subject of selective infanticide.

The Greeks were fascinated by these women: barbarians as opposed to Greeks, who often fought against Greeks. Amazons are the second most popular mythological figures (after Heracles) found on vase paintings.[2] More than a thousand Amazons appear on vases, in fact,[3] and more than sixty Amazon names are painted onto those vases. So what is it about these women – who exist in a space between masculine and feminine, between civilization and wildness, between real and fantastical – which proved so compelling to ancient writers and, in particular, artists? And how did we lose them? Most people could probably name Heracles, Theseus or Achilles, but the Amazons with which each hero was associated – Hippolyta, Antiope and Penthesilea – have been remembered less well. And when they have been, it has rarely been for a good reason.

We should, though, think about the Amazons as a tribe, or group. Because one of the most important things about these women is their collective nature: they are usually found together. It's a stark contrast to the winner-takes-all mentality that pervades the male hero ethos in, for example, the Trojan War. Look at Achilles, in the first book of Homer's *Iliad*: because he feels his honour has been slighted by Agamemnon, he begs his mother (the sea-nymph, Thetis) to intercede with Zeus and have him aid the Trojan – enemy – cause. The Greek soldiers, who were moments earlier his comrades, are now mere collateral damage in his quest for personal glory. Or Ajax, the Greek hero so tormented by losing Achilles' armour to Odysseus (the two men offer competing claims after the death of their comrade, and the Greeks decide in Odysseus' favour) that he attempts a killing spree of his erstwhile friends. Only the intervention of Athene – who confuses Ajax, making him kill livestock while believing he is slaughtering his comrades – prevents him from committing a terrible crime. When Ajax comes to and realizes what he has done, the shame is so great that he takes his own life.

In other words, the heroic mindset for the Greeks who fight at Troy is intrinsically selfish and self-absorbed. There are exceptions (Achilles' devotion to Patroclus, for example, and Patroclus' desire to heal their injured comrades), but the *Iliad* and Sophocles' *Ajax* show us a profoundly individualistic type of hero. And if you want to see what a good leader of men Odysseus is, count how many of the Ithacans with whom he sets sail from Troy make it home alongside him. The answer is: none. Odysseus is a hero because of his own adventures, his own brushes with monsters and mishaps. But he is not a man to stand alongside, unless you have a death wish. Rather, he is a man who can lose a comrade on his travels and not even notice that the poor guy is gone and needs to be buried. Elpenor would lie unburied forever, except his ghost seizes the opportunity of Odysseus' trip to the Underworld and pitches up to complain about his fate.

Unlike these men, Amazons fight alongside one another. When, in Quintus Smyrnaeus' *Fall of Troy*,[4] Penthesilea decides to fight Achilles in the later part of the Trojan War, twelve Amazons accompany her. Quintus lists all their names. It is the Amazons' intensely tribal nature which helps keep them alive in battle – Amazons are generally shown fighting alongside one another on the vase paintings and sculptures we have – but this loyalty can also jeopardize their safety. Although vase painters list the names of dozens of Amazons, we tend to come back to the stories of only a couple. Of these, the best-known today is probably Hippolyta. Hippolyta was a queen of the Amazons, and the daughter of Ares, god of war. Not only does Hippolyta inherit her father's martial skill (the epic poet Apollonius of Rhodes calls her *philoptolemoio* – 'war-loving'),[5] she also has her celebrated belt from him: Pseudo-Apollodorus calls it *Areos zōstēra*[6] – the belt of Ares. It is this belt which Heracles (his name isn't Hercules until the Romans get hold of him) seeks in his ninth labour. And which, somewhat irritatingly, translators have tended to describe as Hippolyta's girdle.

This translation is a bizarre choice even if we are, like Puck in *A Midsummer Night's Dream*, thinking of a genderless girdle which can be put round about the earth in forty minutes[7] (though for many people today, the word 'girdle' implies an undergarment worn by women of my grandmother's generation. One occasionally saw them on washing lines in my childhood: damp instruments of torture). It is an enormous pity to see Hippolyta distorted and diminished by this linguistic shift. She is wearing neither restrictive underwear nor a simple tie around her waist: she is wearing a war belt. The Greek word used to describe her belt is *zōstēr*: the exact same word used to describe the war belt worn by a male warrior for holding weapons. The word for a woman's belt is *zōnē*, which doesn't have martial connotations. Not for the first time, we see that an accurate translation has been sacrificed in the pursuit of making women less alarming (and less impressive) in English than they were in Greek. Euripides, Pseudo-Apollodorus, Apollonius of Rhodes, Diodorus Siculus and Pausanias all use the word *zōstēr*.[8] For all these men, Hippolyta is a warrior, plain and simple.

Or rather, not plain and simple: ornate and highly decorated. Because Amazons separated themselves from respectable Greek norms with their choice of clothing, as well as their all-female society and fighting skill. Unlike Greek men and women, who wore tunics of varying lengths and draperies over bare legs, Amazons wore tunic tops over trousers or leggings.

The British Museum has a wonderful alabastron: a slender pottery perfume bottle, about fifteen centimetres tall, made around 480 BCE.[9] It is decorated with a lovely black and white figure of a woman, her head turned so we can see that her long, curly hair is tied back. She is most probably an Amazon, because she is dressed in the style which we will soon see worn by figures securely identified as Amazons (potters often painted names next to the characters on their pots). She wears a pair of black straight-legged trousers, beneath a tunic top which belts in tightly at the waist. It is a linothorax (a protective garment made from either glued linen or leather) represented by monochrome patterns of lines and dots. In her right hand she holds the Amazons' favoured weapon – an axe – and a quiver is also visible, strapped to her back. The style of her clothing could not look less dated: her weapons are the only things which differentiate her from someone walking through the museum to see this little bottle. That, and the fact that her tunic top would protect her from your weapon if you attacked her.

The tight leg-coverings (and sometimes also long sleeves on their tunics) are shown in incredible geometric detail on red-figure vases. A *krater* in the Metropolitan Museum in New York (attributed to the gloriously named Painter of the Woolly Satyrs in the mid-fifth century BCE)[10] shows an Amazonomachy – a battle between Greeks and Amazons. The Amazons are wearing the most intricate designs on their leggings: chequerboard squares, tight zig-zags, hollow diamonds within a diamond grid. One has an armoured tunic, and another wears a decorated cap. One has the skin of a large cat as a cloak: his paw hangs against her thigh. Two Greek men are fighting these women: they are facing in opposite directions. The one facing to our left, closest to the viewer, is down on the ground. He is cowering behind his large round shield, as an Amazon on horseback thrusts her spear at him. We can see the sole of one of his bare feet; the Amazons have lace-up ankle boots protecting theirs. The other Greek draws back his spear to attack the two Amazons in front of him. Both women have their arms raised as they wield their battleaxes. Follow the scene around the pot and we find men riding a chariot to come and help their comrades.

There are a number of things which are remarkable about this scene. The first is that the Amazons are far more ornately clad than the Greeks. The men's plain tunics contrast with their own finely decorated shields, but the Amazons are a riot of pattern and texture. The second is that this is a pretty even battle and the result is in question. One man is down, one is outnumbered, but more men are coming to join the fray. The men fight alone, as does the Amazon on horseback. The two women on foot fight alongside each other, comrades in arms. This is surely why Diodorus Siculus could say that the Amazons were 'superior in strength and eager for war'.[11] These women aren't fighting because they've been attacked and they have to, they're fighting because they're warriors and they were born to. Another intriguing feature of the painting is the type of axe which two Amazons are wielding. The handle is long and thin, the blade sharply pointed. Amazons were so closely associated with this particular type of weapon (*securis*, to give it its Latin name) that Pliny the Elder tells us that it was invented by Penthesilea, the Amazon queen who fought at Troy.[12] Not only were Amazons respected fighters, but they were innovators in the art of war. No wonder Homer called them *antianeirai*,[13] 'equivalent to men'. Homer also describes war belts, incidentally – the leather and metal belts worn by the great warriors of the Trojan War – and he too uses the word *zōstēr*, the same word other authors use for Hippolyta's belt.

So when Heracles is sent to acquire Hippolyta's belt, this is the object he is looking for. There is assuredly a sexual subtext to a man – and particularly a man so renowned for his multiple, complex and sometimes violent personal relationships – seeking to remove a particular item of clothing from a woman, particularly something worn around the waist or hips. But trying to convey that by translating the word *zōstēr* as something other than 'war belt' costs far more than it is worth; Hippolyta deserves better. Besides, there is often a sexual, indeed a sexually aggressive subtext in Heracles' adventures: we would do well to remember that Heracles is performing his labours only as a penance for the murder of his wife and children during temporary insanity (this part of his story was wisely omitted from the Disney animated film *Hercules*, which is by far my favourite cinematic adaptation of any Greek myth, omissions notwithstanding).

Heracles arrives at the Amazons' home, which is placed most frequently at Themiscyra, on the southern coast of the Black Sea, although they are occasionally placed in Libya. His reception is, perhaps, surprising. The warrior women do not attack him. Instead, he is received by Hippolyta and her women in a scene we can see on a fourth-century BCE pottery fragment held by the Metropolitan Museum.[14] A somewhat uncomfortable Heracles stands, making his case to Hippolyta: his raised eyebrows and wide eyes give him an anxious expression. Amazons surround him, armed with axes, so perhaps this is what is alarming him. Hippolyta sits serenely in front of her guest. She is wearing a belt (it looks like leather studded with metal discs). Perhaps this is the very one he has come to claim.

We can read a more detailed version of this story in Pseudo-Apollodorus' *Bibliotheca*. Eurystheus orders Heracles to bring back Hippolyta's belt for his daughter, Admete. We glean some extra information about Hippolyta here: she rules over the Amazons, a people skilled in war, who live around the River Thermodon.¹⁵ Pseudo-Apollodorus describes their lives as *andrian* – 'manly'. He then repeats one of the stranger myths to appear in the Amazon story: that they ironed one breast to aid the successful throwing of spears or firing of arrows (sometimes it is more dramatic still: surgical removal). This is not a practice with which the Amazons are associated earlier in literature (Pseudo-Apollodorus is writing in either the first or second century CE), or in visual representations. None of the vase paintings mentioned above shows single-breasted Amazons, and none of the Amazons seems to be struggling to cope with her weapon. Indeed, vase paintings often show another female figure – the goddess Artemis, who was renowned for her hunting skills – with a bow and arrow, and she holds the bow at arm's length from her torso. Even the most pneumatic breasts would be no hindrance.¹⁶

So where does the mysterious breast-removal idea come from? The Greeks were enormous fans of what we might call folk-etymology, but a less generous person might describe as nonsense. They loved to find meanings in names through the words which appeared to lurk within them (the obsession that some fifth-century BCE intellectuals had with doing this is mocked magnificently by the comedian Aristophanes in his play *The Clouds*). 'Amazon' was believed to derive from the negating prefix 'a-' and the word *mastos*, meaning 'breast' (we obviously derive our word 'mastitis' from this Greek word). But the name 'Amazon' wasn't Greek: there are several suggestions as to which language it may have been borrowed from, but we don't know its origin for sure. The one thing we do know is that it was a loan-word for the Greeks, a word taken from another language. Attempts to impose Greek meaning onto it were a diversion for intellectuals with too much free time, but nothing more meaningful than that.

No explanation is offered for why Admete might want Hippolyta's war belt, only that she has set her heart on it. Perhaps she has a yearning for something which Pseudo-Apollodorus describes as being a gift from Ares, and a symbol of Hippolyta's supremacy over all the Amazons; perhaps she wishes she too could wear brightly coloured leggings and swing a war axe. So Heracles sets out in his ship, kills a large number of men in assorted fracas en route, and arrives at the harbour of Themiscyra. Considering the reputation for slaughter which must accompany Heracles, Hippolyta behaves in an extraordinarily generous manner. She approaches him, not armed to the teeth and ready to kill this dangerous adventurer, but peacefully, to ask why he has come.

When he explains that he wants her belt, she doesn't argue, or barter. She simply promises to give it to him. This is scarcely the behaviour of the bellicose barbarian women we have been led to expect. Why should Hippolyta give away her prized belt to a man she has never met before, who only wants it as a trinket or status symbol for a girl she has never met at all? The belt was a present from Ares, after all, and as we know from other stories, gifts from gods are enormously valuable to heroes: Perseus required a whole set of them to take on Medusa. And yet Hippolyta is willing to hand over her father's belt without any argument. Later authors would suggest an instant attraction formed between the two heroes, which serves to explain Hippolyta's kindness. The notion that this barbarian woman might simply be generous with her fighting equipment is obviously too strange to stand: there must be romance in the air. But generosity at first sight is all we see in the scene on the Metropolitan

Museum pottery fragment, which is four or five hundred years older than this written account.

The Amazons and the Greeks end up fighting, in spite of this seemingly auspicious beginning. The guilty party is (as so often in Greek myth) the goddess Hera, whose malevolence is both boundless and multi-directional. Her dislike of Heracles is unwavering, caused by the fact that Zeus fathered him with a mortal woman, Alcmene: there are few things that irritate Hera more than the offspring of her husband's many infidelities. To stir up trouble against Heracles in this instance, Hera disguises herself as an Amazon and tells the other women that these *xenoi* – strangers, or foreigners (from which we take the word 'xenophobia') – are kidnapping their queen. The Amazons pick up their arms and hasten to see what is happening to the queen, who has been talking to Heracles on his ship. Heracles, seeing a bunch of armed women approaching on horseback, assumes he has been tricked. Showing his customary calm reason, he asks no questions but simply kills Hippolyta and takes her belt. Plutarch also has him take her axe away with him[17] (those who choose to see the belt purely as a piece of sexual symbolism tend to overlook this part. One hesitates to imagine what a woman's fighting-axe might represent, but I feel confident Freud would be no help at all). Heracles and his men fight the Amazons and then he sails away to Troy. Hippolyta's generosity was worth nothing when set against the paranoia of a murderous man.

Pausanias, in his *Description of Greece*, tells us about the temple of Zeus at Olympia which has the labours of Heracles carved onto it. The taking of Hippolyta's belt was placed above the doors. Additionally, on the base of the throne of the statue of Zeus (a huge gold- and ivory-decorated figure) is a scene of an Amazonomachy. Pausanias looks at this scene of Heracles fighting the Amazons and carefully counts the number of combatants on each side: twenty-nine. He also notes that Theseus is fighting alongside Heracles.

In some versions of their respective myths, Theseus and Heracles team up against the Amazons, as on the relief which Pausanias admires. In other versions, Theseus makes his own separate voyage to the Amazons after Heracles had done the same. The biographer Plutarch discusses these variations in his *Life of Theseus*.[18] In the earliest versions he has found of the story, Theseus receives the Amazon Antiope as a reward for his bravery in fighting her sisters. But Plutarch finds this unconvincing: none of the other men on the Heraclean expedition take an Amazon captive, he explains. Plutarch finds the alternative explanation more plausible. He mentions the author Bion, who claimed that Theseus took the Amazon by deceit (this would be very much in keeping with Theseus' attitude to women, it must be said. As Plutarch drily puts it, there are other stories about Theseus' marriages which had neither good beginnings nor happy endings).[19] By nature, Bion says, the Amazons were *philandrous* – 'fond of men' – and didn't flee from Theseus, but rather sent him gifts as a welcome guest. He invited the Amazon who brought the gifts onto his ship and then set sail with her still on board.

This, then, provides the cause for the second Amazonomachy: when the Amazons invade Athens to try to reclaim their lost sister, Antiope. Plutarch says this Amazon war was neither a minor nor womanish task for Theseus. He did not underestimate the perils of fighting these formidable warriors, and nor should we. The Amazons, Plutarch adds, wouldn't have made their camp nor fought hand-to-hand battles between the Pnyx and the Museion (two hills not far from the centre of Athens) if they hadn't been fearless in conquering the surrounding country. An Amazon invasion, in other words, is impressive. They make sure they control the surrounding area before they take on a city. In spite of Theseus having a whole city of men at his disposal, the war lasts for three months. Cleidemus, one of Plutarch's sources, says that hostilities ended when Hippolyta secured a treaty between the two sides (Cleidemus gives Antiope's name as

Hippolyta, Plutarch explains). And when the tragedian Aeschylus describes the Amazons fighting in Athens, he imagines they built their own citadel on the Hill of Ares, to rival those that Theseus had built;[20] in other words, this Amazon battle wasn't just a scrap or guerrilla warfare, but an all-out siege.

As we have seen with other parts of the Amazon myth, there are multiple versions of this story. Some sources say that the woman who fought beside Theseus (Plutarch has given up on a conclusive name, it seems) was killed by another Amazon, called Molpadia. In other words, this version of Antiope fights against the Amazons who have come to reclaim her. But Plutarch reassures us that the antiquity of this story means we shouldn't be surprised that it wanders about. And wander about it does: Theseus goes on to marry again, a woman named Phaedra. Sometimes it is this which provokes the war with the Amazons, because he has ditched Antiope for another woman. Theseus also has a son by Antiope/Hippolyta, called either Hippolytus or Demophoön.

It is a sign of how popular Amazons were in the ancient world that there are so many contradictory stories about them. It implies that multiple storytellers were creating their myth across different parts of Greece over a long period of time. Perhaps the Athenians felt left out of the Heracles story, so added their local hero Theseus into the mix. And maybe they also preferred a version of the story in which Theseus didn't kidnap Antiope, but rather she fell in love with him when he was besieging Themiscyra alongside Heracles,[21] which she also surrendered to him. It's interesting how the addition of the favourite Athenian male hero doesn't just add romance to Antiope's story, but also makes her a weaker fighter, more prone to betray her sisterhood for the love of a man. Most versions of the Amazons emphasize their solidarity with one another, whether it is painted on a vase, sculpted in a temple, or told in a history, biography or poem. So Antiope's story offers a particular, reassuring counterexample to those who found the idea of women supporting other women to be disconcerting: even an Amazon could be lured away from her true nature by love. Yes, these warrior women were a mighty fighting force, but at least there was the possibility that you could seduce (or kidnap) one and even the odds a bit that way.

Alternatively, you could try to engage an Amazon in single combat, though it might help if you were the greatest warrior the Greek world had ever known. And the best place to do that would be at the third great battle between Amazons and Greeks, which took place in the final year of the Trojan War. As Herodotus puts it, the Amazons were in no wise found wanting during the battles of Troy.[22]

Pausanias was a bit more perplexed by this Trojan expedition. Looking at a sculpture of Amazons fighting Theseus, he wonders that they didn't lose their enthusiasm for danger after earlier defeats.[23] They had lost Themiscyra to Heracles, and then lost the army they sent to Athens against Theseus. Nevertheless, he ponders, they came to Troy to fight against the Athenians and indeed all the Greeks. It's an interesting question. Is it so surprising that the Amazons keep fighting even after they have lost battles? That is what warriors do: win or lose, they continue to fight. The Greeks spent nine years not winning the Trojan War, and in Book Two of the *Iliad*, Homer shows us how keen many of them are to give up and go home. But they stay and keep fighting even so.

We have lost the vast majority of literature written in the ancient world: well over 90 per cent. And among those losses is, or rather was, an epic poem called the *Aethiopis*. It followed on from the *Iliad*, continuing the story of the latter part of the Trojan War. As we have seen, the *Iliad* concludes with the funeral of Hector, the Trojans' greatest warrior, who died at the hands of Achilles in brief, brutal combat. The *Iliad*'s concluding line is, 'And so the Trojans buried Hector, tamer of horses.' For a modern reader, the poem ends by looking forward obliquely to the fall of the city: her mightiest defender is dead, and we know the city cannot hold out against an invading army for very much longer. But there is a Homeric scholiast (a textual critic writing in the ancient world) who tells us something absolutely remarkable about the connective tissue between the *Iliad* and the *Aethiopis*. Some versions of the *Iliad* which he had available to him apparently concluded, 'And so they buried Hector. And then came an Amazon, the daughter of great-hearted Ares, killer of men.'[24] Another variant identifies the Amazon by name, and mentions her mother too: 'And then came an Amazon, the daughter of Otrera, graceful Penthesilea.'

There are reasons to be sad about most of the lost pieces of Latin and Greek literature. But I feel a special pang for the *Aethiopis*, which covered the story of Penthesilea and also of Memnon, the great Ethiopian prince who fought the Greeks at Troy. So much of our understanding of the Trojan War comes from the *Iliad*, which finishes before either of these characters appear. And classics so often stands accused of being limited in its scope (thanks, in part, to the very limited number of schools that are able to offer it as part of the curriculum, as well as the undeniable truth that almost all authors writing in the Greco-Roman world were from a tiny elite of wealthy, educated men). So it is especially painful to have lost a poem which would have shone a much-needed focus on characters who are barely represented at all in the literature we do have. And there is something extra-tantalizing, therefore, in these alternative endings to the *Iliad*, which mention Penthesilea by name, and tell us of her divine parentage. In the Homeric tradition, this is exactly how we are introduced to male heroes: Achilles, son of Peleus and Thetis, for example. Or Agamemnon and Menelaus, who are often referred to as the sons of Atreus. Family connections are a crucial part of how we define a hero, and when that hero has divine relatives (Aeneas, son of Aphrodite, or Sarpedon, son of Zeus), their hero status is that much more impressive. There is a moment in the *Iliad*[25] when Hera asks why the gods should care about Hector, since he is mortal, and was nursed by a mortal woman. She contrasts him unfavourably with Achilles, whose mother was a goddess. While a hero can be of purely mortal parentage, a divine parent is better.

So when Penthesilea is introduced to us as the daughter of Ares, it is meaningful not just because now we know her lineage, but because it boosts her heroic status. The other gods may be less partial than Hera: Zeus explains that Hector was the gods' favourite Trojan because he offered them the most pleasing sacrifices. The king of the gods is less concerned by whose child a hero might be, so much as by how devout and generous the hero has been, a characteristically self-absorbed piece of (relative) egalitarianism. But the gods do tend to look after their own: the Trojan Aeneas is saved on the battlefield by his mother, Aphrodite, for example.

By any measure we might use to define a hero of the Trojan War, Penthesilea scores highly. She is a warrior and, as we've seen, the inventor of the type of axe used by Amazons in battle. She is the daughter of a god, specifically the god of war: there is no finer pedigree for a fighter. She battles the greatest Greek warrior of all, Achilles, which puts her on a par with Hector. Not only that, but she seeks out this battle, unlike Hector, who runs away when he sees Achilles on the rampage in Book Twenty-Two of the *Iliad*. Penthesilea is fighting for glory, just like Achilles. And she is fighting to defend a city, just like Hector. Except that the city she fights for – Troy – is not hers. She chooses this battle, chooses to be an ally to the Trojans after they have lost their most staunch defender, Hector. Homeric heroes usually look out for themselves, but for us, Penthesilea is perhaps a more sympathetic character, one who stands up for the underdog.

So why does Penthesilea choose to fight in someone else's war? Pseudo-Apollodorus gives us an answer:[26] she had accidentally killed her sister, Hippolyta. Obviously, we have looked at Hippolyta's death at the hands of Heracles (and seen that her name is also sometimes connected to Theseus, although that Amazon is usually called Antiope), but here is another version of her story. As noted above, this multiplicity of fates for Hippolyta suggests that she was an enormously popular figure, whose story was told across the Greek world by many storytellers: we find multiple and contradictory versions of Achilles in just the same way. There is more detail about Penthesilea's tragedy in Quintus Smyrnaeus' poem.[27] He explains that Penthesilea was filled with *penthos* – grief – because she had killed her sister by accident. Aiming her spear at a deer, she missed her mark and killed her sister by mistake. As we can see, her name holds the word for grief within it, as though the tragedy was waiting to happen. Fearing the pursuit of the Furies for the terrible crime of killing her sibling, Penthesilea seeks to cleanse herself by fighting and ultimately dying, rendering herself a human sacrifice, a life for a life.

Again, this is an extraordinary decision for anyone to make. When Ajax kills livestock rather than his comrades (he has been made mad by Athene to save the lives of his fellow Greeks), he kills himself rather than live with the shame of his wrongdoing, and the knowledge that his enemies will laugh at him. When Orestes is pursued by the Furies – dark goddesses of vengeance – for the crime of killing his mother, Clytemnestra, he tries to outrun them. They pursue him across the Greek world until (in Aeschylus' play *Eumenides*) they eventually agree for him to stand trial in Athens. Both these men have the option of doing something less self-centred in response to their murdering. Ajax could make amends for the attempted slaughter of his erstwhile friends by, say, defending an outnumbered ally. Orestes could similarly try to assuage the Furies for his crime. But Ajax is too ashamed and Orestes relies on Apollo and Athene (always available to assist a hapless Greek man, it seems) to help him out.

Penthesilea feels a different kind of responsibility for her accidental crime. She blames herself far more than Orestes ever seems to, although he murders his mother in cold blood. So would the Furies pursue Penthesilea with an extra vigour, or is she just more remorseful than other killers? Whatever her reasons, she determines to try to use her death for someone else's good – the defence of the Trojans. According to Pseudo-Apollodorus, Priam, the king of Troy, offers her absolution for her crime.[28] The word he uses is *kathartheisa*, 'to cleanse', from which we derive the word 'catharsis'.

According to Quintus, Penthesilea is accompanied by twelve named Amazons. As is usual with Amazons, she does not fight alone. Again, this is an interesting distinction. Orestes is pursued by the Furies and eventually stands trial alone, although he is aided by Apollo and Athene. Ajax dies alone: his wife Tecmessa cannot save him and his brother Teucer arrives too late to do so.[29] Penthesilea is also guilty of a crime, however accidentally it was committed (the story of Oedipus tells us that ignorance is no excuse when it comes to divine retribution). And yet she is not shunned by her Amazon sisters, she is not abandoned to seek absolution alone. They all ride with her from Thermodon to Troy; they all fight together.

And when Amazons fight, they fight to the death. Pseudo-Apollodorus tells us that Penthesilea kills many Greeks, including Machaon. And Quintus tells us about her battle in a lot more detail. For him, Penthesilea is as much a hero as any man, and he treats her accordingly in his narrative. When she and her twelve Amazon companions arrive, the people of Troy are overjoyed; Quintus compares them to drought-ravaged lands finally receiving rain. Priam – king of Troy – is compared to a blind man seeing light again. This is the salvation he and his people have been waiting for. Thirteen highly skilled warriors are potentially enough, it seems, to swing the odds of the war in Troy's favour. And Penthesilea sees herself as the equal of her male Greek counterparts: she promises Priam that she will take on Achilles and kill him. Quintus calls her *nēpiē* – 'crazy', 'a fool'.[30] Interestingly, it is the same word Homer uses to describe

Patroclus, when he begs Achilles to let him wear his friend's armour and fight in his stead, in Book Sixteen of the *Iliad*. He too is a madman, begging for his own death, though he doesn't know it. Is Quintus deliberately echoing Homer here? It seems more than likely. Patroclus is mad because his request to borrow Achilles' armour will result in his death: he will die at the hands of Hector, once the latter realizes that it is Patroclus he is fighting, and not his more skilful comrade, Achilles. Penthesilea is having her own death foreshadowed by this choice of word, and by the parallels between her and Patroclus. They have confidence in their abilities, which are considerable. But the confidence is misplaced even so, and they will both be cut down by a superior fighter. It is another way in which we are told that Penthesilea is the equal of male warriors: the same language reflects the same situation.

Only Andromache, Hector's widow, is not caught up in the moment. She wants Penthesilea to know that Hector was a superior warrior and he was killed by Achilles, so the Amazon has no chance. It's an angry, grief-filled lament from a woman whose only consolation after the death of her husband is the certainty that Hector was the greatest warrior who ever fought for Troy. The arrival of a new hero who might take on Achilles and win is clearly threatening to Andromache. While she would surely prefer Troy's most powerful enemy to be vanquished, the Greeks to be repelled, her city to win the war, that outcome would be bittersweet for her if it came at the cost of acknowledging that her dead husband was not, after all, the greatest warrior who defended Troy. Her status is dependent upon his, even after his death. And his is vulnerable, now he is dead, to new warriors surpassing him.

Not for the only time in Greek myth, the next part of Penthesilea's story reveals a goddess involving herself in the business of destroying a woman, even though this woman is the daughter of the god of war. While Penthesilea sleeps, the night before going into battle, Pallas intervenes. Pallas is both a name often given to Athene and the name of her foster sister, a daughter of Triton, a sea-god.[31] And it is Pallas – either Athene or her sister – who sends a deceitful dream to Penthesilea, urging her to seek out Achilles and fight him, suggesting that she will be the victor. Unfortunately, Penthesilea believes the dream and wakes up determined to fight.

Then Quintus gives us a scene which is familiar to readers of epic: a long sequence describing the hero preparing for battle, with detailed descriptions of her weapons and armour (all provided by Ares). Quintus tells us about her greaves, made of gold; her bright body-armour; her scabbard, decorated with ivory and silver; her shield, her helmet, her spears. Covered in her glittering armour, she is like lightning.[32] Just in case we might miss the destructive nature of this simile, Quintus underlines that he means it like the lightning Zeus hurls at the earth. She also has a double-pointed axe, of a size which would fell an ox.[33] Interestingly, this was a gift from Eris, the goddess of strife. So just as we have seen with male heroes, like Perseus, Penthesilea has a filial relationship with one god, but receives gifts from other gods too. She is equipped for battle in the same way that Achilles is fitted out for his return to the battlefield in the *Iliad*. After his first set of armour has been stripped from Patroclus' body by Hector, Achilles' mother, Thetis, persuades Hephaestus to make him a new set, with an especially ornate shield. One immortal parent acquires more divine help for their mortal offspring. Another goddess, the nereid Oreithyia, has provided Penthesilea with her horse, whose feet are as quick as a harpy's wings. Quintus tells us she heads into battle *thoē* – 'swiftly'. This time it is Achilles whom she resembles: the hero who is remarkable for his speed. As Penthesilea heads off to fight, Priam prays to Zeus that she will be victorious. He must have done this daily for his son, Hector. But the message he receives from the gods – an eagle, gripping a dove in its talons – fills him with sorrow. At this moment, Priam realizes he will not see Penthesilea return from the battlefield alive.

The Greeks, when they see this new warrior entering the fray, are filled with confusion. With Hector dead, they don't believe anyone can be found to stand against them and fight for Troy. Who could this be? Perhaps a god, they say.[34] They summon up their courage to fight, knowing they too have had the gods' support. The newly invigorated Trojans come forward and the newly alarmed Greeks come to meet them. The Trojan soil, Quintus says,[35] turns red.

And Penthesilea's prowess on the battlefield is on a par with the greatest heroes we read about in the *Iliad*. Quintus lists all the men she kills – Molion, Persinous, Eilissus and several more – as well as the men killed by her Amazon sisters. The battle isn't one-sided though: Podarces, a Greek, kills Clonie, an Amazon. This death angers Penthesilea[36] and she drives her spear into him. He dies moments later, in the arms of his comrades. Again, this is surely meant to make us think of Penthesilea in a heroic light. Anger at the loss of a fellow warrior – and revenge killing of the man responsible – motivates heroes throughout epic poetry. It is an intrinsically heroic emotion, and Penthesilea is revealing herself as a hero inside as well as out. The battle rages on, Quintus says, and many hearts – Greek and Trojan – are stopped on this day. He compares Penthesilea to a lioness,[37] once more echoing the *Iliad* and its descriptions of Agamemnon, Menelaus and, most of all, Achilles; lion similes appear almost thirty times in the poem[38] describing male heroes. Penthesilea strides across the battlefield, demanding to know why the most celebrated Greek heroes – Diomedes, Ajax – don't dare to face her. One Trojan who sees her in this exultant moment thinks she must be Athene, Eris or Artemis. A lioness, a goddess: Penthesilea seems to be beyond human when she fights and glories in her strength and skill.

So inspiring is she that a Trojan woman, Tisiphone,[39] calls out to the other women of Troy that they too should join the battle, just like their menfolk. These women have essentially been held hostage for ten years: they have watched their brothers, husbands, fathers and sons go out to fight the Greeks and not always seen them come back alive.

But there has never been any question of the women fighting alongside them. Women fighting in battle would be profoundly shocking. But that is what the mighty Amazon warrior can do. Penthesilea makes other – ordinary, mortal – women feel strong enough to subvert the vast weight of expectations which circumscribe their behaviour. A large group of Trojan women take up arms, ready to join the fray, but they are dissuaded at the last minute by an old priestess, Theano, who advises caution. She reminds these women that they cannot compare themselves with Penthesilea because she is a daughter of Ares and they are not. They cannot fight like her.

And nor do they need to, because Penthesilea is doing just fine without reinforcements. She continues to cut her way through the Greeks: their cries and screams eventually rouse Ajax and Achilles to join the battle. As the two great warriors put on their armour, they too are compared to lions, but this time like lions slaughtering a herd of sheep in the absence of a shepherd. Achilles kills five Amazons in rapid succession. But Penthesilea is not scared by this terrifying vision. Rather, she hurls her spears at Ajax, but they shatter on his divinely wrought shield and greaves. The Fates have not allowed Ajax to be injured during the war so far, and nor do they today. He pursues the Trojan fighters and leaves Achilles to fight Penthesilea alone.

Achilles rebukes Penthesilea for her confidence, tells her she must be mad, reminds her that everyone falls before him, even Hector. Did she not hear of the time he choked the rivers with corpses? This is a reference, again, to the *Iliad*, where Achilles' killing spree is so terrible and so rapid that the suffocating river gods beg their Olympian counterparts to stop him. It is a shattering image. Achilles hurls his spear at Penthesilea and she is less lucky than Ajax: her blood begins to flow. Even then, she wonders out loud if she could draw her sword and rush at him or if she should go on her knees and beg for her life (again, something male heroes do routinely in the *Iliad* and elsewhere). She has lost her death wish, it seems, now death is imminent.

Achilles drives his remaining spear first into her horse and then into her. She is cut down, Quintus says, like a tall pine tree brought down by the wind. She collapses, her strength broken.[40] When the Trojans see she has fallen, they panic. She was both a warrior and a talisman, as Hector was before her. Achilles taunts her as she lies dying, for having ever thought she could embrace a war which makes even men cower. But as she dies something happens. Aphrodite makes her resemble the sleeping Artemis.[41] She is beautiful even in death and Achilles is suddenly filled with remorse for what he has done. Meanwhile, Ares hears his daughter dying and races to the battlefield to wreak havoc on the Myrmidons (Achilles' comrades). But Zeus issues a warning thunderbolt and Ares retreats.

And then Quintus says something quite extraordinary: Achilles, still gazing at Penthesilea, feels as much love and sorrow as when his comrade Patroclus died. The death of Patroclus is one of the turning points in the Trojan War. The rage his death provokes in Achilles is what compels the great hero to embark on his terrifying killing spree. But before that comes the moment when a comrade brings him the news of Patroclus' death. He collapses to the ground, and his comrade fears he will slit his own throat. Whether Achilles and Patroclus were lovers or merely close companions, Achilles' devotion to his friend is undeniable. The celebrations of Patroclus' life – the funeral pyre, the golden urn for his ashes, the days of games held in his honour – are all provided by Achilles, but only once he has obliterated Hector, the man who had killed him.

And these feelings of love, companionship and intense sorrow are what Achilles feels now, looking down at the body of Penthesilea, a woman he was taunting only moments ago. Thersites, who is critical of the war effort and its commanders, is standing nearby. He mocks Achilles for the feelings he has for this Amazon, and accuses him of being *gunaimanes* – 'woman-crazy'.[42] Achilles says nothing in reply, but reaches out and punches Thersites so hard that the man falls to the ground, dead.

Thersites' response is both terminal and unusual. A kind of love continues to be expressed by the Greeks to Penthesilea, because they give her body to the Trojans for a funeral. This is another remarkable moment: the bodies of the dead – Greek or Trojan – have rarely been treated with this kind of respect during the war. Menelaus had to stand guard over Patroclus' body even after Hector had stripped Achilles' armour from him, so that they could take him back to the Greek camp for funeral rites. And yet Menelaus and Agamemnon give Penthesilea up without question. The fallen Amazon is carried from the battlefield by her enemies.

Scenes of Achilles and Penthesilea were a common theme on ancient vases. Surely the most beautiful, dating back to the sixth century BCE and painted by the master of the black figure technique, Exekias, can be found in the British Museum.[43] The black figure of Achilles – his enormous thighs showing us just how strong he is – stands to the left. His plumed helmet covers his face, only one eye is visible. He is driving his spear down, into the neck of Penthesilea. She is on one knee in front of him. Her shield hangs useless from her left shoulder. Her skin is white (men are often painted black and women white on these types of pots). Her helmet covers only the back and top of her head: her face is visible. Her eye is just a plain black dot, her mouth a small, straight line. But the decorated plume of her helmet matches his, and the bright red interiors of their shields match too. A snake decorates the helmet: it inevitably reminds us of Medusa. And Penthesilea wears a *pardalis* – a leopard skin – hanging down over her tunic, held in place by her red belt. Its paws reach down to her thighs. Blood gushes from her neck. Both Penthesilea's and Achilles' names are inscribed on the vase, next to each figure.

The museum also has a *hydria* – a water jug – which shows the aftermath of this battle.[44] A bearded Achilles is walking from left to right, leaning forward slightly, carrying two spears in his right hand. He has not been inconvenienced enough to lose even one of them.

Over his left shoulder, he carries the body of Penthesilea. Again, she is painted white. Her eyes are closed, her limbs hang limp. While we can see many images of Greek warriors carrying their fallen comrades from the battlefield, this *hydria* is unique in showing a Greek carrying his enemy.[45] Penthesilea is an extraordinary hero, even in death.

We only need to remember how Achilles behaved after he killed Troy's earlier defender, Hector: defiling his corpse by dragging it behind his chariot and refusing to allow his burial. Achilles' treatment of Penthesilea is, in contrast, a model of respect. He carries her body as though she were a comrade, and the Greeks return her to Priam without hesitation: no bargaining, no arguing. Priam and his men burn her on a pyre. The funeral is costly and ceremonial: she is treated as a beloved daughter.[46] They put her bones in a casket and inter them next to the bones of Laomedon, father of Priam and once-king of Troy. It is hard to imagine any fallen warrior being more lauded or lamented than Penthesilea, by friend and enemy alike.

So Penthesilea is no less a warrior because she died so quickly at the hands of Achilles. No matter how great a fighter someone is, Achilles is always better, faster, more bloodthirsty. The act of seeking to fight him at all – given his extraordinary martial superiority – is the sign of a true warrior. And Penthesilea achieves what many warriors strive to achieve throughout the *Iliad*: personal fame and a glorious death. These may seem to us like illusory goals. No death looks glorious up close, least of all one in battle. And glory – the estimation of our peers – is worth what, in the end? Achilles, once dead in the Underworld, tells Odysseus that he would rather be a living peasant than a king among the dead. The glory which he pursued so angrily throughout the *Iliad* was not, in the end, worth dying for.

But that is another poem, and Odysseus is many years away from his visit to the dead; Achilles still lives and breathes. So, by the standards of the heroic code which apply during the war, at least (Achilles doesn't change his mind until after he has died, which is obviously too late in every sense), Penthesilea has lived and died well. She has sought to be purified for the accidental killing of her sister, she has brought hope and inspiration to the Trojans (who will continue to hold out against the Greeks until they are tricked by the wooden-horse wheeze). She has fought as an ally to a battered city, and received the assistance of the gods she resembles. She is buried with full honour beside the king of the city she tried to save. What better hero could she have been?

Fast forward to the twenty-first century and we can perhaps answer that question. Wonder Woman – as played by Gal Gadot in the Patty Jenkins film – is the ultimate warrior. Diana – to give Wonder Woman her actual name – is the daughter of Hippolyta (Connie Neilsen) and niece of Antiope (Robin Wright). Penthesilea is a named (but minor) character in the film. These Amazons live in Themyscira: almost identically named to the Ancient Greek Amazon homeland, but not quite.

Diana grows up wanting to be a great warrior like her aunt, but her mother tries to prevent her training in any kind of combat. Inevitably, Diana trains with Antiope in secret until Hippolyta finds out. She allows them to continue only if Diana trains to be the best Amazon warrior there has ever been. Hippolyta tells Diana the history of the Amazons as a bedtime story: Zeus created them to protect humankind from the ravages of war, which are orchestrated by Ares. He also left them a weapon, should Ares ever return, known as the Godkiller. Diana believes this to be the sword with which she is learning to fight. Hippolyta also tells Diana that she was not born but rather sculpted from clay and brought to life with Zeus' help.

It's an intriguing reworking of the familiar story. Firstly, we might note that Diana has something in common with Pandora: she is made from clay but given an animated existence by a god. A more significant shift is that Ares has gone from being the father of Amazons – and protector, in terms of the armour he gives Penthesilea – to the enemy of Amazons and mortals alike. It is a feature of our times that we now view war as an unadulterated evil. The ancient idea that you might wish to be good at war (as contained in Athene's offer to Paris, in the hope of winning the golden apple), or that skill in defensive war might be desirable, has largely disappeared. Now, better informed about the nature and consequences of war perhaps (though proportionately many fewer of us have first-hand experience of it), we are more likely to desire peace than martial prowess. We particularly tend to feel this about the First World War, during which this film is set. Diana is drawn into the war when an Allied spy, Steve Trevor (Chris Pine), crashes into the sea just off Themyscira, pursued by enemy fighters. She saves his life and he explains the conflict taking place outside Themyscira's enchanted borders. Diana realizes that the huge death toll he describes must be the result of more than human cruelty: she concludes that Ares has returned and only she and her Godkiller sword can destroy him. She decides she must accompany Steve back to London and try to hunt down the war god. Her mother Hippolyta tells her that if she leaves she will never be able to return. But for Diana, her responsibility is clear. She must protect and save those who are dying in the war, no matter what the personal cost.

Again, we see a shift in the role of the Amazons. They are still the warriors we saw in our ancient sources, but they have deliberately held themselves apart from human affairs, although they have been cast in a semi-divine, protective role. Men have not sought them out because they don't even know the Amazons exist. And there is no hint of Amazons as aggressors, a race which will attack to avenge a perceived wrong (as they are sometimes depicted in ancient sources). These modern Amazons don't want a war; they do everything in their power to avoid one. It is a single, lone Amazon who decides she must fight an immortal enemy. In this, she is unlike any of her Amazonian foremothers. She may seem to resemble Penthesilea, heading onto the battlefield to fight Achilles. But unlike Penthesilea with her twelve Amazon comrades, Diana goes alone. She will acquire a gang once she gets to London, but none of them is an Amazon. Perhaps it was a question of emphasis: Wonder Woman might not seem so wondrous if there are a whole bunch of women who can fight almost as well as she can. Or perhaps it is simply another instance of the regrettable tendency in late twentieth- and early twenty-first-century film-making to cast one woman among a gang of men in adventure stories (the original *Star Wars* films are an excellent example, although the phenomenon tends to be known after a small blue Belgian character: the Smurfette).

If Diana's decision to involve herself in a war to try and protect the underdogs has echoes of Penthesilea, Steve Trevor's arrival on Themyscira is also reminiscent of another one of our ancient Amazon stories. He might well remind us of Heracles arriving to try to claim Hippolyta's war belt, but this too is given a modern twist. Rather than deliberately landing on the Amazon island in pursuit of an object, he crash-lands in the sea nearby. It is only Diana's intervention which saves his life, otherwise he would drown. There has been a shift in power – there is no suggestion that Steve would be any match for Diana in combat – and a reversal in emphasis: we don't follow Steve as he embarks on a quest to gain Amazon assistance. This is not his story. Instead we follow Diana, the Amazon, whose life is interrupted by the arrival of a man in jeopardy. It is her choice to intervene and save him, her choice to accompany him to London and then to the trenches, her choice to pursue Ares and save innocent lives. She is protected by divine or superpowerful armour – just as Penthesilea was – and she does not hesitate to risk her own safety for the humans she finds caught up in the war.

But unlike ancient versions of Antiope, Penthesilea and Hippolyta, Diana – the thoroughly modern Amazon – does not die. Not only does she survive both the war and the film, there is a further contemporary twist on the expected narrative. She herself is revealed to be the Godkiller; the sword she wields is nothing more than a sword. And while her final battle is underway, it becomes clear that someone must divert a vast supply of poison gas which will otherwise kill countless civilians. In this Amazon story it is the male hero, Steve, who dies, sacrificing his own life to save others. Just like her ancient counterparts, Diana has fallen in love with the man who came to Themyscira, and he loves her too. But their relationship does not cost her her life. They are both willing to sacrifice their happiness to save humanity, but he dies and she lives.

This development in the role of the Amazon – that she might survive her brush with a male heroic narrative by having her own heroic narrative – is a marked change. And (with almost no exceptions in our ancient sources) it is an extremely recent one too. In 1955, Robert Graves published a poem entitled 'Penthesilea'. It was the same year that he published his *Greek Myths*, so he was certainly immersed in his source material. His Penthesilea is dead at the start of the poem, and her injured body is the recipient of necrophilia by line four. Achilles' behaviour provokes gasps, groans and indignation from onlookers, but apparently he does not care, because he is 'distraught with grief'.[47] The grief is presumably provoked by his 'love of that fierce white naked corpse'. Thersites, an onlooker, issues an 'obscene snigger' and Achilles kills him 'with one vengeful buffet to the jaw'. It's a fury 'few might understand', but Penthesilea 'paused to thank him/For avenging her insulted womanhood/With sacrifice.'

It is a slight poem, but nonetheless grindingly unpleasant. Penthesilea has lost everything about her which made her heroic, a warrior, powerful. She's just a corpse which someone defiles, and this revolting behaviour is then described as love. Still, at least her ghost gets to thank a man who died for mocking this: truly, which of us wouldn't feel our insulted womanhood had been avenged by a man sniggering?

The poem is a succinct illustration of the way female characters in Greek myth have been marginalized by writers in the (relatively) modern world: ancient writers and artists had no problem with a warrior queen who could fight and kill men, whose prowess on the battlefield was equal to any man's and superior to most. It's only in later sources that the suggestion of love between Achilles and Penthesilea appears at all. And even then, that is to add a romantic element to their battle; to connect it, perhaps, to the stories of Hippolyta and Heracles, Antiope and Theseus.

The morphing of love into sexual degradation in this story is a recent phenomenon, and the total erasure of life and character is a depressingly modern shift too. The poem may have Penthesilea for its title, but she is scarcely human in its depiction. Read about her in ancient sources and you get a sense of who she might be, how she might fight, what she might like to wear: basic indications of her character. Read about her in Graves and she is simply a white, naked, abused body, with a dash of post-mortem Victorian modesty to disguise the total failure (or even attempt) to conjure an actual person. It is not the only time a twentieth- or twenty-first-century writer has purported to tell the women's story from Greek myth while in fact making it all about a male character, but it is one of the more egregious examples.

If we are looking for contemporary recreations of Amazon warriors, then Wonder Woman has a Californian counterpart who matches her in courage, strength and skill: Buffy the Vampire Slayer. Not only is Joss Whedon's Buffy the physical and mental match for any vampire – male or female – but she also possesses a highly unusual characteristic in any fighter: she is funny. Wit isn't a characteristic traditionally prized among warriors. They tend to be valued for strength, speed or courage. The wise-cracking fighter is a modern phenomenon, which has really come into its own with the rise of the superhero movie. Cinematic fighters were once strong and silent – Clint Eastwood, John Wayne – or occasionally would allow themselves to be the butt of the joke for the greater good (Christopher Reeve's geeky Clark Kent, all fingers and thumbs).

The vast majority of action heroes are male, and (since the demise of screwball comedy) so are most characters who have funny lines in films of almost any genre. Buffy broke a lot of rules when she appeared in Sunnydale, California, as the Chosen One, ready to fight to save the world, but also ready to try out for the cheerleading team.

Because Buffy is the out-of-towner who moves to small-town Sunnydale from LA, when we meet her she doesn't have a tribe or gang. But by the end of the first episode, she has found one: the Scoobies (as they will come to be known). Buffy's supporting cast are male and female, unlike the all-female tribe of Amazons we saw Wonder Woman grow up with. Buffy fights alongside Willow, Xander, Giles, Angel, Cordelia and, later, Faith, Spike, Anya and Tara. For her countless fans, the whole point of Buffy is that she may be more powerful than the average person, but she is no less human. Just like her Amazon predecessors, she is always impeccably dressed in her version of the best possible warrior outfit: she may wear fewer patterned leggings and big-cat skins, but she more than makes up for it with chic mini-dresses and bicep-boasting vest tops, and a handy bag or pocket in which to store her wooden stake. Her fighting prowess – like that of Penthesilea before her – is tremendously impressive. She can be beaten in single combat, but only by an exceptional warrior (The Master, who is a vampire of prodigious age and strength; Glory, who is a god). In season one, in her penultimate battle with The Master, she drowns, but is revived. The moment she is capable, she goes to fight him again, and this time succeeds in impaling him on a stake.

Buffy's second death, in season five, is particularly poignant. Realizing she will have to die or see her sister Dawn killed, she makes the ultimate sacrifice: she dies for love. It is – as we can see in so many depictions of Amazons on vase paintings – an Amazonian death: a female warrior giving up her life so another woman may live. It's a crucial part of Buffy's mythology, as we see in season six, when she is wrenched from the afterlife and returned to Sunnydale by a powerful magic spell. 'It's do or die,' the Scoobies sing in the seminal musical episode, 'Once More With Feeling'. 'Hey, I've died twice,' Buffy responds. We can surely conclude that death now holds no fear for her. She has become even more like Penthesilea.

Just as her Amazon ancestors appeared in poetry, prose and art, Buffy is a multi-media phenomenon: film, television, musical, video game, comic book and more. There are many reasons the show continues to resonate years after it finished, not least the Amazon-echoing story arc of the final season. Buffy has saved the world many times by season seven and she and her gang decide there is an alternative. By means of a rare artefact and a magic spell, every potential slayer in the world is empowered to become an actual slayer. The Chosen One is now the Chosen Many. Buffy is able to step away from constant demon-slaying because she helps to train up many more young women to fight in her stead. The message is simple: women are stronger together than apart, even ones with superpowers.

And this is what makes Buffy a contemporary Amazon: she may be uniquely talented, like Penthesilea, but she steps away from individual glory. Her status is not threatened by creating more heroic women, quite the reverse: it is cemented. Amazons – even when one is exceptional – are a team, a tribe, a gang, and it is this which Buffy captured so perfectly: an ensemble of women fighting to save us all.

CLYTEMNESTRA

IN THE LATE FIFTH CENTURY BCE, A YOUNG MAN STOOD UP IN THE Areopagus – Athens' most ancient legal court – and accused his stepmother of killing his father. The plaintiff's father had visited a friend, Philoneus, for dinner one night, years earlier. After the dinner, both men fell ill. Philoneus died almost immediately; the plaintiff's father lingered for three weeks. Philoneus' slave was accused of poisoning the wine which she had served to them: she was tortured and put to death. The young man was only a child when this happened, but he tells the jury he promised his father that, one day, he would bring the case against his own stepmother for what he believed to be her part in the crime. His stepmother was defended during the trial by her son, the half-brother of the plaintiff.

The prosecution's case is that this woman conspired with the now-dead slave-woman and persuaded her to commit murder. The young man has no evidence for his claims, but this doesn't prevent him from imagining the moments in which the slave-woman carried out the poisoning, after the food had been eaten. And he doesn't think it was her own idea. Rather, she was carrying out the plan of *tēs Klutaimnēstras tautēs* – 'this Clytemnestra here'.[1]

We don't know the verdict, nor do we have the speech presented by the woman's son in her defence. We can assume the latter would have focused on the lack of evidence, the lack of motive, and the absence of a close connection between the stepmother and the woman put to death for the poisoning. Murder is not something we do lightly on another person's behalf: the entire plot of Patricia Highsmith's *Strangers on a Train* hinges on the sheer unlikeliness of such behaviour. Given that years have passed since the father's death – and given that his half-brother is defending the case against him – it seems more likely that the plaintiff was engaged in a property dispute with his step-family and was using the murder accusation to further his claims, or pressure the family into paying him off.

The only piece of evidence the young man offers – and 'evidence' is a strong word in the context – is the claim that his stepmother had tried to poison his father on an earlier occasion. She counterclaims that the substance she had given his father then was not poison, but a love potion (a mistake also made by Heracles' final wife, Deianeira, in Sophocles' play *The Women of Trachis*). In a society where women had very little freedom and their husbands were legally within their rights to have sexual relationships with other women, the fear of losing your husband (and with him, your home and your children) must have been immense. The incentive to use a love potion was considerable.

So the young man might have compared his stepmother to Deianeira, who inadvertently poisons the great Heracles. He might also have compared her to Medea, whose witchy skills with poison made her one of the more fearsome women in Greek myth. But instead, he compared her to Clytemnestra. Perhaps it's because the actual poisoning was done by another woman, so the comparison with Deianeira or Medea would have been at one remove. Or perhaps the reason for mentioning Clytemnestra was more visceral, given that juries in Athenian courts were all-male. Clytemnestra is the ultimate bad wife, in the same way that Medea is the ultimate bad mother. Clytemnestra was the woman men feared coming home to. Was she craven with lust, driven by revenge, determined to wield power in the *polis* – city – as well as in the home? Whichever version of Clytemnestra's story men read, or saw, or heard, they came across the same troubling phenomenon: a woman who did not know her place.

The version of Clytemnestra's story with which the men in the jury would have been most familiar would – we might imagine – be the power-hungry version we meet in Aeschylus' play *Agamemnon*, first performed in 458 BCE. The play begins with a watchman who is keeping lookout for a beacon: the flaming signal which will tell him that Troy has finally been taken by his king, Agamemnon, and his fellow Greeks. But the man has been ordered to keep watch by Clytemnestra, the wife of Agamemnon and queen of the Argive Greeks. She has been ruling them in his ten-year absence.

This in itself is a highly irregular state of affairs, incidentally. Male anxiety over what women might do in their absence is a theme which runs through Athenian society, no more obviously than in the legal system. Upper-class women were kept cloistered, and would have been unlikely to speak to any men at all, other than close relatives. The fear that a woman might leave the house and catch the eye of a man other than her husband amounted to almost a collective neurosis: the penalty for adultery was more severe than the penalty for rape. The cloistering of women makes it hard to know when they were allowed where, even accompanied by their husbands. But it is a fascinating quirk of fifth-century BCE theatre that the plays of Aeschylus, Sophocles and especially Euripides are full of powerful, frightening women capable of murder, torture and infanticide. Yet, as mentioned earlier, it is more likely than not that women weren't in the audience of the Dionysia to see these representations of their mythological counterparts. The characters themselves were played by men, wearing masks as all characters in Greek plays did. And, equally oddly, men congregated to watch and enjoy these plays in spite (or perhaps because?) of the fact that they featured women behaving so badly. Though there are some indications that this particular play was not often performed after its initial appearance,[2] so perhaps Aeschylus' version of Clytemnestra was too much for all but the sturdiest men in the theatre.

The watchman is overjoyed when he sees the light of the beacon signalling that Troy has been overthrown: finally his long wait is at an end. He hurries inside to tell his queen that Agamemnon has been victorious at Troy, and will be on his way home. The chorus now take centre stage: they are old men, too old to have left to fight alongside their king a decade earlier. They don't yet know the war has been won, and when Clytemnestra enters and begins lighting fires to honour the gods, they ask her what has prompted this flurry of religious enthusiasm. She doesn't answer, and they turn their attention to the past. Specifically they sing of the death of Clytemnestra's daughter Iphigenia, whom they describe in emotive terms – a sacrificial victim, an animal cowering in distress.[3] They tell the whole ugly story: how the Greek army was stranded at Aulis ten years before, and could not find the weather to sail to Troy; how Artemis had to be appeased before the weather would change; how Calchas – their priest – explained that Artemis demanded a sacrifice of blood, the blood of a young woman, of the daughter of Agamemnon, the son of Atreus. They describe Iphigenia pleading with her father when she realized what was about to happen to her. Or rather, what her father was about to do to her. He told his men to gag her, so she could not curse him. Mute, she gazed at her attackers, wishing she could speak.

At this point, when our capacity for horror is almost overwhelmed, the chorus break off. They won't describe the actual moment of Iphigenia's death. It is worth noting that, in this entire passage, they never mention her name. Have they dehumanized her, turned her into a nameless sacrificial victim? Or can they just not bear to add to the pain of remembering this young woman too closely? Either way, they know that her mother keeps her memory alive: *mnamōn mēnis teknopoinos*[4] – 'Rage, remembering, child-avenging'.

There will be many other versions of Clytemnestra in every artistic medium, but there are few who command our sympathy more than this one, at this moment. The sacrifice of Iphigenia is utterly repugnant. Whatever our views on the revenge Clytemnestra will go on to take during this play, and the retribution which will be exacted against her in turn, she is the mother of a daughter who has been slaughtered like an animal. Is it any wonder she nurses an unquenchable rage against the man who committed such a crime? Would we not think less of her if she had simply forgiven Agamemnon and moved on? This is an important question to ask, not least because Aeschylus is unusual in having made the death of Iphigenia so central to Clytemnestra's motivation. Iphigenia died ten years before the day on which the action of the play occurs. And yet it is presented to us, in all its cruelty, right at the beginning of the play. The nightwatchman saw the fire that told him Troy had fallen. He rushed to tell Clytemnestra the news offstage. The chorus then sang, at length, about the death of the young Argive princess. Nothing can happen in the play until we have addressed this unresolved trauma.

When the chorus finish and their leader turns to speak to Clytemnestra directly, he uses an extraordinary phrase: 'I come honouring your power, Clytemnestra.'[5] The Greek word for power is *kratos* – it is the root of words like democracy, autocracy, kleptocracy. It is not a nebulous, vague word, which might imply anything from empty charisma to being a figurehead in her husband's absence. *Kratos* is specific: political might, ruling power. These men don't simply kowtow to Clytemnestra because her husband is their king, they are open in telling her that they respect her power. Clytemnestra responds with a proverb: Let dawn be born from mother night. Motherhood is right at the front of her mind. We can surely conclude that it is never anywhere else, that this powerful woman is motivated, first and foremost, by her relationship to her murdered daughter.

Clytemnestra explains to the chorus that Troy has fallen. She appears already to know more than her watchman could have told her, because she makes a pointed reference to the behaviour of the Greeks inside the city of Troy. So long as they respect the temples and shrines of the Trojan gods, they'll be all right, she says.

Does she know that the Greeks have done the absolute opposite of this, or does she just suspect it because her opinion of Agamemnon and any men he commands is already so low? Presumably the latter, because how could she know that Priam, the ancient king of Troy, had been slaughtered in a temple? How could she know that Cassandra, a priestess of Apollo, had been raped? The Greeks have shown no respect for the gods, and it is hard to avoid imagining a tone of glee in Clytemnestra's words here. This is a woman who has spent ten long years waiting to avenge her daughter. She knows there are limits even to her power. If the Greeks and Agamemnon behaved well towards the gods, perhaps her time would never come, and Iphigenia's murder would go unanswered. But her wishes have come true: the untrammelled cruelty of the Greeks cost Iphigenia her life, and that cruelty has not diminished over a decade of brutalizing combat. How could it?

The chorus respond with another song about the horrors of war and the fall of Troy. And then Agamemnon's herald rushes onstage to announce the king's imminent arrival. Clytemnestra explains that she had known this was coming as soon as the beacons announced the war was won. She cedes no political ground at all: she is ahead of all these men who surround her. The herald and the chorus exchange mutually hostile opinions on Helen (to whom they attribute blame for the war), who is of course Clytemnestra's sister.

Finally, at almost the halfway point of the play, Agamemnon makes his entrance, riding in a chariot. This play may be named after him, but he is not the lead character: Clytemnestra has more stage time and more dialogue. Her husband comes onstage with the booty he has seized from Troy, accompanied by Cassandra, the daughter of

Priam and Hecabe, a priestess of Apollo. Agamemnon offers thanks to the gods for their assistance in razing Troy and in bringing him back home. The word he uses for the destruction of Troy is *diēmathunen* – to grind to dust, to destroy completely. His enthusiastic prayer seems out of place when we recall Clytemnestra's earlier description of the desecration of Troy's temples by his men. Not least because he is accompanied by a priestess, whose body should be sacrosanct. But Agamemnon has made Cassandra his war bride: he has raped her, like the temple in which she served and the city which was her home.

Agamemnon speaks first to the gods, and then to the chorus of old Argive men. He does not address his wife, although she is onstage for at least the second half of his speech (stage directions are an irritatingly modern invention, so we can't always be completely sure when characters appear and disappear). His priority is not a family reunion, but presenting himself to the men of his city. When he has finished speaking, Clytemnestra responds in kind. She too speaks to the chorus, telling them how lonely it is for a woman when her husband goes away to fight a war. We might be suspicious of her motives, but there is a ring of truth in the pain she describes as messengers arrived, one after another, each bearing news of injuries, disasters. If her husband had received all the wounds he was reported to have incurred, she explains, he would have more holes in him than a net.

What are we to make of this speech? We surely don't believe Clytemnestra's portrait of herself as a lonely, wretched woman, lost in a limbo between wife and widow (although this portrayal must have been true for many more Greek wives than not. We'll see the complications which arise from it with Penelope, as she waits twice as long – twenty years – for her husband Odysseus to return home from the Trojan War). We know Clytemnestra has been waiting avidly for his return, has sent out watchmen so that she may be the first to know when Troy falls. Is she describing her behaviour accurately and only lying about her reasons? Did she wait for every messenger as she claims, desperate to hear if Agamemnon was injured? Not because she wanted to hear he was safe but because she wanted to hear that he was not? Did she curse each messenger because they seemed to taunt her: Agamemnon must surely be dead by now, and yet somehow he lives? Or was she sincerely desperate for news that Agamemnon was unhurt, even though her motivation was much darker than anyone has realized? Did she want Agamemnon home safe for one reason and one reason only: so that she could kill him herself?

Then Clytemnestra shows us how devastatingly clever and cunning she is. Finally, she turns to speak to Agamemnon. All these rumours about him were so traumatic for her, she tells him, that more than once she fastened a noose around her neck. Others had to cut her down or she would not be alive today. And that is why Orestes, their son, is not present: he has been sent away for his own wellbeing. He's being cared for by a close friend so he would not witness his mother's suffering.

Thus Clytemnestra offers a pre-emptive excuse for the absence of their son from the palace. Agamemnon must surely have expected Orestes to be here, welcoming his father home (Clytemnestra doesn't need to make the same excuses about their surviving daughter, Electra. Perhaps fathers didn't worry so much about being greeted by their daughters. Or perhaps Agamemnon specifically doesn't think too much about his daughter, having killed her older sister, as we were reminded at the start of the play). Not only does Clytemnestra offer a perfectly good reason for Orestes being absent, she has weaponized her own unhappiness to give her story greater plausibility. She hasn't sent Orestes away because she's a bad mother and doesn't care about him, or because she's a bad wife and doesn't mind if he's not there to welcome his father. She has sent him away because reports of Agamemnon being injured were so frequent and so distressing that her repeated suicide attempts were upsetting for Orestes, so he is elsewhere for his own good. I hesitate to prejudice your reading of the play, but I would say it is at this moment that we might describe Clytemnestra as 'a piece of work'. She just cares too much. Well, we'll see. Oh, and were you wondering why she isn't tear-stained from all these nights spent weeping over Agamemnon's potential injuries? Of course, she has an explanation for that too: she has wept all her tears already, in the long nights when she suffered instead of sleeping.

We might think Agamemnon is rather gullible to fall for all this deceit. And perhaps he is. Nothing about his character as it's presented in Homer's *Iliad* would suggest that we are dealing with a cunning or even moderately clever man: the brains in the Greek camp belonged to Odysseus, Nestor and others. But even if Agamemnon were more immediately sceptical of the words of a woman whose child he once murdered, it would do him little good. He is simply outclassed. We will see a similar dynamic at play between Jason (who is much cleverer than Agamemnon) and his wife, Medea, in Euripides' play.

But then Clytemnestra almost takes things too far. She gestures to her slave-women who have carried their finest tapestries out from the halls of the palace. She tells them to place these gorgeous cloths on the ground so that Agamemnon can walk on them. She doesn't want him to set foot on the dusty earth beneath his chariot wheels, but to walk only on this luxurious purple fabric. This may seem odd to us, but not especially shocking: these tapestries could be like carpets or fancy rugs. But Agamemnon's response shows us that Clytemnestra is in fact asking him to do something deeply transgressive.

He almost accepts the praise which Clytemnestra has offered him as his due. But, he says, it would be more suitable if it came from someone else, and not from his wife. The lavish treatment she is proposing makes him uncomfortable. Walking on these tapestries would be hubristic: it is what a god or a barbarian might do. We see an interesting division in his notion of masculinity here. Luxury is too good for a mortal man and belongs in the realm of the gods. But it is also too exotic, too foreign, too other, and any man indulged in this way resembles a foreigner, a barbarian, not a Greek.

What might the tapestries have been like, to provoke such an extreme reaction from Agamemnon? They are clearly far more precious than carpets or rugs. During the Bronze Age, when this play is set – perhaps the twelfth century BCE, many hundreds of years before it was written – the wealth of a royal house was not held in money, which didn't yet exist. It was held in gold and other precious metals. And it was also held in fine tapestries like the ones Clytemnestra is proposing her slaves throw down on the ground. With no industrial processes, weaving was a formidably time-consuming task. Thin fabrics would have taken longer to create than any other kind: a finely spun yarn needs many more lines of weaving to make the same-sized cloth as could be produced far more quickly using a thick yarn. And patterns would also be much more intricate, because the fineness of the fabric allowed for more detail to be woven into it.

The colour was also a source of their value. Purple-red fabrics were coloured with murex: a sea snail whose secretions are the basis of this dark, regal purple dye. This was imported from the east, probably the Phoenician city of Tyre. The same dye would be used to create imperial purple in Rome, many centuries later. A vast quantity of murex would have been needed to colour the yarn for a large tapestry, and it was an extremely expensive, labour-intensive process to produce it. Clytemnestra and Agamemnon both refer to the enormous cost of the dye – the purple is equal in value to silver,[6] Clytemnestra says. To be clear, the dye alone is this valuable: that's before it has been used on the threads which will be woven into the delicate tapestries.

One more thing to note about murex is that it produced a colour which we might call red, or crimson, or purple. But it would have been a dark, visceral shade. So when Clytemnestra plays on Agamemnon's vanity, tells him his victory is so great that he deserves the cloths beneath his feet, persuades him to walk over them in his bare feet, she achieves two things. The first is for the characters within the play: they see Agamemnon bending to his wife's will, and walking over these priceless tapestries as she has ordered. He is being flattered into behaving like a potentate, while she has won their first exchange in ten years. He does as she commands.

The second is for the audience watching the play. We have seen Agamemnon return home, riding his chariot, carrying his spoils, accompanied by his war bride. And now we see this man step down from his chariot, barefoot, and walk into his palace over a river of glistening red. Even those who don't know his story cannot fail to see that he walks through blood to get home.

As he steps down from his chariot, he exhorts his wife to take care of 'this foreign woman'[7] and magnanimously reminds her that the gods favour kind masters because no one chooses to become a slave. Would this sentiment sound more reasonable coming from a man who hasn't literally enslaved the woman he is describing? Perhaps. But of course, our response is scarcely relevant: Clytemnestra's is the one he should be worrying about. And she is being presented with the actual living proof of her husband's infidelity, and asked to be nice to her. One finds oneself wondering if Agamemnon has ever met his wife before today. Perhaps he had received a blow to the head on the battlefield. Of course we could argue that, in both the Bronze Age when the play is set and the fifth century BCE when the play is written and performed, very different expectations of male and female fidelity were common: Athenian men could have sex with non-Athenian women (with or without payment) and their marriages were regarded as completely secure. Women, unsurprisingly, had no such freedom. But merely because an inequality is the status quo doesn't mean that the person on the receiving end of that inequality is going to like it, least of all when you literally parade the disparity in front of her. And of all women you might not want to further irritate, Clytemnestra should be right near the top of your list.

Agamemnon lingers no longer: he crosses the threshold and enters the palace. This liminal moment – where he is both returned and not yet in his home, ostensibly reunited with his wife but without sincerity or intimacy, victor over Troy and yet vanquished by his wife in the matter of the tapestries, alive and yet doomed – finally comes to its close. The chorus respond with foreboding and it is clear that, while Agamemnon might be too dim to perceive the dark thoughts his wife is nurturing, they are not so naive. When they have finished, Clytemnestra invites Cassandra to accompany her inside. It is the first time anyone refers to Cassandra by name in the play. Agamemnon had called her *tēn xenēn* – 'this stranger', 'this foreigner'. It was another reason for us to be somewhat quizzical about his motives when he asked Clytemnestra to be kind to her. If he is so sympathetic to Cassandra's newly enslaved condition, perhaps he might do her the courtesy of referring to her by name. As it is, she becomes nothing more than a type, an object. Only when Clytemnestra speaks to her do we feel that someone is responding to her as herself, rather than as a foreign-born concubine. And Clytemnestra is certainly interested in Cassandra for who she is as well as what she is – a priestess violated by Agamemnon – but not in a way that could ever be construed as kindness.

Cassandra doesn't reply to Clytemnestra. Does she not hear? Clytemnestra grows impatient and asks the chorus if they can communicate with her. They wonder if there is a language barrier; Clytemnestra loses interest and goes back into the palace. She doesn't have the time or focus to waste on Cassandra, it turns out. The chorus try to speak to the Trojan priestess, but she suddenly cries out to Apollo. Then she asks where she is and, on learning that she is at the house of Atreus (Atreus was the father of Agamemnon and his brother Menelaus), she becomes further distressed. She describes exactly what is about to happen to Agamemnon. He is in a bath, a net or snare awaits him, he is trapped. Her words are confusing but undeniable. The chorus agree that something bad must be occurring. Cassandra prophesies her own death and she and the chorus have an intense exchange about the cause of her troubles (she attributes them to Paris).[8] And then comes a moment which seems to leap out of a horror movie: Cassandra sees Furies dancing on the roof of the palace.[9] These dark goddesses punish wrongdoing, and in particular they punish crimes carried out between blood relatives. The house of Atreus is steeped in just such familial wrongdoing: adultery, child-murder and unintentional cannibalism, just for starters. No wonder the Furies have taken up residence on the roof.

The chorus are astonished by Cassandra's knowledge of the palace history. She explains to them that she was given the gift of prophecy by Apollo, but he also cursed her never to be believed, because she refused his sexual advances. We have no reason to doubt her story and yet we see it disproved as we watch, because the chorus are apparently immune to Apollo's machinations. We believe you, they say,[10] it sounds like the truth to us. She tells them that they will see Agamemnon dead. They ask which man – *anēr* – is committing such an act.[11] You've misunderstood me completely, she replies. And then her vision moves a little further into the future: she will kill me, she says. The two-footed lioness who mates with a wolf in the absence of the lion. It is perfectly clear to us that she means Clytemnestra. The lioness has become the bedmate of the lion's enemy: the wolf. In her husband's absence, we remember that Clytemnestra has been having an affair with Aegisthus, Agamemnon's enemy.

Cassandra throws off her priestly regalia and hurls it to the ground. She no longer belongs to Apollo, she reasons, because he has allowed her to be brought here to die. She can still see the future, although the chorus don't register what she is saying: after Cassandra's death, and because of her, another woman will be killed, as will a man. Those Furies won't be climbing down from the roof of the house of Atreus any time soon, it seems. And Cassandra walks into the palace, to her death.

Only now do we hear what Cassandra has already foreseen: the death of Agamemnon. He cries out that he has been struck, and then again, a second blow. The chorus acknowledge that the king must indeed now be dead. They consider running inside to catch the killers but, as with almost all choruses in Greek tragedy, although they discuss taking action, they don't act. After all, as they say, they can't bring the dead back to life with words.[12] Eventually, the doors of the palace are opened, and Clytemnestra stands before them, with the bodies of the murdered king and priestess beside her. It is interesting to note that, although we heard Agamemnon cry out as he was murdered, we heard nothing from Cassandra: she had accepted her fate even in her final moments, it seems. The chorus are silenced by the terrible sight, and about to be shocked further. Because Clytemnestra is not remotely apologetic for what she has done, which is (from their perspective) to have killed their king. Rather, she revels in the murders. She describes the deed: how she trapped Agamemnon in a snare or net, struck him twice until he collapsed and then delivered a third, final blow. We – like the chorus – only heard him cry out twice, so this implies that he had no capacity to speak after the first two. Rejoice, Clytemnestra tells the chorus, if you can, rejoice. I glory in it.[13] Agamemnon had filled his cup with evil deeds, she says, and now he has come home and drained the dregs.

Cassandra's prediction that Agamemnon would be caught in a snare is not the only mention of some sort of ambush or trickery in the play. Agamemnon appears to have been killed using a trick garment, like a straitjacket. There is a remarkable pot by the Dokimasia Painter, now held by the Museum of Fine Arts in Boston.[14] It was made either just before or just after this play was first performed (the dates are so close that it's not possible to say conclusively that the *krater* shows a scene from the play, nor that the play describes a scene already well known because here is an example of it on this wine bowl). The mixing bowl was produced in Athens, so it is certainly possible to say that, in the middle part of the fifth century BCE, at least some artists in Athens were making the snare a feature of Agamemnon's death. Because here we can see Agamemnon in a thin gauzy robe: his naked body is visible through the transparent fabric. He is reaching forward with his right hand, although at the same time his whole body is leaning back: he shrinks away from the sword in the hand of his attacker. The killer in this version of the story is not Clytemnestra, however, but her lover Aegisthus. She stands behind him, holding an axe. This is one of the most frequent variations in this myth, raising the question: is Agamemnon killed by Aegisthus or Clytemnestra, or the two of them together? For Aeschylus, Clytemnestra claims all the credit for the deed. Aegisthus won't be onstage until two hundred lines after his lover appears with the bodies of Agamemnon and Cassandra. Whether she is boasting of her murderous capabilities or merely describing them with glee, she certainly doesn't want to share responsibility. The Boston *krater* shows us a less shocking version of the story, perhaps: a man killing his lover's husband, rather than a wife slaying her daughter's murderer.

But the gauzy robe which Agamemnon wears in this image is strange. His hand reaches out but the robe stretches around his fingers: he cannot release his arms or hands from within. It almost touches the floor, so it seems to be acting as a restraint. Perhaps this explains his posture: he is leaning back so far that in reality he would fall. His balance is impeded because he cannot use his arms to steady himself. And so, Aegisthus (on the *krater*) or Clytemnestra (in the play) has used trickery before violence. Agamemnon is a returning warrior, after all, so we cannot be surprised if Clytemnestra uses guile to raise her chances of success. It should here be noted that employing trickery to kill or maim an opponent who has superior strength is not a uniquely female characteristic: it is what Odysseus does, time and again.

The theme of nets and woven fabrics runs throughout Aeschylus' play, from the tapestries that Agamemnon walks across to the robe which – if it was like the one on the pot – apparently has the ends of the sleeves sewn together, or perhaps no sleeves at all. The imagery is consistent: Clytemnestra is the hunter, Agamemnon her prey. And weaving, which is the idealized task of 'good' women in myth (we'll look at Penelope, later on, and her weaving and unweaving of a shroud), has become something darker, much more dangerous. Clytemnestra hasn't spent ten years weaving tapestries: she has meta-phorically woven plots and schemes, and literally woven the restraint or straitjacket which she uses to outwit Agamemnon. The wholesome pursuit has been twisted to murderous ends. Even the tapestries which seemingly posed no danger to Agamemnon were turned into a trap when Clytemnestra used them to incite him to an act of hubris.

The chorus continue to respond to Clytemnestra with shock and horror: they tell her she deserves to be banished for her crime. Her reply is coruscating. He's the one you should have banished, she says. He's the one who killed his own daughter, as though she were nothing more than a sacrificial animal. And what did you do about that? Nothing. I tell you what, if you can overthrow me, you can rule this place. If the gods decide differently, you'll learn to live with it.

Make no mistake, this woman is offering to fight a whole crowd of men if she has to. They criticize her again, and she finally lets rip: it was with Justice, Ruin and Vengeance (who are goddesses, not merely qualities) that she sacrificed Agamemnon.[15] Her language is deliberately incendiary. Agamemnon had sacrificed her daughter like an animal; Clytemnestra has treated him the same way. Not only that, but she claims to have had divine assistance in doing so. And then she offers an additional argument, as she turns to the matter of Cassandra. First,

Agamemnon was the darling of Chryseis at Troy, she says (Chryseis was briefly his war bride, before he was forced to return her to her father in Book One of the *Iliad*). And now this bedmate, this lover of his, lies dead beside him. So Clytemnestra, for all her high-minded ideals of avenging her daughter Iphigenia, also has a baser motive: sexual jealousy. But she soon goes back to her original argument: the much-lamented Iphigenia[16] is her motive. He killed her daughter, so she killed him. Her anger extends beyond his death, too. He'll have nothing to boast about in Hades, she says. He'll be welcomed to the Underworld by Iphigenia. The chorus are defeated by Clytemnestra, not just by the havoc she has wreaked, not just by her total failure to be apologetic for it, but by her superior arguments.

Then finally, at the very end of the play, Clytemnestra's lover Aegisthus comes onstage, revelling in the excellence of the day. He explains that his father, Thyestes, had a long-running feud with Agamemnon's father, Atreus. Thyestes tried to take Atreus' kingdom from him, and Atreus repelled his attack. The two men apparently reached a détente and Thyestes was welcomed back into Atreus' house for a feast. But the dinner contained a stomach-churning dish: Thyestes' own children had been murdered and their hands and feet were served up to him. He ate them unknowingly. Aegisthus, his youngest child, survived the bloodbath because he was only a baby when it took place. He, too, is acting in the spirit of revenge: he claims credit for planning the murder. If Clytemnestra is punishing her husband for his terrible acts as a father, Aegisthus is punishing him for whose son he is. Like Clytemnestra, he claims to have acted with Justice on his side. And he too is unapologetic in the face of societal disapproval. Death would seem fine to him, he says, now he has seen this man caught in Justice's snare. The chorus are not persuaded by Aegisthus' arguments any more than they were convinced by Clytemnestra's defence and attack. Aegisthus is unbowed by their criticism and threatens them with imprisonment and starvation. Whatever else drew Clytemnestra and her lover together – sexual desire, a common enemy – we see that they are tremendously well suited in terms of their dispositions. The chorus try to wound him the only way they know how: he planned the murder, they say, but didn't have the courage to carry it out. He left that to a woman.[17]

The chorus are on the verge of all-out combat with Aegisthus and his men, but Clytemnestra will allow no further bloodshed. Again, we are left in no doubt who has taken control of the palace, of the city, in the aftermath of the king's death. Aegisthus may claim to be the mastermind of the day, but when it comes to actual power, it rests in the hands of the queen. She stops Aegisthus – 'dearest of men' – from doing any more damage. The use of this endearment surely helps to persuade the chorus that they have nothing to gain by venting further anger and distress. She tells them to leave. They issue one last barb – you wait till Orestes gets home.

Have the chorus remembered Cassandra's prophecy, that her own death would be followed by the death of a woman and a man? Have they understood that, however much Clytemnestra and Aegisthus believe they were serving the goddesses of Justice and Vengeance, they now may be destroyed by those same goddesses in turn? This is the dark shadow at the centre of the house of Atreus. Every crime committed requires an act of retribution to satisfy the dead: Iphigenia, Thyestes' older children. But every act of retribution then requires another: Clytemnestra's daughter is avenged but her surviving children – Orestes and Electra – are now in an impossible bind, as the *Choephoroi*, or *The Libation Bearers*, the next play in the trilogy, will make clear. If they fail to avenge their father, his spirit will torment them because he has been murdered and his killer goes unpunished. But if they kill his murderer, they themselves will be committing the unforgivable crime of matricide. Retributive justice is all very well, but when such horrors take place within the family, there is no solution which does not worsen the already intolerable position.

Clytemnestra may prevent fighting from breaking out between her lover and the chorus of Argive men, but she ends the play with no hint of humility or apology. Ignore their worthless barking, she tells Aegisthus, effortlessly dehumanizing the old men: they are no more important to her than dogs, their words contain no more merit than animal howls. And she literally has the last words in the play: I, and you, rule this house now. The word order may pain English grammarians, but Clytemnestra means it. I rule the palace, the city, its people, and so do you. Aegisthus is not quite an afterthought, but she certainly isn't giving him top billing. The play concludes with yet another motive for killing Agamemnon: the acquisition of power.

The play is disquieting now, and it must have been even more so when it was first performed. It is hard to measure the impact of something by the absence of work it inspires, but there are surprisingly few vase paintings which show this part of Agamemnon and Clytemnestra's story, even fewer which show the specifically Aeschylean version. Have we just been unlucky in what has survived? Or might there be a reason for the scarcity? These ornate wine cups and bowls were often used by men at parties attended by other men, as well as women who were not their wives. Plato's *Symposium* gives us a very high-minded, idealized version of this kind of night: philosophical discussion, drinking, the arrival of a late guest accompanied by flute-girls. It's not beyond the stretch of our imagination to conclude that perhaps men at these kinds of parties might not be desperate to be reminded of the murderous anger of a wife left waiting at home for her husband. If you wanted a wine bowl decorated with axe-wielding women, you might well choose the Amazons in a battle rather than a raging wife cutting down a single unarmed man.

The Dokimasia pot in Boston shows a different emphasis, as mentioned above: Aegisthus is the killer, Clytemnestra not much more than an axe-wielding cheerleader. But a fourth-century BCE *krater* in the Hermitage Museum[18] in St Petersburg shows a more murderous Clytemnestra. In fact, it shows a naked Agamemnon cowering behind his shield as Clytemnestra bears down upon him with her axe raised above her head, her cloak billowing behind her. This piece was made in Magna Graecia (southern Italy today, but populated with Greek settlements at the time), which raises an interesting question about whether these wine-drinkers enjoyed the sight of a murderous wife more than their Athenian counterparts. And if so, why?

Clytemnestra is usually presented as an archetypally bad wife. The only question tends to be her motivation, which makes her more or less sympathetic, more or less threatening to the society which depicts her. Our earliest descriptions of her are in the *Odyssey*, where she acts (in narrative terms) as a dark reflection of the archetypally good wife, Penelope. The poem follows Odysseus on his extended journey home to his long-suffering wife, while she copes with the invasion of her home by a gang of young men, the disrespect of her son and plenty more. She is held up throughout Greek myth as a model wife to her absent husband. But the story of Agamemnon's homecoming punctuates the poem, not least when Odysseus visits the Underworld in Book Eleven and meets his now-dead comrade. He asks Agamemnon how he died, whether Poseidon had wrecked his ship or whether he'd been killed by men whose livestock he was trying to pilfer. Magnificently, Odysseus manages to conjure up scenarios he himself has experienced and will experience: his heroic self-absorption is an ever-present risk to his own (and his men's) survival in this poem. Agamemnon says no, it wasn't Poseidon and nor was he killed by men defending their land. It was Aegisthus, he says, with help from my wife. He uses the vocabulary of ritual slaughter, just as Clytemnestra will go on to do, in Aeschylus' play. The Homeric version is more of a bloodbath, however: this Agamemnon saw his men slaughtered too, like pigs. He then compares it to a battle, which makes the domestic details all the more shocking: palace tables stacked with food and wine, the floor beneath them covered in blood. He says he heard Cassandra being killed by Clytemnestra while his own life ebbed away. Clytemnestra didn't even look at him as he died, did not even close his eyes and mouth after death. He advises Odysseus to return home cautiously, although he does also suggest that Penelope isn't the murdering kind, 'not like my wife'.

So Homer's Clytemnestra is not quite as terrifying for men as Aeschylus' version: she doesn't kill her husband, although she does stand by as he is killed and has been involved in planning his murder. Obviously for women, and specifically for Cassandra, she is precisely the same degree of murderous. And for the Homeric Agamemnon, Clytemnestra's affair with Aegisthus is the root of her evil. There is no suggestion that this Clytemnestra might be avenging the death of her daughter, or indeed that she might have political ambitions to rule in her husband's stead, both of which were part of her character in Aeschylus. At least as far as Agamemnon tells things here, she was solely motivated by desire for Aegisthus. Clytemnestra is nothing more than an adulteress.

It is this motivation which will come to define Clytemnestra when Roman authors get hold of her. For Ovid, in his *Ars Amatoria* or *The Art of Love*, she is driven by sexual jealousy, which only really manifests itself when she sees Agamemnon's infidelity up close.[19] She stays chaste while she can imagine Agamemnon is faithful to her. She heard the rumours about Chryseis and Briseis (both women whom Agamemnon had claimed as war brides in the *Iliad*). But it is only when he returns home with Cassandra, and Clytemnestra sees the relationship for herself, that she begins her own revenge-affair with Aegisthus. So Ovid is continuing a tradition which deprives Clytemnestra of her status as queen and Fury, but he also removes the responsibility for Agamemnon's murder from her. The implication is that Agamemnon is responsible for his own downfall: if he had had the good sense to keep his mistress away from his wife, he might have lived to a ripe old age.

Of course, Ovid is writing a very different kind of poem from Homer's epic *Odyssey* or Aeschylus' tragedy *Agamemnon*. The *Ars Amatoria* is a bright, racy, jokey guide to having illicit sex in Rome (produced at a time when the new emperor, Augustus, was cracking down on adultery. At least, other people's). So Ovid has every reason to turn Clytemnestra and Agamemnon into a suburban couple whose swinging habits get out of control, rather than treating them with the epic grandeur of our earlier Greek authors. Here we find no reference to Iphigenia, no reference to Clytemnestra's designs on the Argive throne. Ovid knows so much about Greek myth that we know he is being deliberately cheeky here: reducing Clytemnestra – and Medea, a little earlier in the same passage – two famously wronged women who respond with remarkable violence to their abuse – to little more than vexed housewives kicking up a fuss.

The Roman philosopher and playwright Seneca must have read Ovid's treatment of Clytemnestra, because his version of her (in his strange, flawed play, *Agamemnon*) is a similarly sexual being, tormented by her love and intense desire for Aegisthus.[20] She does mention Iphigenia, but not with any particular anguish or need for retribution. As with Ovid's interpretation, the Senecan Clytemnestra is jealous of her husband's sexual conquests while he has been away at Troy: Briseis, Chryseis and Cassandra. But unlike our earlier Clytemnestras, this one is afraid that her husband will punish her for her own indiscretions. She even considers suicide. We have come a long way from the fearless, furious woman created by Aeschylus.

But let us return to Clytemnestra in her raging Aeschylean incarnation. More specifically, let's follow her story through to its end. The second play of the *Oresteia* is *The Libation Bearers*. This is a reference to the offerings made at the tomb of the late Agamemnon by Electra and the chorus some years after the events of the previous play. Clytemnestra has been having bad dreams and she believes the ghost of her late husband needs placating. She has sent her daughter Electra to do the honours. Electra prays for her long-absent brother Orestes to come home and avenge their father. We learn that Clytemnestra still rules with Aegisthus.

But Electra is about to have her wish fulfilled: she identifies a lock of hair left as an offering beside her father's tomb, and she sees a footprint which seems remarkably familiar to her. She concludes that both hair and footprint belong to Orestes, and that her brother must have returned at last. If this seems like a bit of a leap, you are not alone: Euripides mocks this whole recognition scene in his later version of the same story, *Electra*.

But once the siblings are reunited – along with Orestes' companion Pylades – they determine to take action against their father's killer. Orestes has been ordered by no less an authority than the god Apollo to do so. Clytemnestra comes out of the palace to greet these two men whom she believes to be strangers. She welcomes them inside, offers them hospitality. Orestes doesn't identify himself, instead pretending to have met a man who had news for her: that Orestes is dead. Her response is that of a mother who has lost her son, rather than a woman who fears retribution from him. You've stripped away the thing I love, she says: I am utterly destroyed.[21]

Once they get inside the palace, Orestes kills Aegisthus, but wavers before killing his mother. Clytemnestra realizes she is to be killed by someone who has used trickery, just as she herself had used it to kill.[22] For a moment, it seems as though Clytemnestra will talk herself out of trouble: I gave birth to you, she says. I want to grow old with you.[23] He is aghast at her words: after killing my father? You want to grow old with me? She blames Moira – Fate – for Agamemnon's death.

And then she and Orestes share a moment which must resonate with parents and children in less extreme circumstances. You cast me out, he says. She sees things differently: I put you at an ally's house out of harm's way. I was sold into slavery, he replies. Oh really, she says: how much did I get for you? We can surely hear the echoes of parents and teenagers arguing through the ages: they agree on the events which have occurred, but their interpretations of those events are poles apart and neither can see the other's point of view. Mother and son are, in this moment, uncannily alike. But Pylades has reminded Orestes that Apollo demands this retributive killing, and Orestes does as he has been told. Clytemnestra dies reminding him that hounds of vengeance will chase him down.[24]

And so they do. There is one more play to come in this trilogy: *The Eumenides*, which means 'Kindly Ones', a new name for the Erinyes, or Furies (following the theory that, if you give something a nicer name, it may behave less alarmingly). This final play poses and answers one simple question: was Orestes justified in killing his mother? The Furies, who pursue him relentlessly, think he has committed the unforgivable crime of matricide. But Apollo, and then also Athene, take Orestes' side: he had a moral obligation to avenge his father and matricide was the necessary consequence of doing so. Whatever we might feel about the question, the play resolves the issue to its characters' satisfaction: Orestes is acquitted thanks to divine intervention, and the Furies – grudgingly – allow him to continue his life unmolested.

But the play's resolution does raise another question in our minds: why is Agamemnon's life valued more highly – by everyone except Clytemnestra – than Iphigenia's? Why was Agamemnon not pursued by the Furies for the unforgivable crime of killing his daughter? Why was it left to Clytemnestra to avenge her? Why do Electra and Orestes have so much more respect for the wishes of their dead, murderous father than for their living, murderous mother, and indeed their dead, blameless sister? Even if we agree with the conclusion that the trilogy reaches (which is that this cursed family must stop taking matters into their own hands and should instead air their grievances in a court and abide by the verdict – in this case supplied by a goddess), we are surely left thinking that Clytemnestra had a point, way back in the first play, when she asked the chorus why they were so upset by Agamemnon when they were so unconcerned about Iphigenia. It's him you should have banished, she told them.[25] It seems that Clytemnestra seals her own fate when she values her daughter's life equally to the life of a king.

One final note: in Euripides' play *Iphigenia in Aulis*, which tells the awful story of Iphigenia's death, Clytemnestra mentions that she had a first husband, before Agamemnon. His name was Tantalus,[26] and she tells us that Agamemnon killed him and married her himself. She appears to have had no say in the matter of marriage to her husband's killer. And not just her husband. Because Agamemnon also took her baby, an infant which she was nursing when Agamemnon appeared. He wrenched the child from her breast by force and smashed it into the ground. In other words, in this play (and other, later sources will pick it up), Agamemnon kills two of Clytemnestra's children, more than a decade apart.

And while many later authors will drop this element of her story, and focus on her adultery rather than her maternal rage, it is there for us to see in astonishing, dramatized clarity in fifth-century BCE tragedy, and especially in Aeschylus' *Oresteia*. He probably did not invent this aspect of her motivation (it is in an ode by Pindar[27] which was likely composed a few years before Aeschylus' plays were written, although it is possible it was a few years later). So Clytemnestra is a byword in the ancient world, and ever since, for a bad wife, the worst wife even. But for wronged, silenced, unvalued daughters, she is something of a hero: a woman who refuses to be quiet when her child is killed, who disdains to accept things and move on, who will not make the best of what she has. She burns like the beacon she waits for at the beginning of Aeschylus' *Agamemnon*. And if that means men think twice about drinking from a wine cup with her murderous rage depicted upon it, so be it. She would – at least in Aeschylus' depiction – relish their fear.

EURYDICE

There are few more romantic stories in myth than that of Eurydice and her husband Orpheus. It is a miniature saga of the pathos of youth cut short, of the intolerable pain of loss and of a love which survives even death. It is also unusual, because Eurydice doesn't seem to exist in Orpheus' story until the fifth century BCE, and he himself is not particularly well attested before that: he isn't mentioned anywhere in Homer or Hesiod, for example.[1] Let's begin by looking at the best-known version of their story, before hunting round for its antecedents. In this instance, we must turn to the Romans. Specifically, to Virgil, who told the story in the *Georgics*, his poem about country living. It was completed by 29 BCE, after which Virgil would dedicate the last ten years of his life to the *Aeneid*, an epic poem about the fall of Troy and the onward adventures of one Trojan prince, Aeneas. The *Georgics* was composed in a form which is almost impossible to explain. It is ostensibly a guidebook on how to live in the country and be a farmer, but it is also filled with praise for the newly peaceful city of Rome: the terrible civil wars that had punctuated the first century BCE had finally come to an end with the beginning of the imperial system. The first emperor of Rome – Augustus – was patron and friend to Maecenas, who was in turn patron and friend to Virgil. In the *Georgics*, these twin themes of country and city are interspersed with wonderful, fantastical stories which accompany more practical advice on, say, growing arable crops and vines.

In Book Four, Virgil turns his attention to beekeeping. This is no doubt in part because bees were important in a world where honey was the sweetest thing people would eat. It is surely also because Virgil loved insects: bees and ants are a particular source of delight to him. So he begins by talking about the ideal hive, but soon gets sidetracked into the story of Aristaeus, a man who has lost his bees and wants to replace them. Aristaeus seeks out Proteus, the shape-shifting god, in the hope of getting advice to improve his fortunes. But Proteus has harsh words for Aristaeus, who has incurred the wrath of the gods for the terrible crime he committed.[2] Proteus then tells the story of how Aristaeus had attacked Eurydice, the wife of Orpheus. She had run headlong from her assailant, across a river, desperate to escape him. Plenty of translations add in softening vocabulary – Eurydice is shunning Aristaeus' embrace, for example – but this is not in the Latin. Eurydice is trying to avoid being raped. Because of this, while attempting to escape him, she does not see a snake hidden in the deep grass in front of her foot, this *moritura puella*[3] – 'girl about to die'.

Eurydice is bitten by the snake and goes down to Dis, another name for Hades, the Underworld; the god who rules over Hades goes by the same pair of names. Now comes the part of the story we probably know best. Orpheus enters the Underworld, playing his lyre. The shades of the dead appear from the very darkest regions of Hades to hear him play. Even the Furies stop to listen, and Cerberus – the three-headed dog who guards Hades – stands with his three mouths agape.[4] Ixion – who is tormented in the Underworld by being bound to a fiery wheel which never stops moving – comes to rest because the wind that blows him unceasingly is suddenly still. Virgil doesn't mention the part where Orpheus makes his request to be reunited with his wife, but skips straight to the moment when Eurydice is handed over, following behind Orpheus as Proserpina (the Roman name for Persephone, queen of the Underworld) had ordered. But when they are almost back in daylight, a madness overcomes him and he forgets and looks behind him. All his hard work flows away in a moment.

Eurydice then speaks. What great madness has destroyed me, in my wretchedness, and you, Orpheus? The cruel Fates again call me back, and sleep settles on my swimming eyes. And now goodbye. Alas, not yours, I am carried away, surrounded by the vast night, reaching out my helpless hands to you. And then she disappears from his sight, like smoke on the breeze. Orpheus tries to cross into Hades again, but he cannot. He spends seven months crying over this second loss. He continues to mourn his wife and the worthless gift of Hades,[5] and refuses to remarry. Eventually, the women of Thrace are so incensed by this rejection that, during one of their Bacchic revels, they tear him apart. His severed head floats down the River Hebrus, crying, 'Poor Eurydice! Eurydice . . .'

There are several points of interest in this passage. The first is that it is being told for the purposes of censure: of course the gods are punishing Aristaeus, he is responsible for the death of Eurydice and therefore (indirectly) the death of Orpheus. The second is that Virgil spends four lines describing the last moments of Eurydice's life, as she flees Aristaeus. He uses another four lines to tell us that the dryads (tree nymphs, as was Eurydice in this version – they are described as her equals),[6] the mountains and the rivers mourn for her as she dies. Then he uses three more lines to describe Orpheus grieving, playing his lyre alone. The journey of Orpheus into the Underworld takes a lot longer: nineteen lines. But the part of their story which virtually every modern telling dwells on – the ascent, with Eurydice following – is incredibly brief. From the moment when Eurydice is returned to him, through to the moment where he loses her again: this entire section is only six lines long. The onerous condition placed on them – that Eurydice cannot accompany him but only follow him – is dealt with in a single line. The first we hear of the proviso that Orpheus cannot look behind him is when he forgets and does so.

I mention these numbers as a simple way of showing the emphases Virgil places on the different elements of the story. We might be expecting a drawn-out suspense-building narrative centred on the journey back to life, as so many later versions of this story will employ. The dramatic tension is inherent in the journey out of the Underworld, the tantalizing proximity of freedom and reunion. But for Virgil, the *katabasis* (the descent into Hades – from the Greek meaning 'going down') is by far the most interesting part. The detail he paints – of the spirits of the dead flocking to hear Orpheus' song, of the Furies and Cerberus being struck still, of the torment of Ixion coming to a halt – tells us this is the really important scene. The bargain made with the gods of Hades, the specific condition of Eurydice having to follow behind and Orpheus not being allowed to turn and look at her, the journey back up: these elements interest him less. There is no mention of why this condition is placed on them by Persephone, incidentally. The psychological cruelty of it – which we are so familiar with seeing right at the heart of the story of these shattered lovers – is wholly undiscussed. All Virgil says is that Eurydice followed behind, for that was the law (or condition) that Persephone had given them.

In addition, we might note that the only person who speaks in this story is Eurydice. Orpheus is singing when he descends into the Underworld, but we don't have any description of the words and he doesn't speak to Persephone. We also don't have her reply: we're told about the imposed condition rather than hearing it in direct speech. The first time anyone says anything is when Eurydice is torn away from Orpheus and she delivers a five-line monologue bemoaning their fate. Orpheus won't speak until he has been dismembered, and his disembodied head only cries out for Eurydice. Obviously, some of this story takes place in Hades, but it is interesting that only the dead speak, rather than the gods or the living. In terms of dialogue, the focus is on Eurydice and her sorrow at her wretched fate.

A few decades after Virgil wrote this version of Eurydice and Orpheus' story, Ovid follows him in his retelling of Greek myths for a Roman audience, the *Metamorphoses*. But Ovid doesn't seem to want his version of the story to overlap too closely with Virgil's. So he takes Aristaeus out of the picture (though not for issues of taste: the poem isn't short on sexual violence), and ramps up the pathos. His Eurydice is wandering through the grass with a gang of naiads[7] – water nymphs. She is not the victim of a sexual predator, she is with her girlfriends because it's her wedding day. Hymen – god of the wedding ceremony – is present. But Eurydice is bitten by a snake just the same. Orpheus then descends to Hades in record time. Five lines after Eurydice dies, Orpheus is speaking to Persephone (again called Proserpina here). And here we see another major departure from Virgil's version. This Orpheus is given a huge speech, begging the queen of the dead to give him back his wife. He begins with a typically Ovidian flourish, addressing Persephone in all her grandeur and immediately promising he has not come to steal her dog. This is not a purely bathetic moment: Heracles had previously come down to Hades and made off with Cerberus. So Orpheus is explaining up front that he isn't a thief, but a man who wants to reclaim his wife because she was stolen by a snake when she was still young. There is a definite suggestion here (which we'll look at in more detail below) that the young don't 'deserve' to die in the same way that the old do. However unreasonable this may sound to those of us who are no longer very young, it is the first point of his argument: she was young, too young to die.

Then he explains that he tried to suffer the loss, but Love overpowered him. He appeals to Persephone's backstory: weren't you abducted by the king of the Underworld because he loved you? Abduction as a sign of affection is obviously a more acceptable phenomenon in Ovid's time than it is today. But then he makes a more powerful argument: we all come to you in the end, he says.[8] Let my wife have her time and she'll return to you. And then he makes one final plea: if she can't come back with me, I will stay. Rejoice in the death of both of us.

And as he speaks, he plays, and the bloodless spirits of Hades weep. It is an astonishing image. No wonder so many musicians and composers have been tempted to take on this story. Even the thought of it makes me shiver: music so beautiful that the dead cry when they hear it. Now we have a slightly longer version of the glimpsed scene from the *Georgics* as all the torments that are visited upon the inhabitants of Tartarus come to a temporary halt: even Sisyphus pauses to sit on his rock. The king and queen cannot refuse him, so they summon Eurydice. She walks with a slow step, because of her injury.[9] The viper's bite continues to hurt, we might suppose, even after death. Orpheus receives Eurydice on the strict condition (*legem*, as in Virgil) that he cannot look back until they have left the valley of Avernus (the entrance to the Underworld). Otherwise his gift will be worthless – *inrita dona*.[10] These are also the same words used by Virgil in his description. Even as Ovid makes the story his own, he tips his hat to the readers who are paying close attention.

Orpheus and Eurydice make their terrifying ascent. The vocabulary of a single line tells us how difficult it is: *arduus, obscurus, caligine densus opaca* – 'steep, dark, enveloped in thick fog'.[11] Now we see an element of the story with which we're very familiar: fearing he has lost her, Orpheus turns back. Eurydice disappears immediately into the darkness. She reaches out her hands to him, but he can only grab at the breezes. She is gone. The pathos is almost overwhelming, and surely this is why the story resonates so strongly for us today, as it has for hundreds of years of operas, songs and paintings. It is the very fact that Orpheus loves her so much that causes their downfall: her second death, his second loss. If he loved her less, or at least less anxiously, they would make it outside and be free to live and love once again, to enjoy the marriage which was cut short on their wedding day. But, if he had loved her less, he would never have embarked on his terrible journey to the Underworld to reclaim her. The failure of his mission is assured from the moment he undertakes it. There is something cripplingly true about this, isn't there? That we are so often the authors of our own misfortunes because of the same qualities which make us brave, or hopeful, or loving in the first place. This Orpheus hasn't been gripped by madness, he has been afflicted by fear. And because the fear eventually overwhelms him, the thing he feared comes true.

Eurydice doesn't blame her husband, Ovid tells us. Because what could she reproach him for except loving her?[12] She has only time to say farewell, and even that is scarcely audible. This is an interesting inversion of the Virgilian emphasis. Virgil gave Eurydice a short but poignant speech, while Orpheus was silent except belatedly to speak her name. But Ovid has switched the focus to Orpheus, and Eurydice has moved into the margins of the story even before she is taken into the shadows of the Underworld.

And Ovid keeps the focus on Orpheus, just as Virgil did at this same point. We could follow Eurydice back down to Hades, but we don't. Instead we watch as Orpheus tries to persuade the ferryman to take him back across the Styx, but is refused. He doesn't eat for a week, he feeds off grief and tears.[13] Orpheus has now lost interest in women, and turns to (very) young men for love. The rest of the book is a series of songs performed by Orpheus on various mythological subjects. We have to wait for the beginning of Book Eleven for a longer version of the death scene we are familiar with from Virgil: Orpheus is dismembered by maenads, who are prone to religious frenzy, and angered by his rejection of them.

His disembodied head floats all the way to the shore of Lesbos, and a snake makes to attack it. But Apollo intervenes for Orpheus in a way no one did for Eurydice. He turns the snake to stone. At this point, Orpheus goes down into the Underworld for a second time, but now there is no chance of him coming back. He recognizes all the places he'd seen before. And then he finds Eurydice and embraces her with love. They walk together, side by side, Ovid says.[14] Sometimes he follows her as she goes ahead. And sometimes Orpheus goes ahead, safe in the knowledge that he can look back at his

Eurydice. It's such a lovely romantic end to this tragic story that we almost don't notice that, while we are concerning ourselves with Orpheus getting over his fear of losing Eurydice again, we have totally failed to ask if she might prefer it if she didn't have to walk behind him. Dazzled by the enormity of his loss, we have forgotten hers.

These two Roman poets, Virgil and Ovid, shaped the Orpheus and Eurydice narrative, but they didn't invent it. The earliest surviving certain mention of it is in Euripides' play from 438 BCE, *Alcestis*.[15] This unusual play is a tragedy with a happy ending, and tells the story of Alcestis, whose husband Admetus has won a favour from the god Apollo. When it comes to be time for Admetus to die, he can continue to live if, and only if, he can find another person to die in his stead. This is obviously a somewhat double-edged gift: who is likely to offer to die on your behalf? Someone who loves you more than life itself. Chances are, you might well feel the same way about them. In the months or years before the day on which the play is set (the action – as is usual with Greek tragedy – takes place on a single day), Admetus has failed to find any volunteer, except one: his wife, Alcestis.

Now it is the day when Alcestis is due to die. Death appears as a character, coming to escort her down to the Underworld. But before he does, Alcestis delivers a heartfelt monologue on the future she wishes for Admetus and their small children. She tells him he must remember her sacrifice and not remarry: she does not want her offspring to be saddled with a vicious stepmother. This is an early outing for the trope of the wicked stepmother, but we might allow Alcestis her moment of grief: she is about to die, after all. Admetus readily agrees to the condition. He can hardly do anything else, when his wife is dying so that he may live. Alcestis then tells her children that they have heard their father's words: he will not marry another woman.[16]

The whole scene is desperately sad: a young woman, a mother

of children who sit with her as she prepares to die; a husband realizing the greatness of his wife's sacrifice and offering his own sacrifice
in return. We can see the terrible ramifications of the gift Apollo has
given him. Quite understandably, Admetus did not want to die young
(his father is still alive, so he's a relatively young man). But by accepting
Alcestis' offer to die for him, he's depriving his children of a loving
mother, depriving himself of a loving wife. Not only that, but he
doesn't even have the prospect of a second wife, because he has just
sworn to his dying first wife – in front of the chorus and his own
children – that he will remain single after Alcestis' death. We might
rather intolerantly suggest he could have thought of all this a bit
sooner than when his wife is sliding into unconsciousness before their
children's gaze. But Greek tragedy is full of people not realizing
things until terrible consequences unfurl, so perhaps it is not entirely
reasonable to expect greater foresight from Admetus. One of their
children then speaks, but his mother is past hearing. With you leaving
us, the child says, our house is destroyed. I promise this play does
have a happy ending, although at this point it may not seem likely.

Admetus' father, Pheres, soon arrives to pay his respects to his dead
daughter-in-law and sympathize with his bereaved son. But Admetus
greets him with fury, telling him he was not invited to Alcestis' burial.
We don't need you now, he says: you should have sympathized when
I was dying.[17] In other words, Admetus must have been stricken with
some terrible illness of which Alcestis offered to cure him by dying
herself. This does – I think – make him a more sympathetic character.
If he had simply accepted Alcestis' death as the price worth paying to
avoid some nebulous fate on some unspecified day, we might legitimately think he was not really worth Alcestis' sacrifice. But we can
surely all understand how a couple in love could get to this point, how
a woman watching her beloved husband wasting away might feel that
she would rather die herself. How a man in pain might agree. But
there is a horribly arrogant tone to Admetus' next reproach to his

father. He didn't just want sympathy as he was dying, he wanted sacrifice. Admetus is deeply aggrieved because his father did not volunteer to die, that Pheres left the difficult decision to Alcestis. I should be calling her father and mother, he says, bleakly.[18] His argument continues: Pheres is old, he doesn't have long left to live anyway. He's already been king, he has a son who inherited the kingship, his legacy is complete. Well then, you'd better get yourself some other sons, he adds, to bury you when you die. Because I won't. Old men complain about the long span of their lives, say they want to die. But none of them really wants to die: old age doesn't weigh heavily on them at all.

Even the most ardent generation warrior might find Admetus' views somewhat bracing. It's one thing to feel that someone – a parent – should love you more than their own life, but it is quite another to demand it. Whatever sympathy we might have felt for Admetus as a grieving husband is swiftly retreating. What kind of man goes round demanding of his loved ones that they die so that he may live? A monstrously selfish one. And this in turn makes us question Alcestis' sacrifice. Wouldn't her children be better off with their selfless mother than their grasping father?

But Pheres' reply is pretty bracing too. I raised you to succeed me, he says. But I'm not obliged to die for you.[19] Fathers don't have to die for their sons. You delight in life, he adds: do you think your father doesn't? And then he goes on to criticize Admetus for avoiding his due death, for allowing his wife to die in his place. You killed her, he says.[20] The chorus try to get the men to stop arguing, but they are both unrepentant, and they continue to hurl insults at one another.

This intense debate at the heart of the play raises questions with no comfortable answers: what should we expect from our parents, our children, our spouses? Many of us might feel that we would willingly die for those we love, but perhaps, when it came to it, we would also cling to life, as both Pheres and Admetus have done. Would that make us selfish? Or just human?

The assumption underpinning Admetus' argument is exactly the same as that which Orpheus offered in Ovid's *Metamorphoses* when he persuaded Proserpina/Persephone to release Eurydice: she has died too young. It is not just the fact that their love has been sundered which is so awful, but that her life has been cut short unjustly. Would the story of these tragic lovers lose something if they were older? If they were newly married but in their eighties, would we feel the same sense of unfairness? There is something more poignant – isn't there? – in the death of someone very young than in the death of someone very old: it's harder to feel that it's a tragedy when someone who has lived a rich, long life eventually dies, even if they are much loved and mourned. It is still a great sadness, but it's not accompanied by the raging sense of unfairness we feel at the futility of a child or young adult dying.

We mourn differently in each case: when someone dies very young, we feel that they – and we – have been robbed of their potential. We see what should have been their future in glimpses when another young person passes milestones that our loved one never reached. When someone older dies, we feel deprived of experience, of both them and of the huge part they played in our own lives. If we're very unlucky, this grief even sours or obscures the happiness of remembering them.

But Pheres also has a point, doesn't he? You want to live: why wouldn't I? We don't get to impose death on the old, merely because we think they've had their go and now it's our turn. How would Admetus feel if his young son had been offered the bargain by Apollo? Would he have stepped up to die so that his son could live? Or is a longer life expectancy more valuable than a shorter one only if you are the younger man in the equation?

I did promise you a happy ending, so here it is: Heracles arrives to stay with Admetus. There's a brief confusion when he doesn't know that Alcestis has died, because Admetus has ordered his slaves not to mention it. Finally, one of them gives it up and Heracles bounds into action. He hastens to Alcestis' tomb and wrestles with Death, returning with a veiled, silent woman. After some resistance, Admetus accepts that his wife has been returned to him. That Heracles – who, we must remember, will be another surviving visitor to the Underworld, just like Orpheus – has brought back Alcestis. But she cannot speak for three days. She belongs to the gods of Hades until she undergoes a ritual purification.

So how might this story, of a woman who dies to save her husband's life, influence the story of Eurydice? It is our first reference to the Underworld narrative, although she isn't named. When Admetus is responding to Alcestis' big speech (the one where she makes him promise he won't remarry), he builds to a climax of sorrow at her imminent loss. If I had the voice and the songs of Orpheus,[21] he says, if I could charm Persephone and her husband, I would go down and seize you from Hades. And the guard dog wouldn't hold me back, and nor would the ferryman, until I'd brought you into the light again. But I can't do that, so I'll be with you when I die.

It's an interesting example for Admetus to choose, given that Orpheus is ultimately unsuccessful in his attempt to reclaim Eurydice. Presumably, even though this is the earliest version of the story that we can be sure of, Euripides' audience would have been familiar with it from sources which are lost to us: Admetus does a recap of the important bits, but it sounds like he's mentioning an example he thinks we'd all recognize, rather than telling us a story we haven't heard before.

The play has a happy ending precisely because Heracles can do what Orpheus cannot: successfully retrieve a young woman from the greedy maw of Death. And surely that's because Heracles isn't trying to reclaim someone he loves. He seems to have feelings of warm friendship towards both Admetus and Alcestis, but she's not his heart's desire, in the way Eurydice is for Orpheus. Even if Heracles were not such a strongman (who can wrestle Death and come off the winner), and even if he had been later setting out to chase after Alcestis (he catches her at her tomb rather than having to make an actual trip to the Underworld as he will in his final labour: the abduction of Cerberus), he would still stand a better chance of reclaiming Alcestis than Orpheus does of reclaiming Eurydice. Imagine if Heracles had been ordered to walk out of the Underworld and not look back: he would have been fine. He doesn't have the strength of emotion that Orpheus has, so he doesn't have the destructive anxiety that accompanies it. He is a man who can stroll down to the Underworld to steal a novelty dog. This isn't a hero who will be tormented by fear of loss.

And while we're talking about heroes, we should note that, for at least some ancient Greeks, Alcestis is a greater hero than Orpheus. As mentioned in the previous chapter, Plato's *Symposium* – written in the fourth century BCE – presents us with a debate among guests at a dinner party on the nature of eros – love. It's a somewhat more philosophically rigorous depiction of this kind of night out than many of us have experienced, although Aristophanes does have to swap turns with another speaker because he has the hiccups. You can always rely on comedians.

The first speech is delivered by a man named Phaedrus, who says that one defining feature of love is that only lovers will give up their lives for one another,[22] and that's the case for women and men alike. The only example he needs, he says, is Alcestis, who alone was willing to die on her husband's behalf, even though his father and mother were alive. Her devotion to her husband made his parents seem like strangers in comparison. Her behaviour was so impressive to men and gods alike that the gods gave her back to the living world. Whereas Orpheus, he adds, they sent packing. They only offered him a *phasma*, a ghost of his wife, because he was weak, as you might expect from a lyre player. He wasn't brave enough to die for love, like Alcestis, but managed to enter Hades alive. For this, he was made to die at the hands of women . . .

What are we to make of this passage, aside from the obvious fact that Phaedrus is nursing a major grievance against lyre players? Firstly, that Plato has remembered the plot of Euripides' play pretty well, considering he wrote the *Symposium* fifty years or more after *Alcestis* was first performed. Even more so when we think that Plato wasn't born until a decade or so after the original performance. From this, we might conclude that there are still regular performances of *Alcestis*: it has turned out to be very popular. At the very least, Plato expects his readers to be familiar with the example. But he seems to have more than the casual familiarity of an audience-member for a play they have seen once. The argument Phaedrus makes is brief, but he has fully taken Admetus' side in the debate between Pheres and his son. He has no criticism for Admetus' apparent expectation that one of his parents might die in his stead, indeed he shares it. He has only praise for Alcestis and her heroic sacrifice, and offers no censure of Admetus for being willing to accept his wife's death as a price worth paying for his own life.

He is, however, perfectly happy to criticize Orpheus for the lesser calibre of his sacrifice. Phaedrus isn't impressed with Orpheus' musical skill, his ability to charm the shades of the Underworld, to exert the power of persuasion on Persephone and Hades. For Phaedrus, Orpheus is weak because he didn't die for love.

Now this may reflect the prejudices of the author rather than the views of the character. Plato is wildly intolerant of many forms of artistic expression. Only the writing of philosophy is really acceptable in his view: other types of creativity are intrinsically suspicious. But it reveals an interesting attitude which we haven't seen in our other sources: Orpheus' problem is not that he loves Eurydice so much he can't help but break the restriction and look back at her. His problem is that he doesn't love her enough to have died of it. And so Orpheus is found wanting by the gods, just as much as by Phaedrus, at least as far as Plato tells it. He doesn't deserve Eurydice, so he doesn't get her. According to this version of their story, he never has a chance: the Eurydice this Orpheus sees is a mere ghost rather than a reclaimable woman.

Alcestis, of course, is not a ghost when she is returned to Admetus. But she is veiled and mute, so she has a somewhat ghostly quality. Even when Admetus can see her and accept that she has returned to him, he's perplexed that she will not speak. It's Heracles who tells him that she is still sacrosanct to the gods of the Underworld, and that she must remain silent for three days. This, of course, takes us beyond the temporal confines of the play.

In another playwright's hands, we might assume that the author was simply not interested in Alcestis' response, or that – as with so many male writers before and particularly after Euripides – the author didn't think very much about women and so didn't bother to write them any dialogue. But, as I've said elsewhere in this book (and will continue to say whenever the opportunity arises), Euripides is one of the greatest writers of female voices in antiquity and, frankly, in the history of theatre. He is always interested in the perspectives of women, and there is little he enjoys more than giving them fantastic speeches to thrill, distress or horrify his audience. When Alcestis comes back, she raises a question that the play chooses not to answer. Is this what she wanted? She is the eponymous hero of the play, but has her heroic deed – dying for love – been overshadowed by Heracles' heroic deed in wrestling with Death and winning? And, of course, in the days to come we might assume Admetus and Alcestis will be very happy together: given a second chance by the gods because of the power of her love and sacrifice. But surely there might be moments in the dark hours of the coming nights when Alcestis looks across at the sleeping form of her husband and wonders how much she can still love a man who so overtly cared more about himself than he cared about her. *Alcestis* has a happy ending compared to most tragedies, but perhaps that's just because the play ends before the real tragedy has time to play out.

It's curious that the story of Eurydice and Orpheus is so much better known to us than the story of Alcestis and Admetus, when in classical Greece it seems to have been the other way round. We have no record of Eurydice's name, even, until an obscure work called *Lament for Bion*, which was probably written in the first century BCE. It was once thought to be by a slightly earlier poet, Moschos, but is now generally agreed to be by an unknown southern-Italian writer.[23] It is perhaps three hundred and fifty years after *Alcestis* was first performed in Athens, three hundred years since Phaedrus found Orpheus' love for his wife to be wanting in Plato's *Symposium*. But only now does Eurydice have a name, when this poet explains that Persephone allows Orpheus Eurydice's return.[24] Her story certainly begins in Greece, and it's impossible to say for certain when she acquired her name. But our first example of it is from this poet, whose name in turn is unknown to us. Pseudo-Apollodorus also mentions Eurydice by name in his *Bibliotheca*[25] a couple of centuries later. Again, as with the earlier versions of her story, she dies when she is bitten by a snake. Orpheus wins her back with his lyre-playing, as usual, but this time it's Pluto rather than Persephone who imposes the condition of not looking back. And he is even more demanding than his wife: in this version, Orpheus cannot look at Eurydice until they have made it all the way to his house.

We can see hints and echoes of these multiple ancient versions of Orpheus and Eurydice's story in some of their many operatic incarnations. Gluck's 1774 opera, *Orphée et Eurydice*, has more than a touch of *Alcestis* to it. It is a reworking of the composer's earlier version with a libretto by Ranieri de' Calzabigi, who would also later write the libretto for Gluck's *Alceste*. The opera initially follows the story we know so well: Eurydice's death, Orpheus' descent to the Underworld, the return, the look, the second loss of Eurydice. But then, touched by their devotion and despair, the god of love appears and reunites them once again. Love is triumphant, as the libretto says. And unlike Alcestis, this Eurydice never has to wonder if her husband might not love her as much as she loves him: he loves her enough to follow her to Hades, loves her enough to panic and fail, and then loves her enough for the gods themselves to intervene. A truly happy ending.

Meanwhile, in Philip Glass' bonkers 1993 opera, *Orphée*, based on Cocteau's 1950 film of the same name, the proviso about not looking back at Eurydice until long after they have left the Underworld is picked up and played with still further. In the ENO's 2019 production,[26] as in the film, Orpheus and Eurydice couldn't look at each other even once they were back in their home. The story of tragic lovers takes an unexpected swerve into slapstick. Eurydice hides behind doors, Orpheus ducks under tablecloths, all to avoid the fatal gaze. They fail – of course; how could they not? – and Eurydice is reclaimed by the Underworld. In Offenbach's 1858 operetta, *Orpheus in the Underworld*, Eurydice doesn't even merit having her name in the title: an echo of those earliest Greek versions of her story when she goes unnamed. And yet, the opera focuses more on Eurydice than her husband, not least because she gets to dance the can-can in Hades in Act Four.[27]

It's easy to see why composers have been drawn to the character of Orpheus, rather than his wife Eurydice. Who wouldn't want to take on the challenge of trying to create the music that made the rocks and trees want to follow Orpheus, that brought the dead from the darkest reaches of Hades to hear him play? It is the ultimate story about the power of music to change hearts and minds. Even if, for Eurydice, it changes very little and certainly not for the better.

In Anaïs Mitchell's *Hadestown*, which had its London premiere in 2018,[28] we see what happens in an inventive American take on the story. Orpheus is a tormented composer who has found what he believes is a special melody. He meets Eurydice as she is trying to cope with the pressures of poverty: no warm clothes, not enough to eat. There are musical and stylistic hints that this is the Depression, but it is never placed too specifically in time. The pair fall in love and they seem set for happiness. But Orpheus' absorption in his music means he fails to notice that his wife is still hungry and cold, and that the quest for the perfect tune is not keeping them warm. Eurydice is seduced by the basso profondo Hades and makes a voluntary trip to the heavily industrialized Hadestown, before realizing she has made a mistake and is now trapped. Orpheus finally notices he has lost her, and follows her to Hadestown before trying to use his melody to reclaim her. It resonates for Hades and Persephone, reminding them of who they were when they first fell in love. Persephone wants the lovers to be reunited, and intercedes with her husband. But this Hades is as wily as any, and the couple are separated once again when Orpheus cannot resist looking back. The inevitability of tragedy is made explicit in the final moments, when Hermes reminds us that Orpheus and Eurydice's story is 'an old song, it's an old song from way back when'. The tone of the musical is triumphantly modern but the story's appeal is that it has been told over and over again and always ends the same way. Still, Hermes says, 'But here's the thing/ To know how it ends/And still begin to sing it again/As if it might turn out this time.' There's comfort in stories which don't change, even the sad ones.

But – at the risk of disagreeing with the messenger god – the story of Orpheus and Eurydice can and does change in all kinds of unexpected ways. Musical talent doesn't have to reside in the hands and voice of one man, for example. In the 1959 Brazilian film *Orfeu Negro*, or *Black Orpheus*, directed by Marcel Camus,[29] it is democratized. Orfeu (Breno Mello) is a talented musician, but the whole of Rio is filled with incredible music and musicians: it is Carnival time. The film begins in the favela where much of the action will take place. It pulsates with singing, playing and – a huge feature of this version of the story – dancing. Music isn't just something to be listened to here, it's something to move to. After this establishing sequence which runs throughout the credits, we cut to the harbour where a ferry is arriving. On board is Eurydice (Marpessa Dawn), who has come to Rio to stay with her cousin because a man – some sort of predator, though we don't know more – has driven her away from her home.

Eurydice hops onto a tram where everyone seems to be playing or singing something. Orfeu is the tram-conductor: even meeting so casually in a crowded city, we know they are meant to be together. A marching band is playing in the streets, practising for Carnival the following day. Music is representative of both order and disorder in this film. It is highly personal – people playing and dancing for a loved one, or alone – and it is also public, a performance.

By happy coincidence, Eurydice's cousin lives next door to Orfeu. She fits in to the neighbourhood straight away and a local child, Benedito, gives her a charm he has made. Will you keep it even after you die? he asks. It is the first hint we have that all may not end happily for Eurydice. When Orfeu and Eurydice meet again and discover each other's names, he is delighted. I'm already in love with you, he laughs. But I don't love you, she replies. That's alright, he says, you don't have to.

Are they the original Orpheus and Eurydice from ancient times, somehow reincarnated in modern Brazil? There is a strong sense that they are, that this 1950s couple are reliving a story that has happened many times before. We have a hint of this in the opening shot of the movie, when a set of sculpted Greek figures disappear to be replaced by a group of Brazilian musicians. Orpheus and Eurydice are not just statues, but part of a living story.

During Carnival preparations, and on the day of Carnival itself, Eurydice is pursued by a terrifying vision of Death, a monochrome masked man whom she cannot escape. No matter where she is, no matter how ornately she is disguised in her cousin's Carnival outfit, Death cannot be outrun. She races away from him and finds herself on the upper floor of a deserted building, clinging on to a cable so she doesn't fall. But Death still awaits her and she cannot move. When Orfeu arrives, he flips a switch on the wall. The cable snaked around Eurydice's hand is live: she is electrocuted and falls to her death. We might note that there is a touch of *Alcestis* in this narrative as well as the more overt Eurydice story (the snaky cable is a particularly clever touch): Death as a character waiting for a young woman to die so that he may claim her.

Orfeu is bundled away from the scene, but then cannot accept Eurydice is gone. He tries desperately to find her in the Missing Persons office, tracking through one bureaucratic nightmare after another. He comes to a room filled with stacks of paper. The janitor tells him he won't find her there; he must call out for her, and she will come. Orfeu and the janitor go searching elsewhere, passing a guard dog called Cerberus, though he only has one head on this occasion. The janitor then guides Orfeu to a ritual gathering where they try to summon Eurydice: this janitor is surely meant to remind us of Charon, the ferryman who takes the dead across the River Styx. Eurydice is partially conjured into the room, but Orfeu cannot turn around or he will see that it is an old woman who speaks with Eurydice's voice. He leaves and eventually finds Eurydice's body in the mortuary; he carries her in his arms back to the favela. As he climbs near the edge of a sheer cliff, his angry fiancée Mira sees him holding Eurydice. She hurls a rock at him and it hits him in the head: he staggers and falls to his death. Orpheus and Eurydice are reunited after all. Benedito's friend Zeca plays Orfeu's guitar as dawn breaks. Orfeu, they believe, could make the sun rise with his playing, so now Zeca must do the same. A little girl watches him and says, You are Orfeu now. We can only hope that his story will have a happier ending.

Black Orpheus received huge acclaim on its release: it won the Palme d'Or in Cannes in 1959 and the Academy Award for Best Foreign Language Film the following year. The bossa nova soundtrack alone can banish any thoughts of gloom: the merging of Greek myth with Brazilian music works perfectly. It is full of witty references and allegory (Orfeu's friend is called Hermes: he's the one who guides Eurydice to her cousin's house, like his Greek namesake, who is both messenger god and psychopomp – a deity who escorts souls down to the Underworld). And it allows Eurydice to take up as much narrative space as Orpheus, which is rare in any telling of their story before this point. The early parts of the film alternate between her and Orfeu: we follow her off the boat, watch as she helps a blind man to find his bearings, see the way her cousin and the whole neighbourhood take her in. This is intercut with Orfeu and his girlfriend, Mira, who is determined that he should buy her a wedding ring, even though his eyes are on reclaiming his guitar from the pawn shop: the one love he does successfully retrieve. Orpheus and Eurydice's story has more dramatic weight because we see both of them as characters, rather than one character and his muse (which is how they are portrayed so frequently in opera). Because we encounter the idea that they are destined to be lovers, destined to die – they might be this generation's Orpheus and Eurydice, but there have been many more before them and there are countless more to come – we need a sense of them as individuals if we are not to see them as cogs in a sad machine. The vibrancy and complexity of the music, costumes and dance which accompany the familiar tale turn it into something more than a tragedy.

Composers and librettists of staged versions of Eurydice and Orpheus have almost always begun from the same premise: what if I were Orpheus? What if I were the world's great artist, great lover, great persuader, flawed hero? It's easy to see why so many have been drawn to his perspective: this is a story which lends itself to music, and Orpheus is the musician. And it's hardly surprising that this fascination continues when the story is told in paint rather than music: that crucial turning point of the story is literally about the power of the male gaze.

The nineteenth-century German artist Emil Neide painted Orpheus striding out of darkness, towards the light.[30] He carries a highly ornate golden lyre in his right hand and a mighty walking stick in his left. His chest is puffed up and a dark cloak billows around him. Half-crouching behind him in the shadows is Eurydice. She wears a gold armlet of a snake curled around her left bicep, to remind us how she died. The light catches her face just under her eyes: is there the faintest sugges-tion of impatience there? Her preening husband looks enormously pleased with himself, almost as though he has engaged in this whole rescue mission for appearances' sake. She is ostensibly hiding from the light so that if he does turn around he might not see her. Yet I can never quite shake the idea that she's wondering if she could just slink into the shadows and go back down to Hades in peace.

And the image of a man strutting forward so confidently when we know he is about to fail raises an important question about Orpheus too. Does he want to fail? Would he prefer to have Eurydice back in his arms, or to have glory for all time as the great musician with the tragic lost muse? In other words, does he prefer losing the real Eurydice if it means he can create his own version of her without reality sullying his art? Think back to that early version of the story in Virgil, where Eurydice speaks but Orpheus does not. Until his disembodied head is floating down the river, and then he only says her name. Orpheus doesn't have words – only music and song – while Eurydice can speak. But once she is gone, he gets to call the tune.

Readers had to wait a long time for Eurydice to tell the story for herself. But some of the most memorable modern versions of this myth are ones which have done precisely that. The American poet Hilda Doolittle – who used the pen name H.D. – wrote 'Eurydice' in the early twentieth century: it was published in her *Collected Poems* in 1925.[31] This Eurydice is not going quietly. The poem begins with a chilly anger: 'So you have swept me back/ I who could have walked with the live souls above the earth'. The cause of her tragedy is twofold: 'your arrogance and your ruthlessness'. Ovid cheerily told us that Eurydice had nothing to complain of except that Orpheus loved her a bit too much. But while this romantic elision works very well in the context of his telling of the myth, it does always leave me at least thinking: Really? Nothing at all? Eurydice gets bitten by a snake, she is dragged down to the Underworld, she is wrenched out of the darkness and she is still walking with a limp, she is handed back to Orpheus under a strict proviso, she is given the closest breath of freedom, and then she is hauled back down to Hades, dying all over again. Nothing to complain about? She has quite a lot to complain about if you stop thinking about Orpheus and just think about her for a moment. She just doesn't get to complain because no one ever asks her how she feels.

When H.D. takes on the story, she gives Eurydice her voice back: it's telling that the poem – written in the first person – doesn't ever name Orpheus. This really is all about Eurydice. And it's her second death which really hurts: 'I had grown from listlessness into peace,/ if you had let me rest with the dead, I had forgot you/ and the past'. By focusing on Orpheus' perspective at the moment where he loses his love (as virtually every version of their story does), we run the risk of overlooking it from the other side: salvation promised and then cruelly snatched away. Orpheus is left with nothing but his grief and his lyre. Eurydice is left with nothing at all. Although, as H.D. tells it, that's not necessarily a bad thing: 'hell is no worse than your earth'. This poem throbs with rage, as though Eurydice has waited a couple of millennia to get all this off her chest. But it does not end in anger; it ends with a declaration: 'hell must break before I am lost,' she says, in the final stanza. Eurydice may be dead, but she is still triumphantly herself.

And once Eurydice has found her voice, she is loath to give it up. In 1999, Carol Ann Duffy published *The World's Wife*, a collection of poems offering women's perspectives of stories which had usually been told from their husbands' points of view. In 'Eurydice', she gives us a glorious, bristling version of this character who was delighted to find herself in the Underworld: 'It suited me down to the ground.'[32] She invites us to picture her face 'in the one place you'd think a girl would be safe/ from the kind of a man/ who follows her round/ writing poems'. This Eurydice is horrified when Orpheus – whom she views as a self-satisfied stalker – pitches up in Hades to seek her return. She is very much less impressed with Orpheus' talent, having, as she says, 'done all the typing myself,/ I should know.' She has no interest in being his muse, and never did: 'And given my time all over again,/ rest assured that I'd rather speak for myself'.

Duffy nails Eurydice's problem in the traditional versions of the myth: no one ever asks her what she might like. She has no agency in her story, and we don't even know how she feels about it. Orpheus makes his grand *katabasis* in search of her, so we are dazzled by the romantic power of his attachment and the persuasive power of his lyre-playing. But why should Eurydice feel the same way about him that he feels about her? Because she is so frequently silenced, we have just assumed that she does. In one of the finest twists in this excellent poetry collection, Duffy takes the moment of Orpheus' gaze and Eurydice's second death and turns it on its head. Her Eurydice is desperately trying to make Orpheus look back, so she can return to the Underworld in peace. After multiple attempts ('what did I have to do, I said,/ to make him see we were through?'), she finally lights upon the solution. She touches his neck and tells him she wants to hear his poem again. Unable to resist this appeal to his ego, Orpheus turns around and Eurydice 'waved once and was gone'. She finally gets the peace she craves away from the man who bores her with his arrogance and his popular reputation. Eurydice knows the man behind the genius and she would, it turns out, prefer to be dead.

PHAEDRA

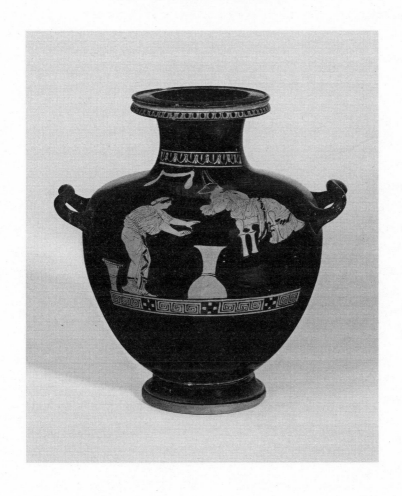

THE WICKED STEPMOTHER IS ONE OF THE OLDEST TROPES IN storytelling. Where would Cinderella be without a vicious step-mother and cruel stepsisters? The story appeals to us on multiple levels: a tragic young woman receives a spectacular change in fortunes (and attendant makeover), and the unkind women who persecuted her get their comeuppance. All this, plus true love and nice shoes.

But Phaedra, the wife of Theseus, makes Cinderella's wicked stepmother seem positively benevolent. Phaedra falls in love with her stepson, Hippolytus. He rejects her and she takes her own life by hanging. She has left a note accusing him of rape. Theseus – finding his wife dead and his son denounced – calls down a curse on Hippolytus which results in the young man's death. Phaedra has achieved what evil stepmothers secretly always desire: the elimination of their love-rival's offspring. Not only that, but she has confirmed the secret (or sometimes overt) belief of so much of our society: that women lie about rape because they are malevolent and trying to entrap or punish innocent men.

This thumbnail sketch of Phaedra is accurate, but only partially so. It ignores a great deal of the source material that we have on her, and adds in no small quantity of our own prejudice: against step-mothers, against female sexual desire and, yes, against women who accuse men of injuring them, rightly and wrongly. Phaedra commits an act of terrible dishonesty and its consequences are catastrophic. But she is not – at least not in one of the most celebrated plays to survive to us from fifth-century BCE Athens – a villain. She is one half of a tragedy, which is not the same thing.

So let's begin with her family history, before looking in more detail at her portrayal in Euripides' play from 428 BCE, *Hippolytus*. Phaedra is one of the daughters of King Minos and Queen Pasiphaë, and so was born and raised on the island of Crete. To describe her family dynamics as complex is quite the understatement. She is the sister of Ariadne, with whom Theseus left Crete after slaying the Minotaur. And both women are the half-sisters of the Minotaur (also known as Asterion).[1] We're usually told the Minotaur is the product of an unnatural fascination exerted by a handsome bull over Pasiphaë, who notoriously had the craftsman Daedalus carve her a wooden cow costume to enable her to trick the beast into mistaking her for an actual cow. But this makes Pasiphaë the guilty party, because who else goes around having bestial urges and then concealing themselves in a bizarre cow-shaped contraption? Actually, as Pseudo-Apollodorus explains,[2] Pasiphaë is the victim of the blasphemy and greed of her husband, Minos. Minos prays to Poseidon that a bull will rise from the ocean (bulls rising out of the sea are a major theme in Phaedra's story, although none of them is summoned by her). In return, he promises that he will sacrifice the bull to Poseidon: he is trying to prove to his subjects that he has the divine right to rule Crete and the proof is that he can ask the gods to grant his wishes and they will. Poseidon hears his prayer and sends him a beautiful bull (the Greek word *diaprepē* is usually translated as 'distinguished,' but this makes it seem like the bull is wearing a monocle, which it is not). Minos then performs a transparently obvious switch, keeping Poseidon's bull for himself and sacrificing a regular, non-oceanic one instead. Poseidon then punishes him by making Pasiphaë develop an intense affection for the bull. And this is when she persuades Daedalus to help her out with the wheeled wooden cow disguise. We can only assume it is more convincing to the bull than it sounds, because their resulting offspring is the Minotaur. This poor creature therefore owes both his existence and his imprisonment to Daedalus, who also builds the labyrinth which contains him. So, not for the first time, we can see that the popular version of a story is missing crucial information. Information that absolves poor Pasiphaë of at least some responsibility. Minos' deceit and Poseidon's revenge are the twin causes of her misplaced passion. As we will see throughout this chapter, you offend the gods at your peril, perhaps more in this myth than in most. And – as the story of Pasiphaë should always remind us – the gods rarely care who they hurt in their pursuit of vengeance.

Theseus famously kills the Minotaur with help from Ariadne, who gives him a spool of thread so he can find his way through the labyrinth and – vitally – back out again. The two elope together or, as Homer has it in Book Eleven of the *Odyssey*, Theseus tries to take her from Crete to Athens.[3] But they don't make it, because Artemis kills her in response to an accusation made by Dionysus. Or – in many versions of their story – Theseus abandons Ariadne on the island of Naxos. In a not-very-heroic manner, he usually leaves while she is asleep.[4] Several sources suggest that Dionysus wanted Ariadne as his bride, but Plutarch offers a couple of alternatives:[5] when she realizes she has been abandoned, Ariadne hangs herself; Theseus left her because he had fallen for another woman, named Aigle.

In his sixty-fourth poem, the Roman author Catullus describes the scene on Naxos as Ariadne wakes up and sees that Theseus has left her. She had abandoned her parents and the embrace of her sister, he says,[6] and Theseus abandoned her while she slept. Interestingly, Catullus uses the word *coniunx*, meaning 'husband', in his description: this relationship is not a trivial one. He describes Theseus as *immemoris* – which is often translated as 'forgetful'. But we can't imagine that Theseus has literally forgotten Ariadne in the course of a single night. Rather, he is heedless of her, or perhaps forgetful of everything she has done for him. He owes his life to her and her labyrinthine assistance, after all. No wonder Ariadne is devastated when she finds he has left her behind. Catullus gives Ariadne furious words of recrimination: Traitor, she says, will you carry your perjury home with you? The speech is dozens of lines long, but its most poignant moment – at least as far as Phaedra's story is concerned – comes early. Let no woman now believe a man who makes her promises, may no woman hope that her man's words are true. Ariadne concludes by calling on the snake-haired Eumenides – Furies – to punish him. Don't let my grief disappear, she says. But, with the same mind he had when he abandoned me here, let Theseus slaughter himself and his family. If she knew who her errant partner was going to marry, would she have stopped short of the final words – *seque suosque* – himself and his own? Ariadne cannot know as she curses him, of course, that one day her sister Phaedra will be included in this description.

Theseus continues sailing back to Athens and experiences a second strange bout of forgetfulness. When he set off on his voyage to Crete, he promised his father Aegeus that he would change the colour of his sail from black to white, if he was returning home safely. Theseus remembers these instructions carefully for ages, but then somehow forgets: as though a gust of wind had blown clouds from the top of a mountain. Aegeus sees the ship returning with the wrong sail, believes his son has died and hurls himself to his death. And so, Catullus remarks, fierce Theseus brought on himself the same kind of grief that he had given the daughter of Minos, with his heedless mind. Catullus explicitly compares Ariadne's loss to a profound bereavement, the grief of losing a father. Loving Theseus turns out to be a very dangerous business.

Given their complicated family history, we might well imagine that Phaedra has a conflicted relationship with her husband. Theseus had, at the very least, conspired with her sister to kill her half-brother. While we may be used to thinking of the Minotaur as a monster, we only have to read Jorge Luis Borges' beautiful short story 'The House of Asterion' to realize that he doesn't seem like that to everyone. And even if we set aside any sororal feelings Phaedra may have had for Asterion, we can see that she still might not feel secure in her marriage. Theseus chose to leave Crete with Ariadne, not with her. No one loves being a second choice. Actually, this is Theseus we are discussing: the number is somewhat higher than two.

And Theseus' wives don't tend to die of old age. Whether or not Ariadne hangs herself, we also have the death of Antiope (sometimes called Hippolyta), the Amazon whom Theseus either elopes with or kidnaps from her home in Themiscyra. As you may remember, sometimes Antiope is killed by another Amazon, but in some accounts she is killed by Theseus during the war waged by the other Amazons for their sister's return. Plutarch also tells us of another version[7] in the now-lost poem about Theseus, the *Theseid*. In it, the Amazons and Antiope attack Theseus on the day of his wedding to Phaedra, and it is during this battle that she dies, killed by Heracles. Plutarch rather sniffily dismisses this variation as a fiction (for Plutarch, the bulk of these stories are ancient history rather than myth).

We must be careful, of course, not to judge ancient characters by modern standards: it is simply a waste of time expecting people who lived thousands of years ago to feel the same way about the nuances of women's lives as we do. So it's worth noting that Theseus is considered a pretty dubious figure by Plutarch himself. Of the story of Phaedra and Hippolytus, he says that historians and tragedians are pretty well agreed on it, so this is probably what happened (unlike the wedding-day bloodbath he is sceptical of immediately before). He doesn't consider Phaedra a villain or a criminal, incidentally. He describes the events of her story as *dustuchias*[8] – catastrophes. But then he goes on to make an even more interesting distinction. There are, he says, other stories about the marriages of Theseus which neither begin well nor have happy endings. But those haven't been performed on the stage.[9] He continues: Theseus is said to have carried off Anaxo . . . and, having killed Sinis and Cercyon, to have taken their daughters by force; to have married Periboia . . . and then Pheriboia, and Iope, daughter of Iphicles; to have abandoned Ariadne because of his desire for Aigle . . . and carried off Helen, filling Attica with war.

Let's just take a moment to look at this catalogue of unpleasantness. Theseus stands accused of being something rather worse than a bad husband, many times over (although he certainly is that. I cannot be alone in wondering if he consecutively marries women named Periboia and Pheriboia because it's less effort to remember such similar names). He abducts Anaxo and later Helen: these are not even euphemised in the Greek. Theseus is a serial rapist, a serial taker of war brides. He doesn't abduct the daughters of Sinis and Cercyon, but he nonetheless rapes them after killing their fathers. And he takes them, Plutarch makes this quite clear, by force – *bia*. This is rape. Helen was either seven or ten when Theseus abducted her, you may remember. In some versions of the story, she has given birth to his daughter before she is reclaimed by her brothers.

And Plutarch makes a concise but vital point at the beginning of this list. These 'other stories' about Theseus' violent sexual history haven't been shown onstage. Professor Edith Hall has argued with characteristic scholarly vigour that she loathes Euripides' *Hippolytus*, because it legitimizes rape myths.[10] By dramatizing a story in which a woman fabricates a claim of rape, we give vastly more prominence to Phaedra's wrongdoing than we do to, for example, Theseus' succession of rapes, forced marriages, kidnaps and child rape, which are still largely undramatized today. Sarah Kane's *Phaedra's Love* – a brutal retelling of the myth that culminates in Hippolytus being castrated and disembowelled, while Theseus rapes his stepdaughter and then slits her throat – is a rare exception. Even Plutarch can see that there is an issue with which stories are told and which are not, and he is writing the best part of two millennia before women will even get the vote. There are a few stories of women making up accusations of rape in Greek myth, Phaedra and Stheneboea being the two best-known. But there are literally hundreds of examples of rape: mostly of women, occasionally also of young men.

Translations and retellings – particularly of Greek myths for children – tend to gloss over this uncomfortable fact. Of course, no one wants to traumatize a child learning about the Greeks for the first time, but the problem with sanitizing these stories is that we develop a skewed perception. When we read that a satyr is attempting to 'carry off' a nymph, to 'seize' a naiad, we are reading euphemisms.

To look at a specific and notorious example, Hades often 'abducts' Persephone, who is eventually reclaimed by her grieving mother, Demeter, for part of the year. The remainder must be spent in the Underworld because Persephone has eaten pomegranate seeds during her stay, so she has to return to Hades every year. This is the price for having consumed food in the realm of the dead. Even people who know very little Greek myth usually know this story: it is one we often learn as children. But the word 'abduct' tells only part of the story. It can make the whole encounter sound more like an adventure from which Persephone is partially rescued, and less like a sustained sexual assault and forced marriage. We focus on the detail of the pomegranate, which makes Persephone complicit or even partly responsible for her own continued and repeated imprisonment. Yet if we read the *Homeric Hymn to Demeter*, we would see that, in this, one of the earliest tellings of Persephone's story, Hades tricks her into eating: he gives her the pomegranate *lathrē* – secretly.[11] She is not told that it could cost her her freedom. Only when she is reunited with her mother Demeter does she discover the consequences: she explains that Hades secretly put the fruit in her mouth, compelled her, by force, to taste it.[12] This image of a young woman being force-fed by her jailor to assure her further imprisonment is genuinely shocking. The *Homeric Hymn* also tells us that Zeus connived with Hades for the latter to take Persephone against her will. There is no way of reading these words and thinking Persephone was not raped. 'Against her will' is quite specific. And Zeus is Persephone's father, Hades her uncle. Two all-powerful male gods, between them responsible for both the world of the living and the world of the dead, conspiring against a young woman to traffic her to the Underworld, rape her, and then hide the truth from her mother for as long as they can: that is a more accurate, if less delightful, way of describing the same story.

Just to be clear, I am not suggesting for a moment that the ancient world isn't packed with its own misogyny: it is. The literature and art which survive today were created in highly patriarchal societies which gave enormous power to a small group of wealthy men. But all too often it is the misogyny of more recent times that we are reading. The *Homeric Hymn* tells us that Persephone is forced to eat against her will; it does not gloss over this element of the story. And yet modern storytellers routinely ignore it. Let's look again at how Theseus fares when his exploits are recounted in Roger Lancelyn Green's much-loved *Tales of the Greek Heroes*, published in 1958. He cheerfully tells us about Theseus killing Sinis and Cercyon (and other 'miscreants'). But he makes no mention of the rape of these men's daughters, which Plutarch knew was worth including in his description. For more modern authors, it seems that murdering villains is fine, but raping their daughters must be overlooked. Of course, we might well feel that a classic children's book is no place for rape: I don't particularly disagree. But these myths are full of violence and we should at least ask why it is the violence against women that is removed in order to make our heroes uncomplicated adventurers.

Because that is certainly what happens to Theseus in Green's version. When we come to Ariadne on Naxos, Dionysus sees her and makes her fall into a magic sleep, 'and when she awoke, she remembered nothing about Theseus, nor how she came to Naxos, but willingly became the bride of Dionysus.'[13] That is – you will forgive me if I am damaging your childhood delight in these stories – enormously convenient for Theseus. We might all wish our bad behaviour could be so easily forgotten. A page later, the new king of Crete sends Theseus 'Phaedra in marriage, so that in spite of his loss of Ariadne, he still married a daughter of Minos.' Well, thank goodness. I was beginning to worry that Theseus was the real victim here.

The stories are charmingly told. They were (and are – the book is still in print) the gateway for so many of us into Greek myth and the classical world. But because we read them as children, we don't always consider them critically: we tend to see them as a neutral, authoritative version from which other versions deviate. And – like all books – they reflect the values of their time. So while I don't want to dissuade you from reading these stories to children, I would urge you to counterbalance the quiet prejudice which lurks within them.

Just in case you were thinking that it's only children's books which are rewritten to make the male characters more heroic and the female characters less injured, incidentally, Robert Graves often did the same thing in his *Greek Myths*. Let's go back to Persephone and Hades. Graves' version of Persephone and the pomegranate has no mention of Hades force-feeding her. Rather, she is denounced by 'one of Hades' gardeners, Ascalaphus,'[14] for having picked 'a pomegranate from a tree in your orchard, and eaten seven seeds.' This owes something to Pseudo-Apollodorus' *Bibliotheca*. But in that version, Ascalaphus' profession as a gardener – which, as far as I can discover, is Graves' invention – goes unmentioned. For Pseudo-Apollodorus, Ascalaphus was witness to Hades/Pluto feeding Persephone a single pomegranate seed. He snitches on her and Demeter pays him back by trapping him under a rock in Hades.[15] Graves omits this last detail, as well as changing the number of seeds Persephone eats (the voluntary consumption of seven seeds is in Book Five of Ovid's

Metamorphoses, but, in that too, Persephone is not told about the rule of not eating until after she has done so) and making it Persephone's sneaky theft rather than Hades' force-feeding. The blameless profession given to Ascalaphus only adds to this: gardeners seem so decent and reliable. These choices may seem minor, but Graves presents his work as scholarly and neutral. It is certainly scholarly, it is anything but neutral: Graves has chosen to tell a composite of the versions in Pseudo-Apollodorus and Ovid and ignore the *Homeric Hymn*, and then he has omitted information about the pomegranate so that Persephone seems more responsible for her own misfortune. Each example may be minor on its own, but across a two-volume collection, they add up. And sadly, Graves' editorial choices rarely work out well for women.

Persephone is just one of a vast number of examples I could have chosen to illustrate this point. But none of the countless rapes which take place in Greek myth makes the slightest difference to Hippolytus of course, who is innocent of any crime. He is killed because of a wrongful accusation of rape made by his stepmother. I thought longer about including Phaedra in this book than about any of the other women, precisely because false rape allegations are such a difficult topic to discuss in a nuanced way. And without inadvertently adding to a problem. False rape claims are incredibly rare and receive far more column inches than they warrant, given their extreme rarity. But omitting Phaedra's story – challenging as it is – seemed dishonest. She is a woman whose story has been told and retold through the ages, just like the others.

The problem is, of course, that Phaedra can be used to legitimize the myth that many women lie about being raped. The truth is very different, however. Accusations of rape that are found or suspected to be false are about 4 per cent in the UK, according to Home Office figures.[16] So 96 per cent of rape allegations are therefore considered – by the Home Office – to be true, even though only a tiny minority of those truthful allegations result in convictions. And these numbers matter: according to the Office of National Statistics, approximately 85,000 women and 12,000 men experience rape or attempted rape in England and Wales each year. Only 15 per cent of them report it to the police. In other words, 85 per cent of those who experience sexual assault and rape never report it. And that shocking statistic should occupy a lot more of our energy than the tiny percentage of false allegations made to the police. For every one false allegation made, 199 rapes or assaults occur, of which roughly 170 go unreported. We should talk about Phaedra, but we cannot allow her to let us lose sight of reality. Which is that rape is experienced and not reported many, many times more often than it is falsely reported.

Now we have some context, let's get back to Phaedra. And specifically, let's get back to her portrayal in Euripides' play. It was, in fact, his second version of *Hippolytus*: the first version does not survive.[17] We do have references to it, however, and these imply that the character of Phaedra was quite different in the two plays. In the first version, it seems that Phaedra was presented as a seductress and adulteress, a villainous woman who harbours a strong sexual desire for a man and acts upon it.[18] But the play was not well received and Euripides rewrote. In this second version, he paints a far more sympathetic picture of a woman tormented by an affliction she did nothing to deserve.

The play begins with the goddess Aphrodite, who explains that, as gods like to be honoured, she shows favour to those who revere her while crushing those who don't.[19] She has a particular problem with a young man named Hippolytus, son of Theseus and the Amazon, because he calls her *kakistēn daimonōn* – 'the worst of the gods'. He spends his days with Artemis instead, who is famously virginal. Because he has wronged me, she continues, I will have vengeance on him today.[20] I've taken care of most of it already, there's not much more to do.

She goes on to explain the details: two years earlier, Phaedra saw Hippolytus for the first time and, in accordance with Aphrodite's plans, was seized by a terrible love for him.[21] Phaedra built a temple to Aphrodite, naming it after Hippolytus. The wretched woman is now dying from the agony of love, and doing so in silence.[22] No one knows what her sickness is. But Aphrodite will reveal everything to Theseus so that he kills his son himself with three curses (or prayers) which he has been given by Poseidon. She describes Hippolytus as her enemy. Phaedra will keep her good name but be killed too. Aphrodite notices that Hippolytus is about to arrive onstage and concludes: the gates of Hades are open for him, this day's light will be the last he sees. With this, she leaves the stage.

It is a blistering way even for Euripides to begin a play. What are we – as a modern audience – to make of this petulant, petty goddess? And what would an Athenian audience in 428 BCE have made of her? A puny mortal doesn't want to get married, or have sex, and this is the mighty goddess' response: total destruction. And destruction at the hands of his own father. And what of the claim that she made at the very start, that she favours those who honour her and punishes those who don't? A few dozen lines later, she is cheerily explaining that Phaedra – who has honoured Aphrodite by building a temple to her – will die as a consequence of the goddess' revenge on Hippolytus. In fact, Phaedra has already been punished with two years – years – of agonizing love. Perhaps this seems like a trivial complaint, but only if we have forgotten the soul-sucking agony of wanting someone we cannot have.

And all of this suffering has been imposed on Phaedra from outside, by Aphrodite. The gods play multiple, layered roles in Greek tragedy, and one of those roles is essentially psychological. While we might say that we have fallen in love or developed a crush on someone unsuitable, the Greeks tended to externalize the causes of such experiences. We fall in love, they were struck by an arrow shot by the god Eros, for example. A sophisticated language of psychology simply didn't exist at the time that Euripides was writing, so things which are internalized for us were often launched upon a Greek from without.

We learn from this opening speech that Aphrodite is absolutely vicious and highly organized in her plans for revenge. She has spent two years preparing to destroy Hippolytus, with no concerns for the secondary victims of her revenge: Phaedra and Theseus. They are simply collateral damage that cannot be avoided. We also learn, much as it may pain those who want to decry Phaedra as a villain, that she is a victim in this plot, just as Hippolytus is. In the whole heartless monologue, there is no more agonizing word than *sigē* – 'she keeps silent'. Could Phaedra not have told her slave-women or a friend (not her sister, obviously, who is one of her husband's exes, if she's still alive) what she was going through? She has not done so, but has suffered in silence, alone. We can surely conclude that Phaedra is profoundly ashamed of her unwanted emotions: this is not the behaviour of a seductress, a scarlet woman. She is not enjoying her infatuation, she is in physical pain. Pain which is killing her.

Hippolytus comes onstage, full of praise for Artemis. One of his attendants makes the suggestion that he should be careful not to slight Aphrodite. But Hippolytus is having none of it. Enjoy your goddess, he says, dismissively.[23] We had no hint that Aphrodite might be willing to change her murderous plot, but certainly Hippolytus seems to be going out of his way to offend her.

Then the female chorus give us some more detail about Phaedra's condition. She has to stay indoors, she hasn't eaten for three days,[24] she won't say what grieves her, but she wants to die. They try to guess what the reason might be: has she offended a god, is she being punished? They don't guess Aphrodite is the cause. Then they wonder if Theseus might have been sleeping in another bed, or perhaps Phaedra might have received bad news from Crete. They are obviously perplexed by Phaedra's sickness, but they seem to be fond of her, and want to be able to help.

Phaedra and her nurse now come onstage. Slaves have to carry Phaedra: she cannot walk. She is feverish, desperate to be outdoors in the forests, hunting deer. Is she remembering her own childhood, on Crete? She wasn't always the wife of an Athenian king. Or is she simply imagining herself alongside Hippolytus, who we know is a keen hunter: he spends his days in the company of Artemis, after all, and she is the goddess of hunting. Or is she going a step further, and imagining herself as Hippolytus? How much of her desire is for him and how much is it to be him? The fantasy comes to an end and she begs the gods to have mercy on her, and let her die. As we already know from Aphrodite, the gods have no mercy, certainly not for Phaedra.

The chorus ask the nurse what is wrong with Phaedra – has she not managed to find out? The nurse says she has tried and failed. But then she makes one last attempt to dig out the truth. She turns to Phaedra with a brutal statement: if you die, you will be betraying your children.[25] They won't inherit their father's property, he will: that bastard son of the Amazon queen, Hippolytus. He'll lord it over your children. Phaedra cries out in sorrow. Does this touch you? asks the nurse. You destroy me, Phaedra replies. I beg you by the gods to be silent about this man. The nurse is triumphant at having brought Phaedra back to herself. Then you don't want to save your children, she asks, and your own life? This cruel onslaught forces Phaedra to admit what is causing her grave illness. We already know from Aphrodite's monologue, of course, that it is a sickness of the heart. Phaedra uses the word 'miasma':[26] both a sickness and a defilement. The nurse presses her further and she finally concedes that it is Hippolytus she loves.

This first quarter of the play is a masterclass in character, even by Euripides' dizzyingly high standards. Phaedra is not – as we might expect her to be from so many later plays and operas – a seductress. She is a reserved, private woman who has spent two years concealing a guilty secret, even from those closest to her (although that is not the same as those she can trust, as the events of this play will make clear). Aphrodite's casual dismissal of Phaedra – her pain and her imminent death – seem all the more heartless once we meet her. We can see from the depictions of both Aphrodite and, later, Artemis in this play that Euripides is a critical thinker on matters divine. He doesn't question the existence of the gods, but he certainly questions their nature. These goddesses are entirely amoral: what they want is the same – as far as they are concerned – as what is right. And anyone who gets in their way will be destroyed.

We are left in no doubt that Phaedra would have gone to her grave without ever speaking to or about Hippolytus and her feelings for him. She does not wish to act on her desire, she simply wishes to die so her suffering can be over. The nurse exploits her weakness, which is her anxiety for the life her children will have after she is gone. Just as Alcestis worried that Admetus might prefer a new wife who would treat her children harshly, here we see Euripides drama-tize the opposite side of the same coin: a stepmother provoked to terrible anxiety that her children will be passed over in favour of her husband's older son (whom the nurse, incidentally, calls *nothon* – 'a bastard')[27] after her death. And this is a real, plausible fear: Hippolytus is older than her children, he might well inherit Theseus' property if Phaedra isn't around to advance her own offspring's cause. We have already seen that Hippolytus is immune to the suggestion that he might prefer not to insult a powerful goddess. If he is impervious to social mores, Phaedra might well be afraid that he would disinherit her children.

Phaedra now delivers her big monologue, telling the chorus and the nurse how she has tried to keep silent, to quash her desire, to wish for death. She wants to shame neither her husband nor her children.[28] If Euripides had written Phaedra as a shameless hussy in his first attempt to tell this story, he has completely changed her in this second version. Shame is an overwhelming prospect for her; she will die rather than incur it. So what goes wrong?

The nurse now offers the kind of tricksy, immoral argument that the comic playwright Aristophanes would have so much fun suggesting Euripides himself believed. How can you, she asks, a mortal woman, resist the power of the goddess of love? When even Zeus is overwhelmed by her? Aphrodite can bend the king of the gods to her will and you try to resist her? Isn't it hubris, to wish yourself stronger than a god?[29] Anyway, men don't solve problems, women have to find the answers. We might think the nurse is as immoral as her argument implies, and perhaps she is. Certainly she is Aphrodite's unwitting servant, the catalyst of all the carnage which is about to unfold. Tempting as it is to condemn her outright, we must remember that she is genuinely fearful that her mistress will die. She makes things infinitely worse – for Phaedra and Hippolytus and Theseus – but she does seem to act with the best intentions.

Phaedra resists her argument, however, and tells her never to speak this way again. You speak convincingly but shamefully, she says.[30] The nurse says she will go and find a treatment for Phaedra's condition. Please don't say anything to Hippolytus, Phaedra begs. Leave it to me, replies the nurse. I'll sort things out.[31] And, of course, she does exactly what Phaedra fears: goes straight to Hippolytus – whom she and we know despises the idea of sex with anyone, let alone his stepmother – and tells him of Phaedra's love for him. As anyone but the nurse could have foreseen, he responds with fury, which Phaedra can hear from the stage. She has destroyed me,[32] Phaedra tells the chorus.

Hippolytus now comes onstage, although he doesn't notice or speak to Phaedra. She can still hear him, however. Before revealing

Phaedra's secret, the nurse had managed to persuade Hippolytus that he must swear to keep silent about it. He willingly made this pledge, but now regrets it and plans to disregard it: my tongue swore, he says, my mind is unsworn.[33]

This line would be quoted by Aristophanes as archetypally Euripidean: what a terrible influence the playwright must have been on the ordinary men of Athens. All able to break their word, because Hippolytus didn't think a pledge meant anything. Except, of course, that audiences are not generally that gullible. And besides, in spite of what he says in this moment of anger, Hippolytus does keep his word. The problem is that Phaedra believes him when he says he will not.

Hippolytus then delivers a long, misogynistic screed: not only is his stepmother evil, but so are all women. They're all sluts and the only reason he is keeping his word to the nurse is because he fears that the gods punish perjurers. He will leave the house until Theseus returns. And he does.

It's a wretched fate to be a woman,[34] Phaedra says, after Hippolytus has gone. Now what? She dismisses the nurse, swears the chorus to secrecy and tells them that she has thought of a way to save her children's reputation.[35] She will take her own life, destroyed by Aphrodite. We are halfway through the play and everything is going according to the goddess' plan. Phaedra leaves the stage, the chorus sing and, as they finish, we hear a slave crying out from the palace that the queen is dead. Phaedra has hanged herself.

At this point, Theseus appears, asking if anyone can tell him what's going on. He rushes to Phaedra's body and finds a note in her hand addressed to him. In this, we discover, she has denounced Hippolytus as a rapist, claiming his attack has prompted her to die by her own hand. Theseus curses his son, testing the apparent gift he has been given by Poseidon (he seems uncertain whether or not Poseidon's curses will work, but we know from Aphrodite's opening monologue that they are part of her plan). Hippolytus now also arrives on stage and finds that Phaedra has lied about him. Theseus is convinced of his guilt and condemns him to exile. Hippolytus – interestingly – doesn't break his oath, in spite of his earlier threat to do so. He maintains his silence about Phaedra's passion for him, as he had sworn he would. He does defend himself, by saying that he despises the idea of love and that, anyway, Phaedra was hardly the most beautiful woman in the world.[36] He swears one last time that he did not lay hands on Phaedra, that he doesn't know what made her take her own life.

This monologue is a really extraordinary piece of writing. We know that Hippolytus is wrongly accused, we know that everything which is happening to him is the product of a spiteful deity who has taken umbrage at his lack of worship. And yet, he is so relentlessly unpleasant that it is genuinely hard to sympathize with him, even as we know he is being wronged. The horrible rant he delivered after the nurse had told him about Phaedra's love for him still hangs over us: he is not just uninterested in sex, he's disgusted by it, disgusted by women wanting it. Of course, it's very much up to a director to decide how that monologue should work: if Phaedra is played by an older woman, it becomes a story of that taboo as well as the fact that they are related by marriage. But not by blood: there would be nothing stopping Phaedra and Hippolytus getting married if Theseus were to die. For an ancient audience her crime is adulterous desire, more than an incestuous lust for a younger man. It is perfectly possible that the two could be virtually the same age. Phaedra is Ariadne's younger sister and her children are still young. And in some later versions of the play, Theseus has been absent for so long that the characters believe him to be dead, which also removes the adultery issue (for an ancient audience – we might still find it troubling) until he reappears, alive after all.

Our distaste for Hippolytus has already been formed in the first half of the play: he is obnoxious when one of his attendants suggests that he owes some respect to Aphrodite, he is hateful when the nurse reveals Phaedra's secret. It is not just Phaedra he despises, but all women, as he explains at length. He threatens to break his vow, which will destroy Phaedra and – she believes – her children's future. And now, Euripides creates this second remarkable monologue, where Hippolytus only speaks the truth: he has been wrongfully accused, he is virginal, and we know he cannot speak further without perjuring himself. He is a little disingenuous once or twice, praising himself for revering the gods[37] when we know that his reverence does not extend to Aphrodite, and swearing he has no idea why Phaedra might have killed herself (although his oath prevents him from saying more).

Yet still – thanks to Euripides' skill and control – Hippolytus has already been so unlikeable that we struggle to care as much as we might at the terrible injustice he experiences. This is true for the characters onstage too: Theseus is unwavering in his belief that his son is a monster. We might think that this is simply indicative of Theseus being a good husband and believing his wife. But he doesn't even consider, for example, that Phaedra's letter might have been written by someone else. Letters are intrinsically untrustworthy in Greek myth, incidentally. Writing in general is treated with great scepticism. The chorus aren't especially helpful either: they think Hippolytus will be believed by his father, but they don't rush in to sympathize with him, even as Theseus and his son argue further. Theseus banishes Hippolytus on the spot, and demands that his men drag the young man away. Then a few moments later, a messenger arrives to tell Theseus that his son is dying, crushed against the rocks when his horses fled in terror from a giant bull that rose from the sea. Poseidon's curse was real, and deadly.

Theseus has no regrets, but concedes that the men may carry his son back to the palace to see him before he dies. Finally, Artemis appears. She tells Theseus that Phaedra had lied, that Hippolytus was innocent. Tells him that his curse was the cause of Hippolytus' death.

Tells him that Aphrodite was the cause, and that she – Artemis – had to allow it to happen, even though Hippolytus was her favourite. She adds that Theseus is not fully to blame, because he acted in anger before he knew the facts. Hippolytus, dying, is carried onstage, and he forgives Theseus. When Artemis explains that the whole awful day has been plotted by Aphrodite, Hippolytus replies: she has destroyed the three of us.[38] Artemis leaves the stage explaining that, just as Aphrodite has killed her beloved favourite, now she will do the same thing in revenge. Hippolytus dies.

There is a melancholy symmetry to this play: the first half ends with Phaedra's death, the second with Hippolytus dying. All parties blame Aphrodite: Phaedra, Hippolytus, Theseus (his final words in the play are a rebuke to the goddess) and Artemis. There is no doubt in any of their minds that she has been responsible for everything that happened. Phaedra is one human agent of destruction: she kills herself and makes her deadly false accusation. But the nurse also takes some responsibility: however well-meaning, her blabbing to Hippolytus is what exacerbates the crisis.

One uncomfortable question is whether Phaedra intends Hippolytus to die. She makes the accusation before taking her own life, which means she can never be interrogated. But although she presumably knows Theseus has a short temper (they are currently living in exile because he had killed a large group of young men, which Aphrodite told us at the beginning of the play), can she know that he will respond as violently as he does? Theseus himself is unsure whether the curses from Poseidon are real or not. He banishes his son, which implies he is doubtful about them: why bother banishing someone if you think they'll be dead from divine wrath in a few minutes? So perhaps – to give Phaedra some benefit of the doubt – she believes Hippolytus will be exiled rather than murdered.

But it is difficult to defend her in the light of what actually happens: Hippolytus does die in a horrific chariot crash. And he is kinder, softer in his dying moments than at any point in the play: he doesn't blame Theseus for cursing him so cruelly, and nor does he blame Phaedra for her lie. He blames Aphrodite, and perhaps (to a much lesser extent) Poseidon – Poseidon's gifts have been bitter to you, his son,[39] he tells his father. So while none of the characters seeks to defend Phaedra's lie, they do not hold her responsible: everyone in the play accepts that Aphrodite has wrought this destruction. In the last moments, Artemis even binds Phaedra's name to Hippolytus': you will be remembered in song, she promises him, and Phaedra's love for you will not be kept silent either.[40] In the Greek, the words 'Phaedra' and 'you' are separated only by the word 'for'. In their deaths, Phaedra finally has the closeness that Aphrodite had made her desire during their lives.

For Euripides, the story of Phaedra and Hippolytus is an object lesson in divine malevolence. The play was awarded first prize by the judges at the Dionysia in 428 BCE, so they were obviously less shocked by this second draft than they were by the ill-received first one. And yet, it was not universally popular. As mentioned above, Aristophanes parodied it several times, specifically that line Hippolytus says to the nurse: My tongue swore, my mind was unsworn. It is a salutary lesson in the way values change through time: what do we care if Hippolytus means what he says? We live in a bureaucratic society where we have paperwork to fall back on if people renege on their promises. But for a fifth-century BCE Athenian audience with limited literate resources (for the most part), the power of oaths and pledges was immense. Zeus himself punished perjurers. If people went around swearing an oath and then refusing to keep it, the whole value system on which their society functioned was in jeopardy. Aristotle even tells us[41] that Euripides was prosecuted for *asebeia* – 'impiety' – over this particular line in the play.

So what happens if the gods are removed from the story? That is a question answered by Racine, whose 1677 play *Phèdre* is probably better known to modern audiences than Euripides' *Hippolytus*. Not least, in the UK, because the title role has been played by both Diana Rigg and Helen Mirren in productions of an adaptation by Ted Hughes. For Racine, the gods are scarcely in the picture at all; they are not characters in the play. And although much of the story remains the same, the shift in emphasis – and the consequences for how the characters experience blame and guilt, in particular – is remarkable.

In this version, Theseus is missing, presumed dead. Hippolytus has a (so far) unexpressed love for a young woman named Aricia, whose family are sworn enemies of Theseus. Hippolytus too is changed: his devotion to chastity is not because he despises all women and sex, but because he only desires one, whom he believes he cannot have. His friend Théraméne teases him for having scorned Venus too often in the past: now he is her sacrificial victim after all. Hippolytus is no slave to Aphrodite / Venus though: he wishes he could erase his father's sexual conquests from memory (Plutarch might have been relieved to see mention of Periboea, Helen and Ariadne here, though Helen's extreme youth when 'stolen out of her bed in Sparta' is glossed over once again).

If Hippolytus is less chaste than he is in Euripides' play, so is Phaedra. She doesn't just build a temple to Venus, but she 'spent half my wealth to decorate it. From dawn to dusk I sacrificed beasts, / Searching their bodies for my sanity.' Here, Hughes is surely referencing the behaviour of another tragic, lovelorn queen: Dido, in Book Four of Virgil's *Aeneid*, who peers into the entrails of sacrificial victims as though she is herself the haruspex, charged with reading entrails and interpreting the future. Phaedra has 'pretended to hate him as my stepson'. In order to disguise her feelings, she really has played the role of the wicked stepmother. A servant named Panope ('all-seeing') now appears to tell Phaedra that Theseus is dead. The nurse (here named Oenone, but we'll keep calling her the nurse to save confusion) is delighted: Phaedra can now declare her love to Hippolytus and marry him. She is free.

Hippolytus has also heard the news about Theseus and for him, too, it means freedom. He goes to release Aricia, who has been held prisoner under his father's orders. The politics of who will succeed Theseus as king of Athens – the consequences for Hippolytus as both potential ruler and potential lover – expand to fill the space left by the absence of those Euripidean goddesses. Hippolytus declares his love to Aricia. But then Phaedra arrives and tells him – in a rather roundabout way – that she loves him. Specifically, she loves how much like a younger Theseus he is. Hippolytus is shocked by her declarations of passion and Phaedra tells him she detests herself 'more than you can ever detest me'. Hippolytus has his sword in hand and she begs him to stab her: 'This heart is utterly corrupt.' The nurse breaks up this painfully awkward scene and Hippolytus tells Théramène they must leave. Théramène explains that Athens has chosen Phaedra's son as their new king: in politics at least, Hippolytus has been outplayed.

Act Three begins with Phaedra writhing in mortification at the disgust Hippolytus clearly felt for her. The nurse consoles her: he hates all women, so at least you don't have a rival. But then news comes that Theseus is alive after all, and will arrive at any moment (as with Greek plays, setting the action in one day does occasionally make for a dizzying pace). Phaedra is devastated: having revealed her love to Hippolytus when she thought she was a widow, she will now stand accused of infidelity. She is especially troubled by the damage this will wreak on her children's reputation. The nurse, however, has a plan.

Theseus arrives with Hippolytus, but Phaedra refuses to speak to him and walks offstage. Hippolytus won't explain, so Theseus goes after his wife to find out what is going on. But at the start of Act

Four, we discover that Theseus believes his wife has been raped by his son: the nurse has already enacted her plan. Theseus criticizes his wife to the nurse only for having tried to spare Hippolytus, having 'deferred his exposure for too long'. It is a huge change in the story: the nurse makes the false allegation, not Phaedra.

Theseus and Hippolytus argue, and Theseus curses his son, just as in Euripides' version. But, here, Phaedra is still alive. Hippolytus storms off, and she comes onstage to admit the nurse's deceit and defend her stepson's reputation. But when Theseus tells her that Hippolytus loves Aricia, jealousy overwhelms her. This man who had been so repulsed by her does have feelings for a woman; she has a rival after all. Having been on the verge of destroying her reputation to protect the innocent young man she loves, she changes her mind. 'I am the only one he cannot stand! And I came rushing here to defend him!'

While we might – again – sympathize with Phaedra's battered emotions, there is no excusing what she does next. She does not tell Theseus of his mistake and instead rages at the nurse: her jealousy means she also wants Theseus to kill Aricia. Ted Hughes gives this monologue absolutely everything: 'My own hands are twitching/ To squeeze the life out of that woman,/ To empty that innocent blood out of her carcase/ And smash her to nothing.'

In Act Five, we find Hippolytus and Aricia trying to work out what they should do, given that Hippolytus is cursed and his reputation is ruined. Hippolytus leaves and Theseus arrives, whereupon Aricia attempts the role that Artemis played in the Euripides version. She tells Theseus that Hippolytus is the victim of slander, but Theseus despises her family and, anyway, she does not have the authority of a goddess so he doesn't believe her. Panope – the all-seeing servant – appears on stage to say that the nurse has thrown herself into the sea and that Phaedra wishes to die. Theseus realizes that his son may be innocent after all, and calls for him to be brought back. But

Théramène appears alone because – as in Euripides – a bull has risen from the sea and wiped out Hippolytus. The king's son is dead. His last words were much as in Euripides: '"The gods have taken my life," he whispered.'

But Théramène and Theseus are much less forgiving: both blame Phaedra for the death of Hippolytus. 'He is your victim,' Theseus tells her. She confesses the lie and calls herself a monster, 'insane with an incestuous passion'. And with her confession, she dies. Theseus wishes that the results of her evil could die with her. But the play ends with him adopting the previously despised Aricia as his daughter.

The central conflict of Euripides' play is essentially linear: where on the line drawn between chastity, personified by Artemis, and overwhelming, indiscriminate sexual passion, personified by Aphrodite, do we place ourselves? For Hippolytus, it's right at one end: total chastity. For the other characters in the play, things are more nuanced. But in Racine's play, the structure has multiple dimensions: Phaedra loves Hippolytus, so pretends to hate him; Hippolytus loves Aricia, so pretends to ignore her; Aricia loves Hippolytus, but is hated by his father, Theseus, who loves Phaedra and doesn't trust Hippolytus. And then there is the nurse, who loves Phaedra but who cannot save herself or her mistress from disaster. The politics of who rules when a king dies, and who is caught out if he then returns alive – this is a major change from the absolutes we find in Euripides. His Phaedra is motivated to make her false allegation by the belief that her children will be ruined if she does not. Racine's Phaedra certainly cares about her children, but she is motivated to let the false allegation stand because of the sexual jealousy she feels for Aricia.

It's interesting that we may find ourselves sympathizing with Euripides' Phaedra more than Racine's. The former creates the slander that kills an innocent young man. But her absolute powerlessness in the face of a divine plot she cannot control or even influence makes her more pitiable than villainous. Whereas Racine's Phaedra is operating on a far more human scale of lust and jealousy, and even though she does not create the falsehood which kills Hippolytus, she stands by it from wholly base motives.

But what if we read Euripides' play in the light of all we know about Ariadne, and Theseus' extensive, destructive sexual adventures? Would it change the way we view his wretched Phaedra? The nurse finally persuades the queen to confess that it is love, specifically love for Hippolytus, which is causing her to sicken almost to death. And she does this by reminding Phaedra that her children will be shunted into obscurity by Hippolytus if she dies while they are still young. By the end of the play, Phaedra is dead, Hippolytus is dead, and her children are Theseus' only heirs. She has – perhaps – achieved her ambition without ever crystallizing it in her thoughts. Theseus' line from his previous wife, or sexual partner, or rape victim (we cannot forget that Antiope/Hippolyta, the Amazon mother of Hippolytus, has a shifting status in Theseus' life, depending on who is telling the myth) has been obliterated. A healthy older son has been removed from the equation so Phaedra's sons can inherit their father's property and titles. Could we read this play as a horrifying revenge on Theseus, for the damage he did to Phaedra's family: killing her brother Asterion (the Minotaur), and abandoning her sister alone on the shores of Naxos? We certainly could. Read this way, Phaedra may still be Aphrodite's pawn (as are all the characters in Euripides' play, except Artemis), but she is also engaged in retributive justice. The play is no less troubling on this reading, but perhaps it acquires an extra dimension. And so does Phaedra, the wicked stepmother who defends her young and destroys all threats to their future, even at the cost of her own life.

MEDEA

THE VIDEO OF 'HOLD UP' BEGINS WITH BEYONCÉ SWIMMING through the rooms of a house filled with water. 'I tried to change,' she says in voiceover. 'Closed my mouth more, tried to be softer, prettier, less awake.' She seems to speak for all the women who have been told they are somehow too much. The actions she lists become more extreme, more symbolic: fasted for sixty days, wore white, bathed in bleach. She moves through the water like a mermaid. 'But still inside me, coiled deep, was the need to know: are you cheating on me?' And then the camera cuts to a huge pair of doors, flanked by four vast Ionic columns: this house or palace is Neoclassical in style. Beyoncé flings open the doors and water floods out around her, flows down a stone staircase. She walks down the stairs in a saffron gown (a colour often worn by young women in Greek myth: Iphigenia was described as wearing one in Aeschylus' *Agamemnon*.[1] There is even a word in Greek – *krokotophoreo* – which means 'to wear a yellow dress'). As she strides through the streets, she acquires a pair of mighty heels and a baseball bat, with which she smashes fire hydrants, CCTV cameras and the windows of assorted cars. 'What's worse, looking jealous or crazy?' she sings. Eventually, she smashes the camera filming her, and drops the bat on the ground. Jealous or crazy? Perhaps she is both. The message is clear: cheat on her at your peril. Her revenge will be public and spectacular. As William Congreve put it, 'Heaven has no rage like love to hatred turn'd, nor hell a fury like a woman scorn'd.'[2]

In 431 BCE, Euripides' *Medea* was performed for the first time at the Dionysia festival in Athens. The story of a woman who asks herself the same question – jealous or crazy – and comes up with a horrifying answer must have sent shockwaves through the city. The set of tragedies to which it belonged came third in competition, out of three. Were the audience shocked by the story of a woman who committed the iciest revenge on her cheating husband? We tend to think that tragedy audiences knew roughly what they were getting when one of the big playwrights tackled a story everyone already knew. But – as we have already seen many times in this book – myths change, and it is rarely possible to say that one story is definitively original and all other versions deviate from that. There is every chance that Euripides made a crucial change to the plot of Medea's story and that is what caused such consternation among its earliest audience. We'll come back to this shortly.

As we saw with Clytemnestra, there were few things more alarming to ancient Greek men than the machinations of a clever woman, and Medea is the cleverest of them all. If Clytemnestra is the worst wife in Greek myth, Medea can lay a strong claim to being its worst mother. But before she becomes that (in the second half of the fifth century BCE), she is already a dangerous figure: clever, female, foreign and magical.

Medea is a barbarian woman, as the Greeks considered her: barbarian meant anyone not Greek. She grows up in Colchis, on the Black Sea (in modern-day Georgia). She is the daughter of Idyia (a daughter of Ocean) and Aeëtes, who is a son of Helios and brother to Circe, the goddess who turns Odysseus' men into temporary pigs. So Medea is, at the very least, a powerful witch, capable of working dark magic for her friends and against her enemies. But Hesiod includes her in his *Theogony*[3] – his account of how the gods were born and the world began – which suggests that he sees her as more divine than mortal. Medea occupies a liminal state between goddess and woman, depending on who tells the story.

Medea

Like Ariadne, Medea is a valuable ally for a man on a mission. In this case, it is Jason whom she assists on his quest to win (or steal) the golden fleece from her father. Jason's story is a classic adventure yarn, told by everyone from Homer (in Book Twelve of the *Odyssey*, Circe recommends a sailing route to Odysseus that avoids the Wandering Rocks, because only Jason had ever made it through them safely) to the 1963 Ray Harryhausen movie, *Jason and the Argonauts*. As is so often the case with these stories, the relatively recent versions often diminish the role played by female characters more than their ancient counterparts. That is certainly true for Medea in the Harryhausen film, which – like everyone of my generation, I suspect – I have probably seen a hundred times.

The goddess Hera (Honor Blackman, proving that even when she was playing someone made of actual wood – Hera is the figurehead on the *Argo* – she could make them sexy) has an interventionist role in this version of Jason's adventures, as she does in Homer.[4] Unfortunately, the film follows the unspoken rule of so many Hollywood movies, and can only expand its focus to include one woman at any given time. Multiple Argonauts can be on-screen at once, and multiple skeleton warriors. But Medea takes a back seat among these Argonauts, because Hera is their protector and aide.

This is a pity, because it means the version of the story that so many of us grew up with marginalizes its most interesting character. It also allows us to believe that men on quests do everything for themselves, when that's rarely the way the story was once told. Every telling of a myth is as valid as any other, of course, but women are lifted out of the equation with a monotonous frequency. And this provides ammunition for those who choose to believe that that's how stories always were and are.

We might remember one of the stand-out moments in the film comes when the Argonauts encounter the bronze giant, Talos. The automaton is roused when Hercules pilfers a brooch pin the size of a javelin from a stash of treasure on the Isle of Bronze (this is Crete, according to Apollonius of Rhodes).[5] Talos attacks the Argonauts and they are helpless to defend themselves against a bronze man with no weak spot. Jason consults his trusty helper goddess, Hera, and she tells him to aim for a plug on the giant's foot. Talos has, it seems, an Achilles heel. Jason does as she says, works open the plug, and lives to fight another day when the giant crashes to the ground, defeated. This puts him way ahead of Hercules' friend Hylas, who is squashed beneath Talos when he falls.

Read the same part of the Argonauts' quest in the *Argonautica*, an epic poem written in the third century BCE by Apollonius, and we see that this Talos is defeated by someone else: Medea. For Apollonius, the bronze man circles the island three times a day.[6] Talos is invulnerable, except for a vein at his ankle. He lobs rocks at the Argonauts, and they are terrified of him. But Medea is not. Listen to me, she says. Only I can overpower this man, whoever he is . . . Keep the ship out of range of his rocks until I have beaten him. Medea is calm when the Argonauts are panicking, she is brave when they are fearful, and most of all, she is powerful. She uses her magic to put the whammy on Talos (I paraphrase Apollonius very slightly – he says 'by the force of her knowledge of potions')[7] and the bronze man grazes his ankle with a sharp rock he is holding. The ichor – which gods have instead of blood – runs out of him like molten lead and he crashes to the ground. This is Medea at her most impressive: using magic to forge a connection to Hades and cause the downfall of this bronze figure that has terrorized a shipful of male heroes. There is something extra-sinister about the way she does it, too. Had she used wit or guile to overthrow their enemy, she would still be impressive. But to make him destroy himself, to have him home in on his only weak point? This is a woman to be reckoned with.

Of course, Medea cannot perform this role in the Harryhausen movie because the plot has been reordered. For Apollonius, the encounter with Talos happens on the way home from collecting the golden fleece. In the film, it is one of the obstacles they face on the way there. But the erasure of Medea's heroic deeds happens several times, irrespective of the order. The film is named for Jason, and we're left in no doubt that he must carry out all the heroic deeds himself, even if a goddess has to intervene and tell him what to do. In order to claim the fleece, Jason fights a Hydra which guards the precious object from marauding adventurers. What kind of hero would Jason be if he couldn't even kill a giant multi-headed snake? Pindar, in his fourth Pythian Ode, has Jason killing a multi-coloured, grey-eyed snake[8] before going on to steal Medea away with him. But for Euripides, Jason doesn't kill a snake of any shade, with one or many heads. You guessed it: Medea does that too.[9] She and Jason are having an almighty row at this point in the play, and even then he doesn't question her assertion that she killed the snake, which she describes as *aupnos* – 'unsleeping'. So it's not like she simply crept up on this mighty reptile while it snoozed. In the film, Medea dies from an arrow wound during Jason's altercation with the Hydra, and has to be revived with the healing powers of the fleece, which shimmers gold as she is brought back to life. This is a much less impressive Medea than that of our ancient sources, who would certainly not let anything as trivial as an arrow stop her.

Perhaps the most terrifying moment for us as children watching this film was when Medea's father Aeëtes sows the Hydra's teeth into the ground, and skeleton warriors rise up to fight Jason. The special effects may look a little shaky now, but I promise that in the nineteen-eighties they were genuinely scary. Again, this moment is in Apollonius, although his chthonic warriors are giants and spring from the teeth of an Aonian serpent, slain long ago by Cadmus, the legendary founder of Thebes. As so often in Apollonius, Medea is the reason that Jason survives his encounter. Before the giants rise out of the earth (they are not skeletal in the *Argonautica*),[10] she tells him that he can use a trick to defeat them: throw a large boulder among them and they will seize on it like wild dogs and destroy each other. In the *Argonautica*, this happens directly after Jason has survived another test set for him by Aeëtes, who orders the young hero to yoke a pair of fire-breathing bulls and plough a field. I'm sure you have already guessed who helps Jason with this impossible task. Medea provides him with a protective salve to rub over his skin, which makes him invulnerable for a day. She digs it out of a box which contains many drugs or potions.[11] The same story appears in Pindar's fourth Pythian Ode,[12] where Medea again provides a potion to make Jason impervious to fire. For Pindar, Medea is a romantic heroine, forced into this by Aphrodite who is helping Jason on his quest and who makes Medea fall in love with him. And for Apollonius too, in the third book of the *Argonautica*, Medea is a love-struck girl. She is persuaded by her sister Chalciope to help this handsome stranger, and much of this book centres on the tension building as we follow Medea's decision to betray her father because she has fallen in love with Jason.

The parallels with Ariadne and Theseus – a daughter who decides to assist a visiting adventurer with the lethal tasks her father has set – are explicitly drawn by Jason,[13] when he asks Medea to bear Ariadne's choice in mind as she ponders whether to help him or obey her father. Medea asks to hear more about Ariadne (who is her cousin – Pasiphaë and Aeëtes are sister and brother), but Jason sensibly changes the subject before Medea finds out what happened to Ariadne after she had chosen to abandon her family and elope with Theseus.

So Medea – even as a young woman – is an interesting double-figure. She is both an innocent, like Ariadne before her, falling for a hero and helping him on his quest, which involves seemingly impossible tasks imposed by her father. She is persuaded by Aphrodite or her sister to help Jason. But in the *Argonautica*, a four-book epic, we have time to see her character develop, and we realize she is no ordinary princess. Ariadne simply needs to betray her family and offer Theseus a spool of thread, but Medea has a whole box full of potions and powers. She is not just an innocent, but also a formidable witch, as the Argonauts discuss before Jason goes to meet her and plead with her for help. Argus tells Jason he has heard from his mother that a girl in the palace (Medea) is highly skilled and has been taught by the goddess of witchcraft herself, Hecate.[14] She can stop full-flowing rivers, or a star in its course, or even the moon. Medea is thus presented as this dual character: young and naive, but simultaneously powerful and strong. And, as we see when the Argonauts meet Talos, she can do things that no one else can: her knowledge of dark magic and her connections with the goddess Hecate make her the most powerful figure on the *Argo* – a ship filled with heroes. She goes toe-to-toe with Talos (actually, in Greek, it is eyes-to-eyes)[15] and her malevolence beats his.

All those heroes who have embarked on quests to battle or overthrow monsters – Perseus, Theseus, Jason – all of them need assistance in their crucial moments. Medea does not: she has learned her skills from Hecate, can summon up her own power when required. This is somewhat different from having a god swan in and help out with a protective hat or special sword. But still, in matters of love, she is scarcely more than a girl, and doesn't even know – at least, as Apollonius tells it – the salutary lesson from her cousin Ariadne's dalliance with Theseus. We have a strong hint from these descriptions of her magical power that Medea is a very valuable ally and a formidable opponent. You would think the person most aware of that would be Jason.

And yet, he will still betray her. And her revenge for this betrayal is what makes her such a memorable figure in both myth and tragedy. When Euripides takes on Medea's story, he creates one of the most intense and dramatic plays of his – and any – time. The reason *Medea* is still performed so frequently today is because it offers one of the greatest roles for a woman in theatre. No less because, when it was first performed in 431 BCE, the title role (as all female roles in Greek theatre) was played by a man.

The play is set in Corinth, and begins with a monologue from Medea's nurse, wishing the *Argo* had never set sail. She wishes Pelias (Jason's uncle) had never ordered him to fetch the golden fleece. She wishes Medea and Jason had never sailed from Colchis (where Medea grew up and the fleece was held) to Iolcus, where Pelias was king: he had usurped Jason's father. If only, the nurse wishes, this hadn't happened, then Medea wouldn't have made Pelias' daughters kill him.

This is – let's be honest – quite a way to be introduced to a character: I wish my mistress hadn't made those young women kill their father. The murder of Pelias is one that requires no magic from Medea, but rather what we might think of as a magic trick, and it was dramatized in Euripides' lost play from 455 BCE, the *Daughters of Pelias*.[16] Medea persuades the daughters of Pelias that she can rejuvenate an elderly ram by chopping him up and boiling him in a large cauldron. A bright young ram emerges from the pot. Can Medea actually rejuvenate a creature through dismemberment and boiling, or does she just substitute a young ram when the daughters of Pelias are looking elsewhere? Either way, they are persuaded by her demonstration to try the same thing on their aged father. He does not emerge rejuvenated from the process. It's part of Medea's story from some of its earliest tellings: Pindar calls Medea 'the killer of Pelias'.[17] There is also a lovely water jar in the British Museum which depicts this scene.[18] The black-figure vase was made around 500 BCE, when Pindar was a boy. A white-haired old man sits to the left of the scene, holding a stick in his left hand. Medea stands beside her cauldron, her head turned back as though she is talking to Pelias, the old man. The ram is positively springing out of the cauldron; his front hooves and horned head look full of life. On the right-hand side of the cauldron, one of Pelias' daughters is gazing at the ram, apparently thinking that her father's frail condition can only improve if they just chop him up and cook him.

So the first thing we hear about Medea in Euripides' play is that she has successfully persuaded some young women to kill their father: already she seems like someone you would avoid making angry. Because of this crime, Jason and Medea are now in Corinth, living in exile. She's popular with the locals and obedient to her husband. So, apart from the small matter of having orchestrated the killing of Pelias, everything is fine. Right?

In line sixteen, we discover that Medea's world has fallen apart. Jason has betrayed her and their children by starting a new relationship with the daughter of Creon, the king of Corinth (she isn't named here, but is usually called Glauce, so we'll go with that). Medea has found herself in a similar position to her poor cousin Ariadne, in other words. She helped the hero on his quest to acquire the golden fleece and depose Pelias. And now she finds herself thrown over for a new heroic-helper, even though Jason isn't on a quest any more. He is still banished from Iolcus, so an alliance with the Corinthian king would clearly be useful. Medea and Jason's relationship has lasted a lot longer than Theseus and Ariadne's, however, as they have two children to show for it.

But no one is going to put Medea into a dreamy sleep and have her wake up with no memory of her marriage. As the nurse explains: she is dishonoured and she is calling on the gods to witness the vows which Jason has broken. She doesn't eat, she lies on the ground in tears. Her friends have tried to reason with her but she won't move, she is like a rock or an ocean wave. She cries out for her dear father, whom she deceived and abandoned to be with this man who betrays her.

Our sympathy with Medea could not be greater: this is a woman suffering profound trauma. We have been reminded that she is dangerous – to Pelias, to Aeëtes – but Medea is still vulnerable. She is in a foreign country, she has no family support. She abandoned her homeland for a man who has now abandoned her: no wonder she is so devastated. And then the nurse says something that makes us sit up in our seats. She hates her children, derives no pleasure from them. I am afraid she's planning something. She is a terrifying woman and no one who engages in hostilities with her will have an easy victory.[19]

This is the first hint in the play, not even forty lines in, that Medea's children are at risk. The grief that she is experiencing is dangerous, destructive, and not just to her. This woman who lies prone and cannot eat is also a potential danger. We're worlds away – as readers or audience – from the dramatic opening of Euripides' *Hippolytus*, although that was produced only three years later. That play began with a goddess declaring her intention to dictate the entire plot, to bring ruin down onto those who have displeased her. *Medea* begins in such a human way: a woman fearing for her mistress and friend because her life has been uprooted by infidelity. It is still so relatable to us, its modern audience. What a fifth-century BCE, (probably) all-male Athenian audience might have made of Medea's predicament is something we'll come to soon.

The children are now brought onstage by their tutor. This gives us a little more background about Jason and Medea: they have children who are old enough to learn from a teacher. Again, it shows us that this relationship has endured far beyond that of Ariadne and Theseus. Medea has more to lose. The nurse and the tutor discuss Medea and her grief, and the tutor has further bad news for the family: he has heard that Creon means to banish Medea and her sons. Surely Jason will stand up for his children? asks the nurse.[20] Old loves are displaced by new loves, replies the tutor. He's no friend to this house.

This is one of the bleakest exchanges in extant Greek tragedy, and that is saying something. How have these two children ended up in such an awful position? A mother who is dangerous and desperate, and a father who literally doesn't care if they are sent into exile? The nurse and tutor agree that it is best not to mention anything about exile to Medea.

We now hear Medea wailing from inside the house, wishing she could die. The tutor takes the children inside, agreeing again with the nurse that he should keep the boys away from their mother. Medea cries out again: Cursed children of a hated mother, would that you would die and your father too, and the whole house fall to ruin.[21] The nurse is upset by this, as we might be. Mothers don't generally go around wishing their children dead. The nurse tells the chorus that it's better to be an ordinary person rather than rich or powerful. And in Greek tragedy, at least, she is right: disaster rains down upon the high-born. You are much better off being the nurse or the tutor if you're hoping to survive to the end of a play. The chorus of Corinthian women express sympathy for Medea: we can see that the nurse was right when she described her mistress as well-liked here. The chorus ask the nurse to bring Medea outside so they can comfort her and perhaps encourage her to be less angry and upset. They call themselves *philai* – her 'friends'.[22]

And now Medea does come outside. We have heard so much about her intense, physical distress: about her lying prone on the ground, deaf to entreaties to get up, to eat. We have heard her crying out in anger and hurt. But when she appears on the stage, she is calmly articulate. This is another indication that she is frightening. Medea is a woman who feels emotions deeply, and yet she can disguise the extremity of her emotions behind a facade of carefully constructed arguments. Throughout this play we will see Medea assume a different persona with each conversation she has: contrite, angry, amenable, humble, raging. All these women are contained within her. No wonder it is a role that actresses clamour to play. Medea is a performer, right down to her bones. And when the occasion demands it, she will always perform.

The monologue that Medea now delivers is one of the greatest pieces of theatrical writing in any language (as is the second, deliberative monologue she delivers later in the play). She begins by addressing the women of the chorus, explaining that she has come out to speak to them because she doesn't want to be thought of as proud or aloof, just because she is quiet or private. People can be very judgemental, she says, even when you haven't done anything. It's especially important for her – a foreigner – to do what's expected of her.[23] Having reminded the chorus – and us – that she knows her place, she appeals to our sympathy. This deed (Jason's betrayal) was unforeseen, she says, sounding like a lawyer who has just noticed an awkward development in a contract negotiation. And then: it has demolished my *psyche* – 'spirit', 'soul', 'life'. Joy has gone from my life, friends, and I want to die. For my husband was everything to me, and he knows it well, and he has turned out to be the worst of men.

Again, look at the contrast with how Phaedra presents herself when we first meet her in Euripides' *Hippolytus*: unable to walk, feverish, desperate to die. And here is Medea, scorned, wronged and absolutely calm as she describes Jason's destruction of her life. Her self-control is as disconcerting as her extreme emotions. What she goes on to say next is so remarkable that it was being quoted at suffrage meetings more than 2,300 years after it was written. Of all living creatures, she says, we women are the most wretched. Her first complaint is that women have to buy a husband: she means with a dowry. Then he becomes the ruler (the word is *despotēn* – owner or master. Our word 'despot' comes from the same root) of our bodies.[24] This makes a bad thing worse, because women don't know if they'll get a good husband or a bad one, and they aren't able to divorce him or reject him.

It's harder still for her, Medea continues, because she is foreign and you'd need sorcery to understand how to treat a man under new laws and customs. If it all works out, terrific. Otherwise, it's better to die. A man, if he gets bored at home, can go out and make his own fun. We have to stay at home with one man. And sure, men will tell you that they have to fight in wars. Well, I'd rather stand three times in the front line than give birth to a single child.

It's different though, for me and you (she's still addressing the chorus). Because you are in your own city, your father and friends nearby. Me, I have no one. I was homeless before my husband scorned me. I was carried off as booty from my barbarian land. I don't have a mother, a brother, no relative I can turn to. So I ask one thing of you: if I can figure out a way of punishing my husband in retaliation for the wrongs he has done to me, keep quiet. A woman is filled with fear, she is a coward when it comes to war. But mistreat her in the bedroom, and no one is more bloodthirsty.

Let's analyse what Medea has just said. Having got the chorus onside at the beginning with her wish to obey their customs, not to be considered aloof or withdrawn, she now appeals to their collective experience. The dowry, to buy a husband. The uncertainty of what you're getting. The disparity in their options: men can fool around outside the home, but women are stuck there waiting for their husband to come back. And if it doesn't work out, divorce isn't respectable for women (unlike men, who can get divorced without difficulty. Although they would have to return the dowry). Perhaps you're wondering if you missed a version of Medea's story in which she marries Jason, respectably, with a dowry and a ceremony: you have not. Medea is employing all her rhetorical skill to build connections between her situation and that of the Corinthian women she wants to maintain as allies. Medea's dowry was the fleece she and Jason stole from her father, their wedding ceremony was Pelias being cooked in a pot. She is presenting herself as an ordinary wife, but she is far from that. Why would we imagine Medea is going to wait at home for her man to come back? She didn't wait for a marriage proposal, she ran off with an adventurer. She is no one's fool.

The line about preferring to stand in battle three times than give birth to a single child is a masterstroke. What better way to bond with the chorus than remind them of the most intense physical experience they have ever known? And Medea is spot on: giving birth in the ancient world was incredibly dangerous. Maternal and infant mortality were part of why life expectancy was so low on average (perhaps thirty-five years).

And then she comes back to her initial point, about being a foreigner, far from home, to further elicit the sympathy of these women who have always lived among family and friends. It would take magic powers to know what to do, she says, carefully glossing over the fact that she does, in fact, have magic powers. We saw it in Pindar's version of her, we have seen it in vase paintings that pre-date this play: Medea is a witch, or a sorceress. Her aunt is Circe, the most renowned witch in Greek myth, thanks to her starring role in the *Odyssey*. She presents herself as a war bride, kidnapped by Jason. But there is no version of Medea's story where that is the case. She always falls in love with him (even if Aphrodite makes it happen).

And then we come to a truly magnificent moment. It's not so bad for you, with your fathers, your friends, your homes: I don't have a mother, a brother, anyone to turn to. Well, that is assuredly true, as far as it goes. Medea does not have a father she can turn to, because she helped Jason steal the golden fleece from him and then sailed away. She doesn't have a mother because she abandoned her home for the man she had fallen in love with. And she doesn't have a brother, because she killed her little brother, Apsyrtos: dismembered him, and threw his body parts into the sea, in order to delay her father as he pursued them while they were making their escape. So while it is technically the case that Medea is brotherless, she really does only have herself to blame.

The speech works brilliantly on multiple levels: if we take her at her word (as the chorus do), we have a thoughtful, elegiac plea for support from woman to women. It's an interesting moment to remember that all these roles were being played by men in fifth-century BCE Athens. If we are more aware of Medea's backstory, we are watching a masterclass in revisionism and rhetorical sleight of hand. Either way, she concludes with her goal achieved: she has begged the chorus for discretion and they make the promise she wants. Whatever she decides to do to pay Jason back, they will keep silent. There is no one watching this play who doesn't believe Medea will do something catastrophic in her revenge.

And now Creon, the king of Corinth, arrives onstage and delivers the news which the nurse and tutor have kept quiet up to now. Medea is banished. Why? she asks. I'm afraid of you,[25] he replies. You're clever and you've been threatening revenge on Jason and his bride, and that's my daughter. So I want you gone now, before you can do any harm. Otherwise I'll regret it later. Medea now switches persona again. It's effortless. She uses his name repeatedly, like a hostage negotiator trying to build a rapport with a kidnapper. She downplays her cleverness: it's just a reputation. It's dogged me all my life. I bear you and your daughter no grudge. Let me stay.

Creon has the measure of her: you speak gently,[26] but you could be planning something terrible. A quick-tempered woman (and the same goes for a man) is easier to guard against than a quiet, clever one. It is agonizing to watch: Creon is completely right, and yet still he underestimates Medea, fails to realize just what she is capable of doing in her single-minded pursuit of vengeance. She is calm, polite, humble, and she makes him believe that he has the better of her. She could not be playing on the weakness of a less-clever, arrogant man any better. He leaves the stage convinced he has upheld his intentions: Medea is still banished. She has, however, persuaded him to give her one day, just to sort things out before she leaves. His final words are chilling: fine, stay for one more day. It's not like you can do the kind of awful things I fear in that time.[27] Should you be in any doubt: she definitely can.

The moment Creon is out of earshot, Medea drops the humility and the subservience. She spits her contempt for him and his idiocy. Do you think I would ever have fawned over him if it hadn't been to my advantage? she asks. Having won over the chorus earlier, she can now treat them as her co-conspirators. Medea has a plan and it is to use the day's grace she has wheedled out of Creon to cause the death of three of her enemies:[28] the father, the daughter and her husband. Her mind is racing with potential plans: fire, stabbing, poison. She wants to be sure she can carry out her plan before she is caught. Poison is the best bet, she concludes.

There is no ethical concern as she makes this decision, it is all about practicalities. Which way can she most successfully carry out her revenge? The idea that this revenge might not be proportionate to Jason's behaviour is nowhere to be found. Medea has already moved on, anyway: where can she go after she has killed the entire royal family of Corinth? If she can find an exit strategy, she will go ahead with the poisoning. If not, she'll just attack Jason and Glauce with a sword and, if she is killed in the immediate aftermath, well, so be it. And then she swears by Hecate that no one will hurt her and be glad of it.

This is central to Euripides' Medea. No matter how many personae she puts on and takes off as she addresses different characters in this play, it remains intact. If you hurt her, she will make you regret it. Her revenge will exceed your original wrong and no one will ever be able to say of her that she let her enemies get away with something. It is no exaggeration to say that this prospect pains her more than anything else. She reminds herself that she is the daughter of a king, the granddaughter of Helios, the sun god. No one gets away with laughing at her.

The chorus sympathize with her about the dishonesty of men and her isolated status as a foreigner. And then Jason walks on. He is gratifyingly ghastly, all pompous opinions billed as common sense, mixed with a total lack of personal responsibility. You see what happens when you get angry, he says. You could have stayed in Corinth if you'd just kept quiet and not made such a fuss. But you had to sound your mouth off, and now you're banished. Still, I won't renounce my loved ones: you and the children won't leave here poor.

It takes a certain sort of person to say this to the mother of his children, after he has decided to marry someone else. Medea hurls abuse at him – *pankakiste*[29] – 'worst of men!' Euripides writes these *agones* – 'debates' – better than anyone. And this one is particularly good: even as the couple take pot-shots at one another, we can sense the sexual attraction between them. Medea lists everything she has done for Jason: saved your life from the fire-breathing bulls, killed the snake that guarded the golden fleece, deceived my father and left my home, persuaded Pelias' daughters to kill him. And now you're throwing me over for a new wife, even though we have sons. If I was childless, she says, I might understand it: men want heirs. What of the vows you made? The gods know you are guilty of perjury. You say you're still a friend to us, so where do you suggest I go? Back to my father's house? Back to Iolcus and Pelias' daughters? The help I gave you cost me my home.

Jason's reply is smooth, completely unapologetic. You're keen to talk about how you helped me, he says. But that was all Aphrodite's doing. She made you fall in love with me. Besides, you haven't done badly out of it. You left a barbarian land and made your home in Hellas (Greece).[30] You're famous here. So yes, you assisted me, but that's what you got out of it. As for my new marriage, it's not about lust. We came here as exiles from Iolcus. So marrying the king's daughter is a really lucky break. It's not because I was bored of you, or wanted someone new. I didn't want more children. I wanted us not to be poor, I wanted my sons to grow up well, I thought this was a good idea, and I thought you'd agree. If you weren't obsessed with sex, you would agree.

The chorus say he speaks convincingly, but they don't agree with him. Neither does Medea: if any of this was true, she says, you would have told me before you did it. The long speeches shrink to a few lines each, and then single lines each, as Jason and Medea settle into the rhythm of their argument.

I would have told you, but you'd have gone nuts.

Sure, call me names, I'm the one going into exile.

That's your fault, shouting your mouth off.

What did you think I would do?

Fine, well, if you need help, let me know.

I will never need your help.

Jason and Medea are a hero and a semi-divine sorceress from a mythic world of fire-breathing bulls, enchanted fleeces and giant snakes. And yet they sound like every divorcing couple we have ever known. To underline the point, the chorus sing an ode to Aphrodite. Because, truly, which of us isn't thinking of the wonder of love at this precise moment?

Then Aegeus – the king of Athens and father of Theseus – appears. He has been to Delphi to consult the Oracle about his continuing childlessness. Medea tells him of her marital difficulties. Aegeus is appalled by Jason's behaviour, particularly the part where he is allowing his family to be banished from Corinth. And Medea sees her exit strategy. I'll help you to interpret the Oracle and have children, she says, if you swear to give me sanctuary in Athens. Of course, he says, but I don't need to swear an oath: we're old friends. I have enemies, she replies. It'll make us both safer if you swear to it. Your forethought is considerable, he says. He doesn't know the half of it.

Once Aegeus has left, Medea revels in her plan. She will beg Jason to let the boys stay, while she goes into exile alone. But this is not the sacrifice it first appears. She will send the children with gifts for the princess – a dress, a crown – which Medea will have coated in poison. Once those have been delivered, she says, I lament what must be done next. For I will kill my children. No one will take them away from me.[31]

It's hard to overstate how horrifying this moment is in performance. We have heard concerns about the children – from the nurse, the tutor, Medea herself – but the hints have been obscure, half-expressed. We have watched Medea's brilliant mind in action: charming the chorus, disarming Creon, demolishing Jason, bargaining with Aegeus. We like her. And then, here it is, like a punch in the gut. This compelling, clever, angry woman is planning something which far exceeds the revenge she has previously mentioned. Killing Jason, Creon, Glauce: these are terrible crimes, but we – like the chorus – have taken her side. Jason is so oily, Creon so pompous, Glauce is just an idea: we haven't met her. These people have wronged her, why wouldn't she want vengeance? It is Greek tragedy, after all: a high death toll is pretty much guaranteed with your ticket. But children? Her own children? She surely doesn't mean it. The chorus try to reason with her, but she is obdurate. Her enemies must not be allowed to laugh at her. You won't be able to do it, they say. It's the way to hurt my husband the most, she replies. The verb is *daknō* – to bite. Medea sends the nurse to bring Jason to her. The chorus sing of Athens and its beauty.

Jason reappears, as plausible, as reasonable as ever: I know you despise me, but I'm here to listen to what you have to say. And Medea switches persona once again, so we see what is surely an echo of their earlier marital reconciliations. It is impossible to watch this play and not imagine them as a couple who have always had rollercoaster rows. Medea's cleverness is highly responsive: she always knows how to perform for her specific audience. This time, she chooses magnanimous self-recrimination. You know what my temper is like, Jason, and we have loved one another for so long. I'm an idiot, picking fights with Creon, with you. Of course you were trying to help us, by starting a new family, creating royal brothers for our sons. I don't know why I was so angry: I should have helped your new bride get ready for her wedding.

I have probably seen this play thirty times: in English, in Greek, set in the Bronze Age, set now. And it is always at this moment that I think the whole thing must collapse. That even Jason – who isn't stupid, and knows his wife – will surely, surely guess that she is playing him for a fool. In *Agamemnon*, we watch a similar scene where Agamemnon simply doesn't realize that Clytemnestra is plotting his imminent murder. But the difference there is that Agamemnon has been away from his wife for ten years, and we never get the impression that they were a close couple. There is always a sense that she outclasses him in terms of intellect, and that he is just about clever enough to realize this and resent her for it. Watching Clytemnestra toy with Agamemnon is like watching a malevolent cat preparing to launch a full-clawed attack on a bad-tempered, rather stupid dog. But Jason and Medea's relationship is a different beast: we can always feel the attraction between them. Jason isn't stupid at all, he's just not in the same league as Medea. Agamemnon fails to read Clytemnestra's intentions because he isn't interested in her, doesn't think about who she is and what she is likely to do. You could accuse Jason of the same problem, but I think Euripides has done something else here. Jason believes Medea because he wants to. Even as she lays it on so thickly – suggesting she might have stood in attendance on Glauce is clearly overdoing it – he wants her to be telling him the truth. He wants Medea to accept his behaviour in the light he has presented it: as a favour to her and their sons. He doesn't want to be the bad guy in their marriage, even though he was willing to see his wife and sons go into exile. And Medea knows that. The easiest person to fool is the one who wants to be fooled.

She calls their children outside to greet Jason, explains that their parents have stopped fighting now. When she sees them, she starts crying: she knows what she plans to do. As do the chorus, who issue a brief plea that the imminent evil should advance no further. Jason so much enjoys being magnanimous to Medea in her apparent accept-ance of her defeat that it costs me actual physical energy not to reach into the pages or onto the stage and slap him. Of course you're angry that I'm marrying again, he says. But I'm glad you've come to accept that it's a good idea. This is the behaviour of a sensible woman.[32] He looks to his sons and imagines them grown up, strong. Medea cries again and he asks what has upset her. Nothing, she replies. I was just thinking about the children.

And now she has Jason disarmed, protective of their boys and sympathetic to her, she makes her move. Her tears have been real enough, but they don't come at the expense of her ever-plotting brain. Even as she weeps, she is putting the next stage of her plan into action. So she begs Jason to intercede with his wife, and with Creon, to allow their children to stay in Corinth. Medea will go into exile, but the children should remain with their father. Jason agrees in principle, though he isn't sure he'll be able to persuade Creon. It's a nice touch from Euripides, because we have seen how easily Medea managed to get what she wanted from Creon, even when he was so angry and frightened by her. Jason doesn't have her persuasive skills.

Your wife could persuade her father, she says. I'll send the children with wedding presents for her, gifts from my grandfather, the sun god. Don't be silly, Jason says: she has a house full of dresses, you keep them. She'll do it because I ask her to, if she cares about me: not because of trinkets from you.

Is there a slight hint of trouble in paradise here? A sense that Jason doesn't have the same connection with his new bride that he had with Medea? There is a faint whiff of disapproval when he says she has a palace full of dresses and gold. Jason – we might remember – was deprived of his kingship by Pelias. Perhaps he has the self-made man's irritation with the privileged classes. And that 'if' is interesting too: if she cares about me, she'll do it because I ask her. Jason knows – doesn't he – that Medea's gifts will very likely sway Glauce, and he would much prefer it to be his charm that makes her do what he asks. Is he slightly annoyed that she doesn't hang on his every word? That his bright young fiancée loves shiny, pretty things and doesn't treat him as the voice of all reason? It must be especially annoying to meet someone young and pliable after being married to someone as clever and manipulative as Medea, and then find out that your second wife still doesn't treat you as the conquering hero you're sure you are.

But Medea knows better than to press this point and aggravate Jason's ego. Even the gods are persuaded by gifts, she says. And gold beats a thousand arguments among mortals.[33] She gives her gifts to the children to take to Glauce. Make sure she receives them with her own hands,[34] she says. Go quickly.

Jason and the children leave, and the chorus deliver a lament which begins, 'Now I have no more hope that the children will live, no more . . .' They weep for Glauce, for Jason, for Medea. The tutor appears onstage with the children and tells Medea that their banishment has been rescinded. She weeps, knowing what this means. He thinks she must be crying for herself, for her own exile from her children. She allows him to believe this, and holds her children close. Now she delivers the second great monologue of this play, in which the warring halves of her character – her love for her children versus her refusal to allow her enemies to prosper – are given full, extraordinary expression.

You still have a city and a home, she tells her sons, but you will be abandoned and I will be wretched. I'll never see you grow up, never see you marry. So it was all futile for me: raising you, the awful pain of childbirth. I dreamed that one day you would look after me in my old age, ready me for burial when I die. I would have been envied by everyone. But now that sweet thought is dead.[35] I will live a life of grief and pain without you. Your beloved eyes won't look upon your mother any more. You're smiling at me, your final smile.

The double meaning in these opening lines is almost unbearable to witness. Surely she cannot do what she has threatened? This woman loves her children. She can't possibly kill them. Medea turns from the children and speaks again to the chorus: What shall I do? My heart has left me, women, looking at their bright eyes. I can't do it. Farewell to my earlier plans. I'll take my children with me, out of the country. How can I hurt them to make their father grieve when I will suffer twice as much myself?

We feel a brief surge of hope that reason, that love has prevailed. Medea does love her children: it is demonstrably clear she loves them in a way Jason does not. He would cheerfully have seen them go into exile so he could marry well and start a new family. His affection for his sons is conditional: there are limits to the inconvenience he is prepared to tolerate for them. Medea is paralysed with love, and even if she were not, she can do the maths. She loves the children much more than Jason does. If she kills them to injure him, she is injuring herself doubly. A clever woman could not conclude that this is the rational choice.

But just as her maternal affection has surged within her, suddenly the darker side of her nature rises up again. What is wrong with me? Am I willing to have my enemies laugh at me, unpunished? I have to do this. What a coward, to let these soft words into my mind. Go inside, children. If it is not lawful for anyone to be present at my sacrifice, leave now. My hand will not relent.

And then, once more, love prevails: Oh my heart, don't do this.[36] Let them be, you wretched creature, spare your children. Let them live and make you happy.

And then anger: No, by the darkest demons in Hades, I will not allow my sons to be mistreated by my enemies. It's too late now: the bride is dying, crown on her head, wearing her dress. I know this.

She says goodbye to her children, but wavers again: your skin is so soft, your breath is so sweet. Go, go! I can't look at you any more.

I understand the terrible thing I am about to do. But anger, the cause of all evils among mortals, is stronger than my resolution.

The children retreat inside the house, but Medea stays outside while the chorus deliver an ode on the virtues of childlessness. The childless live less troubled lives, they think, without the terrible burden of perpetual fear and anxiety. As they conclude, a messenger arrives from the palace. It turns out Medea has been waiting for him. He tells her to flee Corinth. Why? she asks. Because Creon and his daughter are both dead from your poison, the man replies.[37] He describes the scene in detail: the princess taking the dress and crown from their box and putting them on, before the poison floods through her. The crown seems to spew fire onto her head, the dress corrodes her skin. Glauce almost dissolves in agony and her father rushes to his daughter and tries to comfort her. But the poison afflicts him too: after suffering horrific pain, father and daughter both lie dead.

The speech is long, and incredibly gory, but even when the messenger has finished, the chorus maintain their earlier position. They believe that Jason is suffering *endikōs* – 'justly' – on this day.[38] Medea has not yet lost their sympathy. And she has stopped wavering: I must kill the children as quickly as I can and leave Corinth. Otherwise, someone else, an enemy, will kill them. They will die, so, since they must, let it be by my hand, I who gave birth to them. Arm yourself, my heart. Come, wretched hand, take the sword. Take it. Crawl towards this awful moment in your life. No more cowardice, no more remembering that they are your children, your beloveds. For one brief day, forget your children. And then you can cry. For you love them, even though you kill them.

I am a wretched woman.

And with these words, she disappears into her house. We can only watch in helpless horror. Medea's logic is superficially reasonable, but it has led her to a terrible conclusion. Of course it is all too likely that, having killed the entire royal family of Corinth, Medea's children are at risk of a vengeance killing. She and Jason have already had to flee Iolcus, after instigating the murder of Pelias. There is something in what she says: it would be better for her to kill her children – as quickly and painlessly as possible – than for a baying Corinthian mob to find them first. And yet, would there be such a mob? The women of Corinth have sympathized with her throughout this play, have kept her secrets and supported her. Is Medea right to fear that her children would die? Or is she just making an excuse to herself, justifying what she wants to do – kill their children to injure her husband – with a quasi-altruistic argument?

The chorus sing a desperate ode to Helios, the sun god, Medea's grandfather. Can he really look down upon such an awful scene? But even as they describe Medea as a Fury,[39] they qualify it with *talainan* – 'pitiable', 'wretched'. They still feel sorry for her. And then they – and we – hear Medea's children crying out for help: What shall I do, where do I go to escape my mother's hands? The second child responds: I don't know, beloved brother. We are destroyed.

The shock of this scene – of children screaming for help as their mother slaughters them with a sword – is in no way diminished by the fact that we only hear it, rather than see it. The chorus are appalled, and ask each other if they should go inside and intervene to save the children. Choruses are usually bystanders, commenting on the action. Their suggestion in this play that they might leave the stage to help Medea's children is striking. The children scream again: For gods' sake, help us; we are in danger from her sword.

It is worth mentioning at this point that there are gendered expectations of murder in Greek myth. Women traditionally commit murder – when they do – with poison, as we have seen Medea do already. She is a renowned witch, expert in all kinds of potions. When she wants to kill her love rival, she uses a traditional woman's weapon to do so. But when it comes to killing her children, she does something different. She picks up a sword – a man's weapon, never used in a domestic setting unless something deeply transgressive is taking place. We have already heard her say that she has to forget the children are hers for a day. When she picks up a sword to use against them, she is doing more than that: she is both forgetting that she is a mother and forgetting that she is a woman.

The chorus realize that they are too late to save the boys now. They react by singing an ode about Ino, the only other mother they can think of who killed her own offspring, and that was when she was mad, cursed by Hera. After killing them, Ino leapt over a cliff. The chorus are not suggesting that Medea is mad: they know that she is perfectly sane. But the act she has chosen to commit is so extreme that their only paradigm is a woman driven mad by a malevolent divinity.

Now Jason arrives from the palace, raging about Medea. She cannot expect to go unpunished for her killing of the king. But then he clarifies his feelings: I don't care about her, I'm here to save my children's lives, from those who want vengeance for their mother's murderous acts.[40] We might have been sceptical of Medea in the previous scene, when she said she must kill her sons so a stranger didn't do it instead. But it turns out that she was right: Jason also believes an avenging mob are coming to kill his children.

You don't know the half of it, the chorus tell him. What is it, he says: I suppose she wants to kill me too? Even now, he is underestimating Medea. Knowing her as well as he does, as well as anyone does, he still cannot imagine the extremes to which she will go. The chorus break the news to him: Your sons are dead, by their mother's hand.

Jason can scarcely believe it. He demands that someone opens the doors of the house so he can see for himself. But he is too late, because Medea appears high above him, above the house itself, on a chariot provided by her grandfather, Helios. She has the bodies of their children with her.

In the fourth century BCE, Aristotle would criticize this plot point in his *Poetics*:[41] he disliked the 'mechanical' element of Medea being flown off the stage on a high platform. It is a stage technique that is usually reserved for a god or goddess at the end of a play (hence the phrase *deus ex machina* – 'a god from a machine', *mekhanē* in Greek). I cannot emphasize enough how significant this is in the context of this play. We may find Medea's behaviour horrific and unforgivable, but Euripides is showing us that the gods have endorsed it. They have provided her with a literal means of escape from Corinth's angry mob.

Jason is unable to accept what he sees. He calls her 'most hated by gods, by me, by mortals'. And yet, there she is, in her chariot provided by the gods. He stands helpless on the ground, a broken man: his fiancée, his king, his sons all dead. Objectively – if we can be objective about such an emotive subject – who does it look like the gods despise? Jason and Medea's final exchanges are sadly familiar to anyone who has watched a divorcing couple tear each other apart, and weaponize their children against one another (even though the children usually – happily – survive the process). He calls her names, she gloats over his futile rage. He tells her she has caused herself the same pain that he is experiencing, she tells him it was worth it. He blames her villainy, she blames his treachery. The gods know who started it, she says. He demands the return of his sons' bodies for burial. She refuses: she will bury them herself in the temple of Hera. With one final twist of anger, she prophesies his death: Jason will receive a blow to the head from a piece of the *Argo*, his own ship. It is not how a hero would wish to go. It only adds to her apparent apotheosis: she can even see the future now.

One last flurry of insults passes between them: he calls her a child-killer, she tells him to go and bury his wife. He wails over his lost children, she reminds him that he will be a childless old man. He yearns to hold them and love them, she remembers that he was perfectly content to see them sent into exile. His belated affection does not move her at all. Jason cries out to Zeus, but he is far too late; Medea is leaving

Corinth for good. The chorus are left to make one final observation: the gods make many unexpected things happen. No kidding.

So, given that this play is an undeniable masterpiece, why might it have proved so controversial when it was first performed? Remember that it came third in competition at the Dionysia in 431 BCE. Surely the audience can't have been shocked by the story, which they must have known very well? In fact, though, it is all too likely they did not. We know of two rival traditions in which Medea's children die in completely different ways. Were they both well known to Euripides' audience? It's impossible to say for sure, but it would go some way to explaining why his play was, apparently, so shocking when it was first performed, although it would soon go on to become extremely popular. The first of these traditions is one that both Medea and Jason raise in the Euripides play: the children are killed by vengeful Corinthians. According to the scholia who write about Euripides,[42] the Corinthians then start the rumour that Medea had killed her own sons. In a lovely twist (which is almost certainly apocryphal), the scholia also tell us that Euripides was paid five talents by fifth-century BCE Corinthians to place the blame on Medea and let them off the hook. The second tradition is that Medea kills her children by accident: she takes them to Hera's sanctuary as soon as they are born, believing the goddess will make them immortal.[43] But instead, the children die.

So while we can't be certain that Euripides was the first writer to make Medea's infanticide deliberate, it is probable. In which case, no wonder his audience was appalled. They must have turned out expecting a bit of light Corinth-bashing, or perhaps a hapless woman being thwarted by the cruel goddess Hera. And instead they got the terrifying prospect of a clever, violent, rage-fuelled woman: the wife of their collective nightmares.

It is important to note that at no point in Euripides' play is Medea anything other than sane. The decisions she makes might horrify us, but she makes them after long, reasoned deliberations. I emphasize this because it is so rare to see a contemporary production of *Medea* which does not make her mad in the final scene. It's a completely understandable choice: modern audiences might well struggle with the idea that Medea can slaughter her children, causing herself a lifetime's worth of grief in the process, and do so without being insane. We want to believe that someone could commit such a catastrophic crime only if she is out of her mind. An additional problem is the *deus ex machina* that so troubled Aristotle. How do you convey to a modern theatre audience all the symbolism inherent in this? That Medea has somehow morphed during the play from an abandoned wife, face down on the ground, howling over her treacherous husband, to an immortal or almost-immortal figure? That the act of killing her children has not broken her, as we would expect, but made her more powerful than ever? There is a gendered element in this disbelief, of course: cinema audiences had no problem believing that Keyser Söze became his most terrifying form when he decided to kill his family rather than allow himself to be threatened with their loss, in *The Usual Suspects*. The temptation is to roll the (to our eyes) oddity of the chariot appearance into our expectations of madness as a prerequisite for a woman to kill her children, so that the final scene is a destroyed woman hurling futile abuse at her ex-husband. But for Euripides – and for ancient artists – Medea is far from that.

There is a magnificent *calyx-krater* (a large wine-mixing bowl) from Lucania in southern Italy, which depicts the scene of Medea escaping Corinth in her chariot.[44] This piece was made around 400 BCE, just thirty years after Euripides' play was performed in Athens. This version of the scene has the children's bodies left behind on an altar, being mourned by a white-haired older woman, presumably the nurse. Jason appears to the left of the scene: he is just arriving to discover that his sons are dead. In front of him is a small, skipping dog. And flying above the scene in a chariot pulled by glorious coiled yellow serpents is Medea. Her ornate dress, and headdress, remind us that this is a barbarian woman. But she looks every inch a goddess as she flies stony-faced through the air. Her chariot is surrounded by a huge nimbus, reminding us of its divine origin (which explains how it can fly, given the snakes don't have wings). In perhaps one of the greatest digital curatorial comments in any museum in the world, the Cleveland Museum of Art website used to list the description of the pot – 'Here Medea flees the scene after murdering her children on a flying serpent-pulled chariot' – under the heading, 'Fun Fact'.[45] I salute this curator.

Much as it may pain our sense of justice, Medea really does get away with murder. She leaves Corinth for Athens, just as she had planned to when Aegeus arrived during the play. In some versions of their story, she is present in Athens to act against Theseus when he arrives to find his father, Aegeus (although, for Apollonius in the *Argonautica*, Theseus and Ariadne's relationship predates Jason and Medea's). In many versions of Medea's story, she has children who survive: Pausanias lists several alternative names,[46] and Herodotus also thinks she has a son who survives.[47] Diodorus Siculus tells us that these inconsistencies are the fault of tragedians: the problem is they like things to be marvellous[48] or miraculous.

Medea has long been used as a frame to describe women who exhibit violence against their offspring, no matter how appropriate the comparison might be. There is even an opposing theory to the Gaia thesis: that instead of a Mother Earth which nourishes and cherishes us, we instead inhabit a planet determined to extinguish us. It is called the Medea Hypothesis.

Toni Morrison's Pulitzer Prize-winning novel, *Beloved*, has been considered a Medea narrative, because it tells the story of a woman who kills her own daughter. I am more sympathetic to Medea than most, but even I wouldn't suggest she has anything like the same justification for killing her sons as a woman trying to prevent her child being taken back into a life of slavery. Margaret Garner, on whose story Morrison's novel was based, was described as 'The Modern

Medea' in Thomas Satterwhite Noble's 1867 painting of her, held by the National Underground Railroad Freedom Center.[49] If we take Medea at her word when she says it is better to kill her children herself than have them killed by a hostile hand, then perhaps we can justify the connection. But Medea spends a great deal of Euripides' play saying that she will kill her children to take revenge on those who have scorned her and believe they have done so with impunity. She exterminates Jason's line: no children to keep him company in his old age, and no great likelihood of remarriage; who would agree to marry Jason after she heard what had happened to Glauce? This is a far cry from a woman making a desperate choice – as Garner did – to save her child from the horror of a life in slavery, at the cost of the life itself.

Medea's story is unusual because it maps so easily onto contemporary lives: most of us don't know what it's like to accidentally kill our fathers and marry our mothers, but most of us do know what it is like to feel abandoned and betrayed. Even if our response is – hopefully – somewhat more measured than Medea's. A story that could easily seem so alien – giant snakes, magic, boiling people in pots – is made so human by Euripides that it is still performed all over the world. The visionary Japanese director Yukio Ninagawa staged an all-male production which played in cities across Japan for twenty years. His stated goal[50] was to show Japanese women that they could be as strong and straightforward as Medea. And though she is far from straightforward to the characters within the play, she is straightforward to us, the audience. We always know what she is thinking, feeling and planning, because she tells us. She is a complex character with multiple internal forces pulling her in different directions, but that is why she seems so real, so human. Unlike the externalized forces of divinely wrought desire which afflict Phaedra, or the cruelties of fate which condemn Jocasta, Medea is ravaged by her own psyche. For all her witchy powers, she is a woman in crisis, lashing out at those who have hurt her.

And this is why Medea's story seems so real, no matter how much she can call on a divine chariot to escape her enemies. No wonder her story has been retold so successfully by women, from Christa Wolf's excellent *Medea*, which keeps the story in its Greek frame, to Ludmila Ulitskaya's expansive *Medea and her Children*, both of which were published in 1996. Ulitskaya's Medea is a childless matriarch: she lives in a house to which her countless nephews, nieces and their offspring make an annual summer pilgrimage. This Medea – the last Greek in her Crimean village – discovers her husband's betrayal long after he is dead. Her response is not to destroy her family, but to reach out to them and allow them to console her. Perhaps she is the inheritor of one of Medea's most important characteristics: her brain. As Ulitskaya puts it: 'Medea had a saying, which Nike was fond of quoting: "Cleverness covers any failing."'

Let's go back to Beyoncé, looking every inch a priestess of Hecate as she strides down the steps of her water-filled temple in her saffron-yellow gown. What's worse, looking jealous or crazy, jealous and crazy? she asked us. It's an excellent question for Medea, not least because of the verb Beyoncé uses. She's not worried about whether it's worse to be jealous or crazy, but whether it's worse to *look* jealous or crazy. She, like Medea, is acutely troubled by how she appears. The moment Creon leaves the stage, Medea tells the chorus that she was only pretending to be self-effacing, to diminish the virtues of her cleverness, so that he would bend to her will. She will not let anyone see her be weak, unless she can correct their misapprehension immediately, by either words or murder. Been walked all over lately, Beyoncé concludes, swinging her baseball bat at a car windscreen: I'd rather be crazy.

PENELOPE

I F HELEN OF SPARTA WAS SO DANGEROUSLY DESIRABLE THAT MEN travelled across Greece to bid to be her husband, and the loss of her was enough to start a war, can we imagine any woman who could stand beside her and not be found wanting, at least in the male gaze? What of the one man who travelled to Sparta to woo Helen, but somehow found himself doing a deal to marry someone else?

Odysseus was no different from any other Greek king when it came to a potential marriage to Helen. He travelled from his home island of Ithaca to the palace of Tyndareus in Sparta, as did men from across the Greek world. Each hoped to claim Helen as his bride. But when Odysseus arrived in Sparta, and saw the situation for himself – the number of suitors, the likelihood of arguments and fights – he removed himself from the contest and came up with one of his many ostensibly bright ideas. According to Pseudo-Apollodorus,[1] it was Odysseus who proposed that all the suitors should swear an oath to fight for the return of Helen to her future husband, if she were ever to be abducted. As far as it went, of course, this oath was an excellent plan: no Greek was prepared to risk all-out war with so many other Greeks, so none of them abducted her. Paris – a non-Greek – was a small glitch which neither Odysseus nor anyone else had foreseen. Odysseus was not a man to let a good idea go to waste, and he offered his suggestion to Helen's stepfather, Tyndareus, in exchange for the latter's assistance in helping him win the hand of Penelope. Helen's semi-divine beauty was so astonishing that wars were fought over her. But one man, seeing Helen in all her magnificence, preferred someone else: the daughter of Icarius.

Penelope was not as keenly sought as Helen, who could boast the king of the gods as her father. But, at least according to Pausanias in his *Description of Greece*,[2] she was the object of many men's desire: Icarius apparently set up a foot race for her suitors, which Odysseus won. Perhaps Tyndareus helped him to cheat in exchange for the suggestion about Helen's suitors. It would certainly be in keeping with Odysseus' character for him to use subterfuge to achieve his desired outcome. Pausanias mentions another fascinating detail:[3] Icarius did not want to lose Penelope after her marriage. First, he tried to persuade Odysseus to stay in Sparta instead of taking his bride home to Ithaca. When that failed, he tried to persuade Penelope to stay by following the chariot in which she and Odysseus travelled. This is a very strange scene: the bride's father pursuing her and her new husband, and begging them not to leave him. Odysseus seems to have tolerated it for a while, and then asked his wife to choose whether she travelled with him or stayed behind with her father. In the first of a series of opaque manoeuvres which we must try to interpret, Penelope says nothing, but veils her face. Her response may be wordless, but Icarius understands her perfectly, concluding that she wants to leave with Odysseus but will not express that desire for fear of seeming immodest. He allows her to leave with her husband and sets up a statue to Modesty to commemorate this moment in his daughter's life. Penelope, we can see, is more than a match for her father. And she seems to have found the right husband in Odysseus, whether he won her by speed of foot or speed of thought. He chooses her, and then she chooses him.

The happy couple have one child, a son named Telemachus, who is only a baby when Paris and Helen elope to Troy. Although Odysseus had withdrawn from the contest for Helen's hand, he does still seem to have been bound by the oath sworn by her suitors, because he is dragooned into leaving Ithaca and fighting for Helen's return. Again, Pseudo-Apollodorus is our source:[4] he tells us that, when the Greeks arrived to take him, Odysseus pretended to be mad in order to avoid going to war. It almost worked, but Palamedes, another crafty Greek, suspected the deceit and made to attack the infant Telemachus. At this point, Odysseus had to give up the pretence of lunacy to defend his son. But even these few stories about Odysseus and Penelope's early relationship seem to tell us they are well-matched. They both want the same things, and they both tend to use subtlety to achieve them. Neither of them embraces directness if there is a roundabout route to take instead. It's hard to imagine them quarrelling, and easy to imagine them laughing together at the folly of others.

The reason we have so few stories about Odysseus and Penelope together is not because poems, plays and pottery have been lost, as is so often the case. Rather, it is because the majority of Penelope and Odysseus' marriage is spent apart: Telemachus is only a baby when Odysseus has to leave to fight at Troy. He besieges the city for ten years, and then spends another decade trying to get home to Ithaca. In literature and art, Penelope has been idealized for millennia for her patience, endurance and loyalty during the twenty-year period while her husband is away. She raises their child alone, she does her best to maintain his kingdom and she doesn't remarry, even when everyone thinks he must be dead.

It's enough to make you wonder if the ideal wife is one you scarcely even see, let alone spend any real time with. Because there is no doubt about it: Penelope has been presented as a perfect wife for as long as her story has been told at all. And yet, her wifely qualities are what, precisely? If we were considering the characteristics we might look for in a long-term partner, we would probably think of compatibility – emotional, psychological and sexual – as being pretty key. And though we might get that impression of Penelope and Odysseus from their brief pre-war relationship, we see little evidence of it because they are separated so early in their marriage, and for so long. Penelope's wifely virtues as we see them in Homer's *Odyssey* are being a single mother and being chaste (and also chased, but we'll come to that shortly).

This portrait of Penelope is often contradictory; she changes depending on whom she is talking to and who is influencing her at any given moment. The *Odyssey* is a poem which depends upon the unreliability of various figures, Odysseus most of all. He is sometimes disguised by Athene as a battered old beggar, and sometimes made extra-handsome by the same divine intervention. Sometimes he tells the truth about himself, sometimes he lies. Sometimes he lies by telling stories about Odysseus while pretending to be someone else. Partly because of his unpredictability, we find ourselves trying to unpick how much Penelope knows or guesses about him, when and whether she is being sincere or ironic. His untrustworthiness rubs off on our reading of her. Or perhaps they're a good couple because she is like him, as prone to dishonesty as he is.

We first meet her in Book One, when she is listening to a bard singing about the journeys home which the Greeks have been making from Troy, and how they have been cursed by Athene. To clear up any confusion: Athene was highly pro-Greek and anti-Trojan during the ten-year war. But in the fall of the city, her temples were profaned: Cassandra, for example, was raped by Ajax as she clung to Athene's statue, meaning that the rules of sanctuary were disregarded even before the rape affronted Athene further. As a result, Athene set herself against many of the Greeks, particularly Ajax. (This is, confusingly, a different Ajax from the one who slaughters livestock and kills himself, whom we met earlier on). But Odysseus – always Athene's favourite – kept her support even when the other Greeks had squandered it. So when Penelope hears this particular song, she is understandably distressed because she cannot know that Odysseus still has the goddess' favour.

Penelope

Homer introduces her with her patronymic: the daughter of Icarius, wise Penelope.[5] The very first thing we learn about her character, therefore, is that she is clever, or thoughtful (*periphrōn* can mean both). It is a word which Homer will use to describe her many times. Whatever else we conclude about Penelope, we know she is smart. She had heard the bard singing from upstairs and come down to hear him better. She is accompanied by two female attendants. Her house is – as we learned a few lines earlier, during Telemachus' conversation with the disguised goddess Athene – filled with suitors. More than a hundred men have made their way to Penelope's palace during the latter part of Odysseus' absence. They obviously stayed away during the war itself, because news returned from Troy with reasonable regularity telling them that their king was alive and well and would be returning home. But in the ten years that have followed the war, the stories which have made it back to Ithaca have become somewhat threadbare. Telemachus has just been instructed by Athene to go looking for his long-lost father, and travels to Pylos and Sparta to question Nestor and Menelaus (their respective kings) about Odysseus' potential whereabouts. As we already know from the very start of the poem – which begins with a council of the gods during which Athene demands that Odysseus be allowed to return home – Odysseus is held captive (willingly or unwillingly – another part of his story open to interpretation) by the nymph Calypso on her distant island of Ogygia. He has spent the past seven years as her husband-in-all-but-name. Finally, Athene feels that the gods must let him return to Ithaca.

So stories about Odysseus' adventures have dried up, because for seven years he has been about as far from Ithaca as possible. Many people have assumed he must be dead, which is what has motivated the suitors to descend on Penelope, all bidding to become her second husband. They have moved into her palace, and are eating and drinking their way through her supplies. The more she delays, the more they consume, and the more they reduce the value of her property (which is also Odysseus' property and Telemachus' inheritance). All this would obviously stop if she would simply pick one and marry him. But she has not given up on Odysseus, even if everyone else seems to have done so.

Penelope attends the suitors, looking like a goddess among women.[6] She holds a veil in front of her face and stands by a pillar. Even this description might baffle us a little. How does she resemble a goddess if she is veiled, when goddesses are not? What can the suitors even see of her? Is she tall? Goddesses often do appear to be taller than mortals. Or are these just literary niceties? Penelope is the wife of the hero so she must resemble a goddess?

Penelope is obviously no longer young, even if we assume she was a teenager when she married Odysseus, which is plausible. He has now been away for twenty years: she is the mother of a young man who is twenty or twenty-one (though Telemachus often seems younger than this. The story requires him to be not fully adult, or he would not be in such need of his father. Equally, were he to seem more adult, more in charge of himself and his emotions, Odysseus might not have a role to take on when he returns). Penelope must therefore be at least thirty-five and perhaps a little older. As we have seen from the many images of girls – *korai* – on Greek vases and sculptures, compared with the comparatively few images of older women (none, or almost none, of Jocasta), this was not considered an especially desirable age for a woman to be, relative to being of just-marriageable age. And yet, Penelope is like a goddess. A cynical reader might think the suitors have all pitched up in the palace of Ithaca with the goal of becoming its king, and that the route to achieving such status is to marry its queen: who she is, what she looks like doesn't matter to them. But Penelope is presented to us – this first time we meet her – as almost divine.

She is, however, entirely human in her first words. She begs the bard to stop singing sad songs about the Greeks being cursed by the gods on their journey home. He knows plenty of happy songs, she says. Sing one of those instead of this heartbreaker. She already misses her husband, who is famous across Greece.

Again we might wonder if Penelope is actually impressed or excited by her husband's fame, or whether this is another literary convention; Odysseus is the poem's hero, so we want to be reminded that he's a big deal. Or does it reveal something more intrinsic to her character: she loves Odysseus, at least in part, because he is so renowned? Is that recompense for his long absence? Either way, she doesn't want to hear any more about persecuted Greeks trying to make their voyages home.

But Telemachus responds by criticizing his mother.[7] It isn't the fault of the poets that bad things have happened, he says. This one is just singing about how things are. Toughen up and listen: it's his newest song and it garners him the most praise. And, anyway, Odysseus isn't the only one who didn't make it home. If we are wincing at the unsympathetic tone adopted by this young man towards his distressed mother, we're about to wince again. Go back to your loom, he tells her, and tell your slaves to do the same. Talking is men's business, and mine especially; I am the master of this house. Penelope looks at him with astonishment[8] and retreats inside.

What might we make of this exchange? Even allowing for the fact that Bronze Age gender relations are very different from ours, Telemachus seems to be unusually brusque with his mother. Do they not get on? Does he not care that she is so clearly upset about her missing husband? There is something psychologically plausible about his response. The man she misses is unknown to Telemachus. He misses the idea of his father, and perhaps the name, the fame, the security of having a powerful parent. But he doesn't miss his actual father, because he can have no memory of a man who left when he was a baby. Why would he not have some resentment towards this absent father? As mentioned above, Telemachus often seems younger than his years and this is surely the response a teenage boy might have to his father: missing him and resenting him at the same time. And, equally, his response to Penelope implies a conflict. He wants to take care of her, perhaps, and see himself as the man of the house. But this house is full of slightly older men who threaten him – literally and metaphorically – with their plans to marry his mother and displace him in Ithaca's line of succession. The suitors plot to kill him during this poem: he is afraid, and with good reason. Fear often makes us lash out at the person whose fault it isn't. Telemachus can't take on more than a hundred suitors without coming across as rather foolish and naive. So he criticizes his mother – in front of the suitors who court her – instead. Feeling that his own status, as prince of Ithaca, is in jeopardy, he takes his anxiety out on his mother.

Telemachus' emotions seem to reveal an interesting social point, too. During his earlier conversation with the disguised Athene, the goddess had revealed her own irritation with Penelope: let her marry one of the suitors, she said, but she can go back to her father's house to do it. In other words, Athene (in whom we might sense a hint of sexual jealousy: she is devoted to Odysseus, but her enthusiasm doesn't always extend to his wife) doesn't care what Penelope does, so long as Odysseus' palace and property remain his, and Telemachus remains next in line to succeed him. But the fear implicit in Telemachus' angry words suggest that Athene's view of Penelope's potential remarriage isn't reflected by reality. The suitors certainly think – and so, it seems, does Telemachus – that if Penelope remarries, the power and property of the king of Ithaca will be acquired by her new husband. She will not retreat to her father's house in disgrace, this woman of middle years. She is queen of Ithaca and whoever marries her will become king.

In other words, Penelope's power is as contested as her behaviour. A goddess suggests that she might be bundled back to her father, but the mortal men of Ithaca view her differently. And as for Telemachus, his harsh words also seem to be contradicted a few hundred lines later. In the second book of the poem, he follows Athene's advice to set sail and try to find news of Odysseus. But he instructs Eurycleia – the nurse of Telemachus and Odysseus before him – to keep his voyage secret from Penelope. Don't say anything to my dear mother, he tells Eurycleia,[9] until she notices I'm missing. Keep quiet for twelve days so she doesn't start crying and ruin her pretty face.

This is an intriguing shift in their relationship: one minute Telemachus is snapping at his mother, completely unprovoked; now he is trying to protect her feelings. His contradictory attitude is reflective of a conflicted young man who wants to protect his mother and yet finds her infuriating. The notion that she might not miss him for twelve days is quite something too. Is that because Penelope will be confined to the women's quarters and so wouldn't see her son for days at a time? Or is it because Telemachus often disappears for a few days without warning? We must be careful not to read our own values into the Homeric world: we would undoubtedly think it odd if a mother and son living in even a reasonably large house didn't see one another for twelve days at a time. But Bronze Age Ithaca is not now, and however much the psychology of this mother–son relationship rings true, the practicalities are not the same. When Penelope finds out in Book Four[10] that her son has gone off on his own quest, she does indeed start to cry.

And then she gets angry. For a few moments, she cannot speak. Then she berates her womenfolk for keeping this information from her. If she had known Telemachus was planning to go away, she says, she would have made him stay or he would have left over her dead body. Eurycleia admits that she had kept Telemachus' voyage a secret, and explains that he was trying to avoid upsetting her. Penelope is somewhat mollified and retreats to her chambers to bathe and sleep. Athene – whom we have already seen show quite a brisk attitude to

Penelope – now softens a little and sends her a dream: Penelope's sister Iphthime appears to her as she sleeps and tells her that Athene is guiding Telemachus. Penelope asks if Odysseus is dead or alive, but the spirit cannot tell her. The book ends with the suitors plotting to kill Telemachus, so we know that Athene's support for the young man might well be the difference between life and death.

It is not until Book Five of the *Odyssey* that we find out how our hero might feel about his wife, after almost twenty years without her. Odysseus has spent seven years trapped with Calypso on the island of Ogygia. She is finally persuaded by Hermes to send Odysseus on his way. Calypso is resentful about it, in particular about the fact that Odysseus wants to return to his wife, specifically,[11] not just his home. I'm prettier and taller than your wife, she tells him (I should confess that it is at this moment I really fall for Calypso. Who hasn't wanted to believe they are at least taller than a love rival?). Odysseus agrees that his wife is not as beautiful as the goddess. Is this honesty – goddesses are surely more beautiful than any mortal – or is it tact? She is mortal, he concedes, and you are divine.[12] At this point we also discover that Calypso had offered to make Odysseus immortal if he would stay with her as her consort. And still he chooses the grief-stricken path back to Penelope. No wonder Calypso wants to console herself with her greater height.

The bond between Odysseus and Penelope is an unusual one. It is – evidently – not a two-way street as far as sexual fidelity is concerned. Calypso is not Odysseus' first dalliance, although she is the longest-lasting. He has also spent a year living with Circe. One year, seven years: these can hardly be dismissed as casual affairs. Meanwhile Penelope has a house full of young men, who both outnumber her and could physically overpower her. But even the suggestion that she might marry one, back in Book One, left Athene snorting in anger: let her go back to her father's house, if that's what she wants. Not for the first time in literature and society, and assuredly not for the last, there is one set of standards to which Penelope must adhere, and a very much looser set for Odysseus. And yet, in some ways, Odysseus does remain faithful to his wife. He shares another woman's bed, but he doesn't share her idea of their future. She offers him something of enormous value – immortality, for which all heroes strive, one way or another – and he rejects it. He would rather return to his less beautiful, mortal wife. Homeric heroes make huge sacrifices for even a brush of immortality: Achilles specifically chooses a short, glorious life that will result in fame which outlives him (a kind of immortality) rather than a longer, less famous existence. And here is Odysseus, offered eternal life but rejecting it. And all for the chance to return to a woman he has not seen for twenty years. A divorce lawyer might not call this fidelity, but it is something.

Sadly, we can only imagine how Penelope might feel if she heard this exchange between her husband and Calypso. Would she be hurt by the easy admission that she is less beautiful than the nymph? Or would she admire her husband's wiliness: he needs Calypso's assistance to build a new boat on which he may leave. If he flatters her, he is more likely to find himself in a seaworthy vessel. Would Penelope be angry that her husband has shown so much less sexual restraint than she has, or would she expect nothing else? They are a couple of their time, after all. She would surely be touched that her husband rejects immortality just for the opportunity to take to the seas again (he has already undergone multiple maritime disasters at this point), with the goal of returning to her. One has to hope she never finds out that the first person Odysseus meets on his journey back to Ithaca from Ogygia is a young princess, Nausicaa. He washes up, naked, on a beach in front of her.

But what does Penelope do while Odysseus is making his erratic journey home? The short answer is, she weaves. Way back in Book

One, when we first met Penelope, we saw Telemachus tell her to be quiet, stop crying and go back to her weaving. This could be a suggestion made to any respectable woman in the Homeric tradition: women weave. Even Helen weaves, and she is – as everyone is keen to stress, even her – a terrible wife. But for Penelope, weaving plays an integral part in her story, and her freedom from unwanted entanglements with the suitors: the literal saves her from the metaphorical. And just as Agamemnon's homecoming was dictated by Clytemnestra's weaving – the strange straitjacket which she uses to paralyse him – so is Odysseus' homecoming decided by Penelope's weaving. Both women use this most traditional skill for deceitful purposes: the difference is that Penelope is using deceit to help her husband, while Clytemnestra used it against hers.

The story of Penelope and her weaving is told three times by three different people at three different moments in the *Odyssey*, with almost unvarying language. We can see that it is an important plot point, from the repetition alone. So let's look at it in more detail. The first time we hear it is in Book Two, when Antinous – the most obnoxious of Penelope's suitors – is speaking to Telemachus. Don't blame us suitors for hanging around the place. Blame your dear mother: she's the cunning one.[13] He goes on to explain that Penelope has cheated the suitors for almost four years: she promised she would remarry once she had woven a shroud for Laertes, Odysseus' father. Laertes – to be clear – is not dead at the point when Penelope makes this offer; indeed, he survives beyond the end of the poem. But making a shroud for a not-yet-dead father-in-law is a perfectly respectable thing for Penelope to do: it means that, when he does die, he will be laid out appropriately. To do less would be disrespectful.

The suitors agree to this bargain, and Penelope begins her task. But here is the cunning part: by day she weaves the shroud, by night she secretly unravels it. Astonishingly, this trick deceives the suitors for more than three years. One wonders how they could be deceived for quite so long (did they believe it was an especially massive shroud? Did they think basic woven garments took ten or twenty times longer to make than they actually did? Sadly, Antinous does not say). Even in the fourth year, the suitors didn't tumble to the trick: one of Penelope's maids snitched on her. For those of us who have ever wondered if Penelope might have been a little tempted by one or more of these young men who occupy her home for so long, this seems to be a valid textual reason why she might not have remarried: these suitors are idiots. And she has been used to a relationship (albeit long ago) with Odysseus, a man who is assuredly not stupid. So, in this fourth year of weaving and unweaving, Antinous continues, the suitors caught Penelope in the act of undoing her work and forced her to finish the shroud. Now her delaying strategy is concluded, she must choose one of them.

There are a couple of points to consider in this story. The first is one that is all too often overlooked. Weaving is not something you can unravel quickly, like knitting or crochet (where each stitch is looped into another stitch, so if you remove the last one from your knitting needles or crochet hook and pull on the thread, the whole thing can be undone very easily). Weaving is a much more laborious process to undo: every line of fabric must be unmade by passing the shuttle over and under the threads in the exact same way it was made. Penelope has taken on a Sisyphean task: to make a few inches of cloth every day, to undo it again every night. The sheer physical effort involved in such a thankless task – staring at the threads by torchlight, hunching over the loom – is considerable. And that is before we consider the psychological strain of spending years making something and then undoing it, over and over again. In order to avoid giving up on Odysseus, Penelope has effectively sentenced herself to years of hard labour.

The second point is to ask whose shroud Penelope is weaving. It is ostensibly a shroud for Laertes, but is it really a shroud for Odysseus?

She has delayed remarriage for several years by this point: the war must have ended five or six years before she began the project. She knows that she cannot delay indefinitely, only postpone the inevitable in the hope that Odysseus makes it home before she finishes. So is she weaving the shroud for her marriage to a man she loves, or loved long ago? She bursts into tears repeatedly in the *Odyssey*: doesn't this suggest a woman who is under enormous emotional strain? There are parallels, as mentioned above, with Clytemnestra. But Clytemnestra is using her weaving prowess to create a trap for her husband, Penelope is using hers to try and avoid being trapped herself.

The second time the story of the weaving and unweaving is told, it is three-quarters of the way through the poem, and this time it is Penelope who relates it to an interested stranger who has arrived at her palace. We know the stranger is the disguised Odysseus (enchanted by Athene so Penelope doesn't recognize him. Although after a twenty-year absence, perhaps she would not have known him anyway). But Penelope believes she is talking to an old beggar. I weave deceit, she says,[14] before explaining the whole story, almost word-for-word as it was told in Book Two. There could be no more perfect phrase to describe this couple than *dolous tolopeuō* – 'I weave tricks' or 'deceit'. That is another difference between Clytemnestra and Penelope: Clytemnestra works against her husband precisely because they are in no way alike. He could sacrifice Iphigenia, whereas she never could; he is gullible where she is conniving. But for Penelope and Odysseus, deceit is their unifying characteristic. He can barely open his mouth without fibbing; why would his wife value honesty? She adds details which Antinous did not mention: I can't find another scheme to avoid marriage,[15] she says. My parents are urging me to remarry. In this pair of lines, we can hear a terrible isolation in Penelope's words. She has held out as long as she could, alone, and used up every idea she had. We already know she has a somewhat erratic relationship with Telemachus, who has lied to her, hidden from her and shouted at her during this poem. And now we discover that her parents are also keen for her to marry again. The energy it must have taken to hold out against all the suitors, a recalcitrant child, parents who seem to have sided with her enemies: and all that on no sleep because she has stayed up till all hours unweaving a shroud in the dark. No wonder she cries.

This weaving scene is – directly and indirectly – the inspiration for many visual representations of Penelope. There is a lovely example of a fifth-century BCE red-figure *skyphos* (two-handled wine cup) in the Archaeological Museum of Chiusi in Tuscany.[16] Penelope sits on a hard chair, ankles crossed. She wears a long draping robe, which gathers over her feet; her toes peep out from under the hem. She has a veil over her hair, too: her posture and dress are equally demure. But her right elbow rests on her right thigh, and her bowed head rests on her right hand. Her eyelids droop: she is clearly exhausted. A young man – Telemachus – stands in front of her, holding his pair of spears. Is he speaking to her, or trying to get her attention? The pot is slightly damaged so we can't read his expression. But either way, it doesn't seem to be working. Behind her, we see the reason for her fatigue: a loom on which is woven a length of fabric. The pattern is intricate: Pegasus and Medusa are travelling across the cloth, from left to right, at a gallop. The speed and movement of these tiny figures in the background are a direct contrast to the stillness and exhaustion of Penelope in the foreground. Their energy has come at the cost of her own.

Penelope is almost always shown sitting down. Visitors to the Musée d'Orsay can see a mid-nineteenth-century interpretation of Penelope, by Jules Cavelier.[17] This gleaming white sculpture echoes the version of her we saw on the Chiusi pot, but this Penelope is very definitely fast asleep. She, too, has her legs crossed as she sits in an upright chair. But her hands are in her lap, and her head has drooped so far forward that your neck aches to look at her. She, too, is worn out by her night-time unweaving, and has simply had to give in to it and sleep.

She is awake in the American artist David Ligare's picture, *Penelope*, from 1980.[18] This modern Penelope sits on a chair, its curved legs casting shadows across a tiled floor. She is outside, facing the sun, her head turned towards the viewer. She looks pensive, rather than tired, and the sea is calm behind her. Her legs are crossed in the characteristic pose, but her left foot rests on a small grey brick. The painting has an almost photographic quality, and yet it is full of references to other, ancient art: is the brick beneath her foot a jokey reference to the plinths on which ancient statuary is often placed? Or is it a modern echo of the small footstool shown on a beautiful grave marker in Athens' National Archaeological Museum?[19] This particular grave stele is attributed to the fifth-century BCE sculptor Callimachus, and shows Hegeso – an Athenian woman – sitting on a *klismos*, a chair with exactly the same curved legs as the one Penelope sits on in the Ligare painting. Either way, the painting offers us a calm, thoughtful Penelope, her hands resting neatly in her lap, the underside of her right foot dirty next to the hem of her long white dress.

But two depictions of Penelope show her in a more active light, actually doing the thing that she is famous for rather than thinking about it or sleeping to recover from it. The first is Dora Wheeler's tapestry, produced in 1886, *Penelope Unraveling Her Work at Night*.[20] This Penelope is bathed in golden light; we can see a small lamp behind her which illuminates the scene. She is wearing a plain, sleeveless, white shift dress which is tinged to a warm cream colour by the light. A red bodice fits over it, and her bare arms are stretched wide. Her brown hair is tied in a loose bun, and her brown eyes are full of concentration. Her head is turned away from us, towards her loom. The lamp catches the underside of her jaw, which is set, determined. Penelope is hard at work: both her hands are wrapped in the warp yarns, which run from top to bottom of a woven cloth. The fingers of her right hand are splayed as she keeps the loose threads from tangling. Her left hand is clenched in the fabric: this is not an easy job. Her arm muscles and shoulders are toned from the physical demands of the work. There is something intrinsically pleasing about seeing a woven representation of this most famous story about weaving. Wheeler's tapestry – which was based on a pastel drawing[21] she made in 1885 – is somewhat degraded by time, but it is beautiful nevertheless. And there is something equally special about seeing Penelope in action, rather than seated in passive exhaustion. The daughter of a textile artist herself, Wheeler obviously knew and cared about the effort Penelope was making and the skill required, not just the weariness it would provoke.

The second Penelope in action is by New Zealand artist Marian Maguire. In her 2017 work, *Penelope Weaves and Waits*,[22] she creates a Penelope in acrylic who resembles one we might see on a red-figure vase painting. Penelope is painted in a terracotta hue, perched on a stool, black curly hair tied back in a scarf. She leans in towards her loom with the weft thread and spindle dangling between her hands. The partially completed weaving is a bird in flight: its movement and freedom contrast with Penelope's weary posture. However tired she is, she does not pause for a rest: her gaze is fixed on the thread in front of her. Maguire's piece is a painted sculpture, so her Penelope sits in the centre of a wooden fireplace: the implication is that she is the heart of the house. Painted on both sides of the surround, in front of Penelope and behind, are ten grasping hands reaching towards her. These represent the suitors, grabbing at Penelope as she turns to deceit to try to keep them at bay. Above her, along the mantel, are twelve sets of dangling feet. These are the slave-women hanged by Telemachus, when Odysseus finally returns and takes his revenge on all the men and women who have – as he perceives it – worked against his interests in the *Odyssey*'s concluding blood-drenched books. Everything Penelope does has consequences for all the people to whom these disembodied limbs belong. One of her women gives her up to the suitors, who then demand that she stop tricking them and finish the shroud, as we discovered all the way back in Book Two from Antinous. And yet all of them will die in the aftermath of her completing it. If they only knew, they would be begging her to continue with her delaying tactics.

The third time the story is told by Homer is in the final book of the *Odyssey*. We are in the Underworld and Amphimedon – one of the now-dead suitors – is telling the story to Agamemnon. If we hadn't picked up on the parallels between Penelope and Clytemnestra before now, we can hardly miss them in this context: a man murdered by his unfaithful wife in conversation with a man murdered by the husband of the faithful woman he wanted to marry. Amphimedon and Agamemnon knew each other before the war, it turns out. Agamemnon asks where all these strong young men have come from, flocking down to the Underworld all at once. Agamemnon assumes it must have been a shipwreck, but the answer, of course, is that Odysseus and Telemachus slaughtered the lot of them. The *Odyssey* has an astonishingly bloody conclusion: over a hundred suitors slain, and the twelve slave-women who were deemed to have conspired with them hanged from a single length of rope. Amphimedon explains the whole story, beginning with the third rendition of Penelope and her loom. From his perspective, of course, the weaving and unweaving turned out to be lethally deceitful. He complains that Penelope didn't want to marry any of them but wouldn't tell them to leave. And while we might feel some sympathy with him (he is dead, after all), we might also think about the two previous times we have heard this story. Of Penelope telling the disguised Odysseus that she had run out of tricks and would have to remarry, and Antinous telling Telemachus that they had caught his mother out when her slave-woman snitched on her. How was Penelope meant to empty her house of all these men, when they were threatening the life of her son and destroying his future inheritance by eating and drinking their way through her supplies? Would they really all have left if she had told them she had no plans to remarry? Would her own parents have allowed it?

We must draw our own conclusions about what Penelope wants, because the ways in which Homer presents her are contradictory. In Book Eighteen, for example, she is inspired by Athene to show herself off to the suitors. Should we see this as Penelope indulging in an understandable desire for praise from this posse of young men? Or should we conclude that Penelope tends to avoid the suitors unless Athene intervenes? That it is Athene who wants Odysseus' wife to seem desirable to other men, rather than Penelope's choice?

There is no doubt about one thing, however. The shroud which Penelope made has not been used as a winding sheet for the still-alive Laertes. It has not served as a metaphorical shroud for the end of her marriage to Odysseus: the happy couple have been reunited. In fact, as is underlined by the dead Amphimedon narrating this story for the final time, the shroud was for him, and the other suitors, and the slave-women, all killed by Odysseus and Telemachus. Even while Penelope was making it, she cannot have known that this massacre was coming. But she finished her weaving, and the deaths followed soon after. An evil spirit brought Odysseus home,[23] Amphimedon says. Homecomings aren't always happy endings.

Agamemnon certainly wastes no time on sympathizing with Amphimedon: true to form, he immediately takes the story and makes it all about him. He doesn't even reply to the dead suitor, he addresses his response to the absent Odysseus. Lucky you, son of Laertes, he says. You have a wife of great virtue, who remembered you for so many years. The fame of her virtue will never die, he adds: the gods will compose a poem about her. And then, after seven lines praising Penelope and envying Odysseus, he turns things back to himself. Not like my wife, who killed her husband, he says. Amphimedon's sad story doesn't touch Agamemnon at all, save to make him envy the man who killed him, a hero who returned home to a faithful wife.

There are other questions about Penelope which the *Odyssey* raises: when does she recognize her returning husband? When she proposes the suitors compete, in Book Twenty-One, to string Odysseus' bow and shoot an arrow through a set of axe-heads? Does she know then that the kindly beggar she has been talking to is really her husband? Has she found a way to arm him with precisely the weapon he needs to even the odds against a numerically superior enemy? Or is it just good luck: she knows the bow is difficult to string (and anyway, it is Athene who puts the bright idea of the contest into her head),[24] and she is simply using this as another way of distracting the suitors and delaying her agreement to marry one? Is she teasing Odysseus or testing him in Book Twenty-Three, when she asks Eurycleia to move their marriage bed (he long ago carved it from a living tree which grows through the palace, so the bed cannot be moved)? Does she really doubt that the man who has entered her home in disguise, listened to her woes, befriended her son and turned into a spree killer is her husband? Athene has disguised Odysseus – improving and worsening his appearance as the situation requires – so perhaps she really doesn't know for sure that he is her man. Perhaps she fears he is an imposter. Or perhaps – irritated that Odysseus had revealed his true self to his son, his nurse and his swineherd before he reintroduced himself to his wife – she is simply giving him a taste of his own medicine. Why should their reunion be entirely on his terms?

Penelope is not unknowable by accident. Homer has deliberately shown her opaquely: remember when we first met her, in Book One, she was hiding her face behind a veil. She is an enigma, praised by men who largely don't know her as the ideal wife. When Agamemnon describes her virtue at the end of the *Odyssey*, who is he talking about? A woman he met once, twenty years ago, when he and Palamedes came to Ithaca to collect Odysseus and force him to join the war effort. Is he really praising Penelope, or just envying Odysseus having a wife who isn't Clytemnestra? His preference for women other than his wife dates back to long before the latter murdered him, incidentally: in the first book of the *Iliad*, he cheerfully tells his men that he prefers Chryseis (his newly acquired war bride) to his wife.

And this is the great difficulty in finding Penelope among the praise heaped upon her by men. Are they describing her, or merely describing their idealized conception of what a wife should be? Which seems to be one who is competent, self-sufficient and conveniently far away. One who either doesn't know, or at least doesn't complain, that her husband has adventures (sexual and otherwise) with seemingly little recollection that he has a wife at all. And one who doesn't do the same herself. Are they valuing her for nothing more than her chastity? Or, more specifically, for her chastity in the face of so many men apparently desiring her?

What happens if we take that chastity away from her? In the *Bibliotheca* of Pseudo-Apollodorus, in his final passage on the Trojan War, he considers some alternative versions of Penelope's story and Odysseus' homecoming: it's said by some sources, he says, that she was seduced by Antinous, and sent back to her father by Odysseus because of this. In Arcadia, she was seduced by the god Hermes and gave birth to another god, Pan. Or Odysseus killed her when he found she had been seduced by another of the suitors, Amphinomus. Penelope's chastity is vital to the value men place on her, but there are versions of her where she is different: less perfect, less chaste. We just tend to forget about them because the versions of her story which have been preferred through history are the ones in which she never wavers.

There is a second element to Agamemnon's praise of Penelope, of course. We are witnessing a misogynist tradition which dates back millennia: praise one woman in order to criticize another. Penelope is a model of virtue against which other women fall short. For Agamemnon she is the ultimate good wife, everything his own wife was not. By lauding Penelope, he has found a new route by which he can reach his desired goal: to complain about Clytemnestra. Praising Penelope for qualities he can only know by repute is not insincere or inaccurate, but it is also not particularly relevant to who Penelope is.

For more detailed imaginings of Penelope, we can turn to two authors in particular: one ancient, one modern. Ovid composed a letter from Penelope to Ulysses (the Latin version of Odysseus' name) in his *Heroides*. This Penelope is not an opaque creation, defined only by the way men value her chastity and apparent lack of murderous instinct. She begins her letter to her long-absent husband by explaining that she doesn't want him to reply, but rather, to return. She is wildly unimpressed by the heroics he displayed in the *Iliad*, referencing Book Ten, where Odysseus and his friend Diomedes attacked the Thracian camp at night. She accuses him of forgetting about her and Telemachus[25] when he embarked on these dangerous excursions. And even though the war is long over, for me, she says, Troy still stands.[26] She makes no secret of her impatience, her anxiety and the pressures being exerted on her by her father to remarry. She complains about the suitors and Odysseus' servants conspiring with them to eat up all their livestock. She reminds him that his son needs a father if he is to grow into manhood. Finally, she concludes with a damning pair of lines. When you left, I was just a girl, she says. If you came back right now, you would see an old woman.

She is – as women imagined by Ovid so often are – a highly nuanced character. She displays real human emotions of a woman in her position: anger, fear, worry, impatience, self-pity. It's harder to imagine Agamemnon demanding the gods create a poem about this version of Penelope, because she is not merely a cypher of good wifely behaviour, but a woman with complicated feelings and demands of her own: come home, Ulysses, I need you.

A similar instinct – to create a three-dimensional Penelope we can see clearly, rather than the veiled enigma of Homer – is at play in Margaret Atwood's wonderful short novel, *The Penelopiad*, published in 2005. The title is a clear nod to ancient epic poems which take the names of men or cities as their focus: the *Iliad*, the *Aeneid*. This is a slender epic about a woman, and told by her too. Like Agamemnon and Amphimedon in the final book of the *Odyssey*, this Penelope tells her story from the Underworld. And like Ovid's Penelope before her, she does so in the first person, so we can hear this hidden woman speak out. The book retells the story of the *Odyssey*: of the suitors, the weaving, the drawn-out recognition between husband and wife. The chapter titles alone reveal Penelope's amused, self-centred, caustic world view: 'Helen Ruins My Life', 'The Suitors Stuff Their Faces', 'Home Life in Hades'. This is the woman we have longed to meet, who isn't at all saintly, but is quietly watching and judging the behaviour of those who surround her. No matter how tart she now is with the dead suitors, however, Penelope is haunted even after her own death by the murder of her slave girls. This moment – commemorated on Marian Maguire's fireplace sculpture too – has always haunted Atwood, according to her author's note.[27] Perhaps, rather than call it a retelling of Homer, I would do better to describe her novel as a necessary addition to Homer, who spends well over four hundred lines describing the killing of the suitors. Once they are all dead, the slave-women are forced to carry the bodies of these men outside, before cleaning their blood from the furniture. The women are then hanged by Telemachus: it takes Homer only ten lines to describe their deaths.

When the question arises – why retell Greek myths with women at their core? – it is loaded with a strange assumption.

The underpinning belief is that women are and always have been on the margins of these stories. That the myths have always focused on men and that women have only ever been minor figures. This involves ignoring the fact that there is no 'real' or 'true' version of any myth, because they arise from multiple authors across multiple locations over a long period. The version of a story we find in the *Iliad* or the *Odyssey* is not somehow more valid than a version we find in a fifth-century BCE play or on the side of a vase merely because it is older. Homer drew on earlier traditions just as the fifth-century BCE playwright Euripides or the sculptor Phidias did. When Euripides wrote about the Trojan War, he centred his plays on the female characters: Andromache, Electra, Helen, Hecabe, and two Iphigenia plays, offering different, contradictory versions of her fate. Sometimes the stories centred on men have been taken more seriously by scholars. The *Iliad* was for a long time considered grander, more epic than the *Odyssey*, because the former is full of war and the latter is stuffed with women and adventures. The nineteenth-century writer Samuel Butler even suggested – with debatable seriousness – that the *Odyssey* must have been written by a woman, so packed was it with female characters. What on earth makes us believe that the *Iliad*, where Helen is a relatively minor player, is somehow more authentic than Euripides' *Helen*? If Ovid could see that the stories of Greek myth could be told just as well from women's perspectives as men's, how did we forget? When people ask why tell the stories that we know best from the *Odyssey* from Penelope's perspective, or Circe's perspective, they presuppose that the story 'should' be told from Odysseus' point of view. Which means the answer to this question should always be: because she's in the damn story. Why wouldn't we want to hear from her?

Conclusion

When the contents of Pandora's jar escape into the world, we have tended to see this as something bad. As discussed in Chapter One, for ancient authors, the contents of the jar aren't always themselves evil; in some versions of the myth they are good. But those versions haven't prevailed as the favoured narrative, perhaps because we find it easier to believe that things aren't as good as they used to be. There is an enormous temptation to believe in some sort of declinism: that things are always getting slightly worse. And when Zeus sends Pandora to mortals (the price he sets against fire, which Prometheus stole for us), he intends her to cause trouble.

But the question remains: is the trouble something she does, by opening a jar? Or is it something she is? Pandora is the first woman; thanks to her (according to Hesiod), the carefree age of men comes to an end. But you'll forgive me for suggesting that an all-male age with no women (and no fire) sounds incredibly boring. Of course it was carefree, what the hell would anyone care about?

Pandora is an agent of change, and the embodiment of the will of Zeus. She is not an unmitigated evil, as her box-opening reputation might have you believe. She is dual: *kalon kakon*, beautiful and ugly, good and evil. What Pandora brings to mortals is complexity. And that is true of all the women in this book: some have been painted as villains (Clytemnestra, Medea), some as victims (Eurydice, Penelope), some have been literally monstered (Medusa). But they are much more complicated than these thumbnail descriptions allow.

Their stories should be read, seen, heard in all their difficult, messy, murderous detail. They aren't simple, because nothing interesting is simple.

We do not live in a world of heroes and villains, and if we believe we do, we should really consider the possibility that we haven't thought about things properly. We cannot hope to make sense of our stories or ourselves (myths are a mirror of us, after all) if we refuse to look at half of the picture. Or – worse – don't even notice half of it is missing. This book is an attempt to fill in some of the blank space.

Acknowledgements

GEORGE MORLEY IS THE SMARTEST EDITOR A PERSON COULD HOPE for, as well as being a generally wonderful human being in all regards. I'm so glad she wanted this book. Peter Straus is the Platonic ideal of agents: I was crazy-lucky the day he took me on, and I still am. He is in complete denial about how awesome he is, so feel free to tell him if you ever bump into him.

The book was edited during lockdown. There are possibly better address books than mine for such an eventuality, but it's hard to imagine whose. Roslynne Bell, Paul Cartledge and Patrick O'Sullivan all used their quarantine time to read and make corrections. They saved me from carelessness and/or stupidity more times than I care to think: remaining mistakes are mine, of course. Chloe May was my super-patient desk editor, Marissa Constantinou read the manuscript alongside George, Susan Opie was the copy-editor.

Edith Hall, Philippa Perry, Tim Whitmarsh, Tim Parkin, Emma Bridges, Tim Marlow, Francesca Stavrakopoulou, Adam Rutherford and Shaun Whiteside all offered their expertise without hesitation. I saw every version of *Eurydice* I wrote about with Julian Barnes (I'm pretty sure I neglected to mention the one where we skipped out early and had cocktails instead of Act Three). A huge gang of nerds – classicists, writers, musicians, historians, scientists – offered their favourite versions of each of these women when I asked for suggestions. I wish I'd had space to include everything; it all informed my thinking around the work I did include. Sometimes they reminded me of things I'd forgotten, often they introduced me to work I didn't know. It was a wonderful way to broaden the focus of this book and I can't thank them enough.

Pauline Lord runs my gig diary like an actual machine, and without her I would just be sitting on a bench at a distant railway station wondering where I live. Matilda McMorrow looks after my social-media existence and generally makes sure I don't get lost in the woods. Christian Hill runs the website beautifully, as he has for (I think) twenty years. I'd be lost without them. Mary Ward-Lowery and I made two series of *Natalie Haynes Stands Up for the Classics* for Radio 4 while I was writing and editing this book, James Cook told us to make it how we had to when the Radio Theatre was closed. I spend so much time working alone, it is wonderful to have a collaborative project to make with people who care about it so much.

Dan Mersh read every chapter as I finished it. He must surely have thought he'd be off the hook from that by now, but no: thank you, always. Helen Bagnall is a wonderful friend, always full of imagination and ideas. Damian Barr is both magnificent and almost impossibly generous. Robert Douglas-Fairhurst is my touchstone each day. Helen Artlett-Coe is the lawless desperado I need. Michelle Flower checks in on me with pictures of cats: this is vital to my wellbeing. So many of my friends reached out and took care of me while I wrote this, and again while I edited it. They were solitary times, during which I very rarely felt alone.

Sam Thorpe, Jenny Antonioni and everyone at TMAP kept me from crumbling under the stress of trying to write a book while doing a seventy-date tour of its predecessor. They didn't stop doing that when we couldn't go into the dojo, either, they just took it online instead. Well, warrior women have to learn to fight somewhere.

My lovely family kept me on an even keel too: thanks to my mum (if you're reading this after a book festival appearance, you have already met my mum), my dad, Chris, Gem and Kez.

Notes

PANDORA

1. Hesiod, *Works and Days*, introduction xiv.
2. Louvre Museum.
3. Sir John Soane's Museum.
4. http://www.sothebys.com/en/auctions/ecatalogue/2014/british-irish-art-l14132/lot.207.html.
5. Hesiod, *Theogony* 585.
6. Ibid 570.
7. Ibid 585.
8. Ibid 587.
9. Hesiod, *Works and Days* 57.
10. Ibid 80–3.
11. Ibid 96.
12. Theognis, frag 1. 1135.
13. *The Aesop Romance.*
14. Aesop Fable 526 (Gibbs)/123 (Chambry)/312 (Perry).
15. Metropolitan Museum, Drawings and Prints.
16. https://www.britishmuseum.org/research/collection_online/collection_object_details.aspx?objectId=461830&partId=1.
17. https://www.ashmolean.org/sites/default/files/ashmolean/documents/media/learn_pdf_resources_greece_focus_on_greek_objects_teacher_notes.pdf.
18. Hurwit, Jeffrey M. (1995), 'Beautiful Evil: Pandora and the Athena Parthenos', *American Journal of Archaeology* 99.
19. Pausanias, *Description of Greece* 1.24.7.
20. Thucydides, *The History of the Peloponnesian War* 2.45.2.
21. The phrase used for women is *attike gune* – 'a woman of Attica', which is a geographical description, but removes the civic context present in the word 'Athenian'. Jones, N. F. (1999), *The Associations of Classical Athens: The Response to Democracy* (Oxford and New York: Oxford University Press) 128.

22. https://www.huffingtonpost.co.uk/entrypulp-fiction-fan-theories_n_5967174.
23. Hesiod, *Theogony* 585.

JOCASTA

1. Antiphanes, frag 189.3–8, cited Wright, M. (2016), *The Lost Plays of Greek Tragedy, Volume 1: Neglected Authors* (London: Bloomsbury Academic), p. 214 + Taplin http://www.engramma.it/eOS/index.php?id_articolo=3303.
2. Wright, p. 97.
3. Sophocles, *Oedipus Tyrannos* 858.
4. Ibid 981–3.
5. Ibid 1071.
6. Ibid 707ff.
7. Ibid 713.
8. Homer, *Odyssey* 11 271.
9. Ibid 274.
10. Pausanias, *Description of Greece* 9.5.10–11.
11. Euripides, *Phoinissai* 20.
12. Ibid 30–1.
13. Ibid 44.
14. Ibid 619.
15. Martin, R. P. (2005), 'The Voices of Jocasta', *Princeton/Stanford Working Papers in Classics*. Available as of March 2020 at https://www.princeton.edu/~pswpc/pdfs/rpmartin/050503.pdf.
16. Lille Stesichorus Antistrophe.
17. Athenian red-figure kylix, attributed to the Painter of Oedipus (ca. 470 BCE), depicting Oedipus and the Sphinx, Vatican Museums, inv. 16541.
18. Sicilian red-figure *calyx-krater* (ca. 330 BCE) possibly depicting Oedipus, Jocasta and their daughters, Syracuse, Museo Archeologico Regionale Paolo Orsi inv. 66557.
19. Hall, E. (2016), 'Oedipal Quiz – Little Boys in Greek Tragedy', The Edithorial. Blog available as of March 2020 at https://edithorial.blogspot.com/2016/05/oedipal-quiz-llittle-boys-in-greek.html
20. A red-figure Apulian *loutrophoros*, mid-fourth century BCE, by an artist close to the Painter of Laodamia, Basel, Antikenmuseum, inv. S21.
21. Cabanel, Alexandre (1843), oil on canvas, *Oedipus Separating from Jocasta*, Capentras, Musée Duplessis.
22. https://en.wikipedia.org/wiki/File:Toudouze_oedipus.gif.
23. Aristophanes, *The Frogs* 1188ff.

Notes

HELEN

1. *Orestes* 352, *Andromache* 106.
2. Asimov, I. (1992), *Isaac Asimov Laughs Again* (New York: HarperCollins), p. 200.
3. Homer, *Iliad* 3 418, 426.
4. Euripides, *Helen* 21.
5. Epic Greek Fragments, *Cypria*, 11, MLW.
6. Euripides, *Helen* 256.
7. Gantz, T. (1993), *Early Greek Myth: A Guide to Literary and Artistic Sources*. Vol 1 (Baltimore: The Johns Hopkins University Press), p. 289.
8. Plutarch, *Theseus* 31.2.
9. Diodorus, *Bibliotheca Historica* 4.63.
10. Gantz, p. 289.
11. Euripides, *The Trojan Women* 890–4.
12. Gantz, p. 566.
13. Ibid; e.g. Pseudo-Apollodorus.
14. Homer, *Iliad* 6 344ff.
15. Euripides, *The Trojan Women* 901–2.
16. Ibid 914ff.
17. Homer, *Iliad* 24 28–30.
18. Euripides, *The Trojan Women* 935–6.
19. Ibid 943–4.
20. Ibid 950.
21. Ibid 1022–3.
22. 10–50 million, approximately. Dr Adam Rutherford, WhatsApp conversation.
23. Gantz, p. 575.
24. Euripides, *Helen* 34.
25. Ibid 42–3.
26. Ibid 81.
27. Gantz, pp. 574–5.
28. Plato, *Republic* 9.586c.
29. Euripides, *Helen* 588.
30. Homer, *Iliad* 24 804.
31. Ibid 24 761–75.
32. Homer, *Odyssey* 4 219ff.
33. Book of Jasher 44 15ff.
34. Russell, J. R., (1986), 'Ara the Beautiful', *Encyclopædia Iranica*, available as of March 2020 at http://www.iranicaonline.org/articles/ara-the-beautiful-.

35. Tacitus, *Histories* 3.45, *Annals* 12.36, 12.40.

36. Christie, Agatha (1930), 'The Face of Helen', in *The Mysterious Mr Quin* (London: Collins).

37. Hartley, B. (2014), *Novel Research: Fiction and Authority in Ptolemy Chennus*, Ph.D. thesis (Exeter), 94ff.

38. Homer, *Odyssey* 4 277–9.

39. Photius, *Bibliotheca* 149b 3–38.

40. Wright, M. (2018), *The Lost Plays of Greek Tragedy, Volume 2: Aeschylus, Sophocles and Euripides* (London: Bloomsbury), pp. 87–8.

41. http://www.liverpoolmuseums.org.uk/walker/exhibitions/rossetti/works/beauties/helenoftroy.aspx.

MEDUSA

1. Nietzsche Aphorism 146, tr. by Shaun Whiteside.

2. Hesiod, *Theogony* 274–6.

3. Ibid 276–8.

4. Ibid 279.

5. Pindar, Pythian Ode 12 16.

6. Ovid, *Metamorphoses* 4 794ff.

7. Ibid 798.

8. Stavrakopoulou, Francesca (forthcoming: 2021), *God: An Anatomy* (London: Picador).

9. Homer, *Iliad* 5 741.

10. Ibid 11 36.

11. Homer, *Odyssey* 11 634.

12. Pindar, Pythian Ode 12 21.

13. Homer, *Iliad* 11 37.

14. *Prometheus Bound* 798–9.

15. https://www.theoi.com/Gallery/P23.1B.html.

16. Ovid, *Metamorphoses* 5 250.

17. Pseudo-Hyginus, *Fabulae* 63.

18. Pseudo-Apollodorus, *Bibliotheca* 2.36–42.

19. Hesiod, *Shield of Heracles* 222.

20. Ibid 224.

21. Ibid 227.

22. https://www.metmuseum.org/art/collection/search/254523.

23. https://www.britishmuseum.org/research/collection_online/collection_object_details.aspx?objectId=461872&partId=1.

24. Pseudo-Apollodorus, *Bibliotheca* 2.4.3.
25. Gantz, p. 489.
26. Pseudo-Apollodorus, *Bibliotheca* 2.45–6.
27. Ovid, *Metamorphoses* 4 617–20.
28. Pindar, Pythian Ode 12 8.
29. Homer, *Iliad* 5 114.
30. Ovid, *Metamorphoses* 11 85–193.
31. Ibid 11 125–6.
32. Wright, vol. 2, p. 61.
33. Ovid, *Metamorphoses* 4 741.
34. https://collections.mfa.org/objects/154107.
35. Pseudo-Apollodorus, *Bibliotheca* 2.46
36. http://www.museivaticani.va/content/museivaticani/en/collezioni/ musei/museo-pio-clementino/Cortile-Ottagono/perseo-trionfante.html.
37. https://www.metmuseum.org/en/art/collection/search/204758.
38. https://www.reddit.com/r/justlegbeardthings/comments/9vcppc/ be_thankful_we_only_want_equality_and_not_payback/.
39. *Orange is the New Black*, Season 3, episode 12, 'Don't Make Me Come Back There.'
40. Book of Judith, Ch 12–13.
41. Pindar, Pythian Ode 10, 47–8.
42. Ovid, *Metamorphoses* 5 209.
43. Book of Judith, Ch 16, v 26.
44. https://www.gq.com/story/see-rihanna-as-a-topless-medusa-on-the-cover-of-british-gq?fbclid=IwAR1iGwZPDG99bxRtckveo8AnbooTB m_C_RdKS-75inxprJ_4Gw-D3v5POSo.
45. https://thelegomovie.fandom.com/wiki/Medusa.
46. Pausanias, *Description of Greece* 2.21.5.
47. *medousa* is the feminine form of *medōn*, Liddell and Scott.
48. Pseudo-Apollodorus, *Bibliotheca* 3.10.3.

THE AMAZONS

1. Mayor, A. (2014), *The Amazons: Lives and Legends of Warrior Women Across the Ancient World* (Princeton: Princeton University Press), p. 85.
2. Ibid p. 31.
3. Ibid pp. 191, 280.
4. Quintus Smyrnaeus, *Fall of Troy* 1.40.
5. Apollonius of Rhodes, *Argonautica* 2.778.

6. Pseudo-Apollodorus, *Bibliotheca* 2.5.9.

7. Shakespeare, *A Midsummer Night's Dream*, Act 2, Scene 1.

8. Euripides, *Herakles Mainomenos* 415; Pseudo-Apollodorus, *Bibliotheca* 2.5.9; Apollonius of Rhodes, *Argonautica* 2.777; Diodorus, *Bibliotheca Historica* 4.16; Pausanias, *Description of Greece* 5.10.9.

9. https://www.britishmuseum.org/collection/object/G_1864-1007-253.

10. https://www.metmuseum.org/art/collection/search/247964.

11. Diodorus, *Bibliotheca Historica* 3.53.4.

12. Pliny, *Natural History* 7.57.

13. Homer, *Iliad* 3 189.

14. https://www.metmuseum.org/art/collection/search/250814.

15. Pseudo-Apollodorus, *Bibliotheca* 2.5.9.

16. https://collections.mfa.org/objects/153654.

17. Mayor, p. 219.

18. Plutarch, *Life of Theseus* 26ff.

19. Ibid 29.

20. Aeschylus, *Eumenides* 685.

21. Pausanias, *Description of Greece* 1.2.1.

22. Herodotus, *Histories* 9.27.4.

23. Pausanias, *Description of Greece* 1.15.2.

24. *Aethiopis* frag 1 (Loeb, *Greek Epic Fragments*), p. 114.

25. Homer, *Iliad* 24 56ff.

26. Pseudo-Apollodorus, *Epitome* 5.1.

27. Quintus Smyrnaeus, *The Fall of Troy* 1.18ff.

28. Pseudo-Apollodorus, *Epitome* 1.5.

29. Sophocles, *Ajax*.

30. Quintus Smyrnaeus, *The Fall of Troy* 1.96.

31. Pseudo-Apollodorus, *Bibliotheca* 3.12.3.

32. Ibid 1.153.

33. Ibid 1.159.

34. Ibid 1.216.

35. Ibid 1.227.

36. Ibid 1.238.

37. Ibid 1.315.

38. Alden, M. (2005), 'Lions in Paradise' in *Classical Quarterly*, vol. 55, no. 2, pp. 335–42. https://www.jstor.org/stable/4493342?seq=1#page_scan_tab_contents.

39. Quintus Smyrnaeus, *The Fall of Troy* 1.406.

40. Ibid 1.629.

41. Ibid 1.664.

42. Ibid 1.726.
43. https://www.britishmuseum.org/collection/object/G_1836-0224-127.
44. https://www.britishmuseum.org/collection/object/G_1836-0224-128.
45. Mayor, p. 300.
46. Quintus Smyrnaeus, *The Fall of Troy* 1.800.
47. https://www.poeticous.com/robert-graves/penthesileia.

CLYTEMNESTRA

1. Antiphon 1, 17
2. Macintosh, F. et al. (2005), *Agamemnon in Performance 458 BC to AD 2004* (Oxford: Oxford University Press), p. 59.
3. Aeschylus, *Agamemnon* 136.
4. Ibid 155.
5. Ibid 258.
6. Ibid 960.
7. Ibid 950.
8. Ibid 1156.
9. Ibid 1190.
10. Ibid 1214.
11. Ibid 1252.
12. Ibid 1360–1.
13. Ibid 1394.
14. https://collections.mfa.org/objects/153661.
15. Aeschylus, *Agamemnon* 1431–3.
16. Ibid 1526.
17. Ibid 1644.
18. https://www.hermitagemuseum.org/wps/portal/hermitage/digital-collection/25.%20Archaeological%20Artifacts/36020.
19. Ovid, *Ars Amatoria* 2 399–408.
20. Seneca, *Agamemnon* 118.
21. Aeschylus, *Choephoroi* 695.
22. Ibid 888.
23. Ibid 908.
24. Ibid 924.
25. Aeschylus, *Agamemnon* 1419.
26. Euripides, *Iphigenia in Aulis* 1149–52.
27. Pindar, Pythian Ode 11.

EURYDICE

1. Gantz, p. 721.
2. Virgil, *Georgics* 4 453ff.
3. Ibid 458.
4. Ibid 483.
5. Ibid 519–20.
6. Ibid 460.
7. Ovid, *Metamorphoses* 10 7ff.
8. Ibid 10 32.
9. Ibid 10 49.
10. Ibid 10 52.
11. Ibid 10 54.
12. Ibid 10 61–2.
13. Ibid 10 75.
14. Ibid 11 64–6.
15. Gantz, p. 722.
16. Euripides, *Alcestis* 371–3.
17. Ibid 633.
18. Ibid 646.
19. Ibid 682.
20. Ibid 696.
21. Ibid 357ff.
22. Plato, *Symposium* 179b.
23. https://www.theoi.com/Text/Moschus.html.
24. *Lament for Bion* 114.
25. Pseudo-Apollodorus, *Bibliotheca* 1.3.2.
26. https://www.eno.org/operas/orphee/.
27. https://www.eno.org/operas/orpheus-in-the-underworld/.
28. https://www.nationaltheatre.org.uk/shows/hadestown.
29. https://www.imdb.com/title/tt0053146/?ref_=fn_al_tt_1.
30. http://www.sothebys.com/en/auctions/ecatalogue/2018/european-art-n09869/lot.79.html.
31. Bruzelius, M. (1988), 'H.D. and Eurydice' in *Twentieth Century Literature*, vol. 44, no. 4, pp. 447–63.
32. Carol Ann Duffy, 'Eurydice'.

Notes

PHAEDRA

1. Pausanias, *Description of Greece* 2.31.1.
2. Pseudo-Apollodorus, *Biblotheca* 3.1.3ff.
3. Homer, *Odyssey* 11 321–5.
4. Pausanias, *Description of Greece* 1.20.3.
5. Plutarch, *Life of Theseus* 20.
6. Catullus 64.
7. Plutarch, *Life of Theseus* 28.
8. Ibid.
9. Ibid 29.1.
10. http://edithorial.blogspot.com/2015/05/why-i-hate-myth-of-phaedra-and.html.
11. *Homeric Hymn to Demeter* 372.
12. Ibid 413.
13. Green, R. L. (2009 reissue), *Tales of the Greek Heroes* (London: Puffin Books).
14. Graves, R. (1955), *The Greek Myths*, vol. 1 (London: Penguin Books).
15. Pseudo-Apollodorus, *Biblotheca* 1.5.3.
16. Anon (nd.) Rape Crisis England and Wales, 'About sexual violence: statistics.' Available as of March 2020 at https://rapecrisis.org.uk/get-informed/about-sexual-violence/statistics-sexual-violence/.
17. Gantz, p. 286.
18. Ibid.
19. Euripides, *Hippolytus* 5–6.
20. Ibid 21–2.
21. Ibid 28.
22. Ibid 39–40.
23. Ibid 113.
24. Ibid 135.
25. Ibid 305.
26. Ibid 317.
27. Ibid 309.
28. Ibid 420–1.
29. Ibid 474–5.
30. Ibid 503.
31. Ibid 521.
32. Ibid 596.
33. Ibid 612.
34. Ibid 669.

35. Ibid 717.
36. Ibid 1009–10.
37. Ibid 996–7.
38. Ibid 1403.
39. Ibid 1411.
40. Ibid 1430.
41. Aristotle, *Rhetoric* 1416 a28–35.

MEDEA

1. Aeschylus, *Agamemnon* 239.
2. Congreve, *The Mourning Bride*.
3. Hesiod, *Theogony* 992.
4. Homer, *Odyssey* 12 72.
5. Apollonius of Rhodes, *Argonautica* 4.1637.
6. Ibid 1644.
7. Ibid 1677.
8. Pindar, Pythian Ode 4.249.
9. Euripides, *Medea* 482.
10. Apollonius of Rhodes, *Argonautica* 3.1054.
11. Ibid 3.804–5.
12. Pindar, Pythian Ode 4.221.
13. Apollonius of Rhodes, *Argonautica* 3.997.
14. Ibid 3.529.
15. Ibid 4.1670.
16. Wright, vol. 2, p. 194.
17. Pindar, Pythian Ode 4.250.
18. https://www.britishmuseum.org/collection/object/G_1843-1103-59.
19. Euripides, *Medea* 36.
20. Ibid 74–5.
21. Ibid 113–14.
22. Ibid 182.
23. Ibid 222.
24. Ibid 233.
25. Ibid 282.
26. Ibid 316.
27. Ibid 355–6.
28. Ibid 374–5.
29. Ibid 465.

30. Ibid 536.
31. Ibid 792.
32. Ibid 913.
33. Ibid 964–5.
34. Ibid 973.
35. Ibid 1035–6.
36. Ibid 1056.
37. Ibid 1126.
38. Ibid 1232.
39. Ibid 1260.
40. Ibid 1304–5.
41. Aristotle, *Poetics* 1454b.
42. Gantz, p. 369.
43. Pausanias, *Description of Greece* 2.3.11.
44. https://www.theoi.com/Gallery/M26.1B.html.
45. https://www.clevelandart.org/art/1991.1.
46. Pausanias, *Description of Greece* 2.3.6–11.
47. Herodotus, *Histories* 7.62.
48. Diodorus, *Bibliotheca Historica* 4.56.
49. http://www.thomassatterwhitenoble.net/new-page-1.
50. Smethurst, M. (2002), 'Ninagawa's Production of Euripides' *Medea*' in *The American Journal of Philology*, vol. 123, no. 1, pp. 1–34, https://www.jstor.org/stable/1561998?seq=1.

PENELOPE

1. Pseudo-Apollodorus, *Bibliotheca* 3.10.
2. Pausanias, *Description of Greece* 3.12.
3. Ibid 3.20.10.
4. Pseudo-Apollodorus, *Epitome* 3.7.
5. Homer, *Odyssey* 1 329.
6. Ibid 1 332.
7. Ibid 1 346ff.
8. Ibid 1 360.
9. Ibid 2 372.
10. Ibid 4 705.
11. Ibid 5 210.
12. Ibid 5 218.
13. Ibid 2 88.

14. Ibid 19 137.
15. Ibid 19 157–8.
16. http://www.beazley.ox.ac.uk/XDB/ASP/recordDetails.asp?id=F322BAD4-652B-4E56-AFE7-E51A636F2E81&noResults=&recordCount=&databaseID=&search=.
17. https://www.musee-orsay.fr/en/collections/works-in-focus/search/commentaire_id/penelope-23467.html?no_cache=1&cHash=0c0b8e3261
18. davidligare.com/paintings.html.
19. https://www.namuseum.gr/en/collection/klasiki-periodos-2/.
20. Held by the Metropolitan Museum, New York: https://www.metmuseum.org/art/collection/search/16951
21. Peck, A. and Irish, C. (2001), *Candace Wheeler: The Art and Enterprise of American Design, 1875–1900* (New Haven: Yale University Press), p. 145: https://books.google.co.uk/books?id=n2r1mG-z0UAC&pg=PA147&lpg=PA147&dq=Penelope+tapestry+new+york&source=bl&ots=gQLNphwqxq&sig=ACfU3U0CkHVYd1qaLuMYU3SQfS3YEZ-qPA&hl=en&sa=X-&ved=2ahUKEwj7rqm4qszmAhWSiVwKHUqrCIEQ6AEwEX0ECAoQAQ#v=onepage&q=Penelope%20tapestry%20new%20york&f=false.
22. https://www.marianmaguire.com/2017---odysseus--penelope.html.
23. Homer, *Odyssey* 24 149.
24. Ibid 21 1.
25. Ovid, *Heroides* 1.41.
26. Ibid 51.
27. Canongate paperback edition, p. xxi.

Further Reading and Other Sources

A FEW NOTES ON THE TEXT AND SOURCES. FIRSTLY, AS YOU WILL doubtless have noticed, I play fast and loose with transliterating and translating names from Greek and Latin. Sometimes I go for a Greek transliteration (Heracles, though really it should be Herakles), sometimes I go for the Romanized version (Oedipus), sometimes I go rogue with the English version (Helen). There is no system, no coherence: just years of thinking of characters and writers by certain forms of their names and a reluctance to change, I suppose.

The translations in this book are all mine: I rarely go formal unless it feels necessary. My versions of Aeschylus and Euripides in particular are closer to actual speech than lofty theatricality (this is my transparent bid to be allowed to translate them for the stage at a future date). I own a lot of Greek and Latin texts, but many, many more are freely available online: Perseus is my website of choice, and there are others. They are a wonderful resource, provided by academics who have made the world a better, more democratic place to study. I won't offer a list of which editions or textual traditions I followed, because this isn't an academic book and no one ever asks me for more details about these things.

I am often asked, though, which translations are good. It's a hard question to answer, because I tend to use ones which I have owned since school or college, because they're already on my shelves. Occasionally I replace an old one with a new one. (Emily Wilson's translation of the *Odyssey* is obviously wonderful, so I ditched my previous versions for hers. I say 'ditched', but I think I own four different translations of the *Odyssey*, for no good reason. Inexplicably, I only have a Greek edition of the first twelve books and use Perseus for the rest. There is no logic to my library.) As a general rule, Penguin Classics and Oxford World's Classics are what I have, and they're usually pretty good. I own dozens of Loeb editions, which are sometimes more erratic in the quality of the translations, but always useful when there's a tricky bit of Greek. There are lots of old translations available for free online, but be warned: they can be pretty impenetrable.

Non-ancient books which made this book possible include: Emma Bridges & Djibril al-Ayad, *Making Monsters*; Lillian E. Doherty, *Gender and the Interpretation of Classical Myth*; Timothy Gantz, *Early Greek Myth*; Edith Hall, *Greek Tragedy* (as well as her terrific essays and blog posts about everything from Phaedra to Jocasta); Mary R. Lefkowitz, *Women in Greek Myth*; Adrienne Mayor, *The Amazons*; Matthew Wright, *The Lost Plays of Greek Tragedy*; Froma I. Zeitlin, *Playing the Other*. It feels perverse to try to distil a lifetime of reading into a manageably short list, so I am only offering the books which lived on my desk for weeks at a time while I was writing this book. The rest are just occupying bits of my brain which I probably need for other things. Too late now.

A fullish list of the artworks mentioned (including their place of residence at the time of writing) is below (thanks to Roz, who did literally all the hard work here). Any omissions are mine; I hope you'll forgive me.

PANDORA

Cousin, Jean (ca. 1550), *Eva Prima Pandora*, Paris, Louvre, inv. RF 2373.
Howard, Henry (1834), oil on mahogany panel, *The Opening of Pandora's Vase*, London, Sir John Soane Museum, inv. SM P6.
Rossetti, Dante Gabriel (1871), oil on canvas, *Pandora*, private collection.
Athenian *kylix* attributed to the Tarquinia Painter (ca. 460 BCE) depicting the creation of Pandora, London, British Museum, inv. 1881,0528.1.

Bonasone, Giulio (1531–76), engraving, *Epimetheus opening Pandora's Box*,
   New York, Metropolitan Museum, inv. 64.682.102.
Athenian red-figure *calyx-krater* attributed to the Niobid Painter (ca. 460–
   450 BCE) depicting Pandora, London, British Museum, inv. 1856,1213.1.
Athenian red-figure volute *krater* attributed to the Group of Polygnotos
   (ca. 450–420 BCE) depicting the creation of Pandora, Oxford, Ashmolean
   Museum, inv. AN1896-1908.G.275.

JOCASTA

Athenian red-figure *kylix* attributed to the Painter of Oedipus (ca. 470 BCE)
   depicting Oedipus and the Sphinx, Vatican Museums, inv. 16541.
Sicilian red-figure *calyx-krater* attributed to the Gabil Gabib Group (ca. 330s
   BCE) possibly depicting Oedipus, Jocasta and their daughters, Syracuse,
   Museo Archeologico Regionale Paolo Orsi, inv. 66557.
Apulian red-figure *loutrophoros* attributed to an artist close to the Painter
   of Laodamia (ca. 340 BCE) depicting Alkestis and her children, Basel,
   Antikenmuseum, inv. S21.
Cabanel, Alexandre (1843), oil on canvas, *Oedipus Separating from Jocasta*,
   Capentras, Musée Duplessis.
Toudouze, Edouard (1871), *Farewell of Oedipus to the Corpses of his Wife and
   Sons*, Paris, École nationale supérieure des Beaux-arts.

HELEN

Tintoretto (ca. 1550–55), oil on canvas, *Leda and the Swan*, Florence,
   Galleria degli Uffizi, inv. 3084.
Leonardo copy, e.g.: da Cesto, Cesare (ca. 1505–10), oil on wood, *Leda and
   the Swan* (after Leonardo), Salisbury, Wilton House, Collection of the
   Earl of Pembroke.
Copy of a lost painting by Michelangelo (after 1530), oil on canvas, *Leda
   and the Swan*, London, National Gallery, inv. NG 1868.
Rossetti, Dante Gabriel (1863), oil on panel, *Helen of Troy*, Liverpool,
   National Museums.

MEDUSA

Winged gorgoneion, bronze shield apotropaion/decoration (first half of the sixth century BCE), Olympia, Archaeological Museum, inv. B 110.

Athenian red-figure Panathenaic amphora, attributed to the Berlin Painter (ca. 490 BCE), Medusa, Munich, Staatliche Antikensammlungen, inv. 2312.

Athenian red-figure pelike, attributed to Polygnotos (ca. 450–440 BCE), Perseus beheading the sleeping Medusa, New York, Metropolitan Museum, inv. 45.11.1.

Klee, Paul (1939), pencil on paper, *Forgetful Angel* (Vergesslicher Engel), Bern, Zentrum Paul Klee.

Athenian red-figure kalpis *hydria*, attributed to the Pan Painter (ca. 460 BCE), Perseus flees with Medusa's head, London, British Museum, inv. 1873,0820.352.

Apulian red-figure bell *krater*, attributed to the Tarporley Painter (ca. 400–385 BCE), Athene holding Medusa's head, Boston, Museum of Fine Arts, inv. 1970.237.

Canova, Antonio (1800–06), marble, *Perseus Triumphant*, Musei Vaticani, inv. 969 and New York, Metropolitan Museum, inv. 67.110.1.

Cellini, Benvenuto (1545–55), bronze, *Perseus with the head of Medusa*, Florence, Piazza della Signoria, Loggia dei Lanzi.

Garbati, Lucuano (2008), fiberglass and resin, *Medusa*.

Donatello (1455–60), bronze, *Judith and Holofernes*, Florence, Palazzo Vecchio.

Gentileschi, Artemisia (1611–12), oil on canvas, *Judith slaying Holofernes*, Naples, Museo Nazionale di Capodimonte.

West pediment, Temple of Artemis at Corcyra (ca. 590–580 BCE), limestone, Medusa, Chrysaor and Pegasus, Corfu, Archaeological Museum.

THE AMAZONS

Athenian white-ground alabastron (ca. 480 BCE), attributed to the Group of the Negro Alabastra, Amazon, London, British Museum, inv. 1864,1007.253.

Athenian red-figure volute *krater* (ca. 450 BCE), attributed to the Painter of the Woolly Satyrs, Amazonomachy, New York, Metropolitan Museum, inv. 07.286.84.

Apulian red-figure volute *krater* fragment (ca. 330–310 BCE), attributed to the Baltimore Painter, Hippolyta and the Amazons with Heracles, New York, Metropolitan Museum, inv. 19.192.81.1.7,42,46,55.

Athenian black-figure neck amphora, signed by Exekias (ca. 540), Achilles and Penthesilea, London, British Museum, inv. 1836,0224.127.

Athenian black-figure *hydria*, attributed to the Leagros Group (ca. 510–500 BCE), Achilles carrying the body of Penthesilea, London, British Museum, inv. 1836,0224.128.

CLYTEMNESTRA

Athenian red-figure *calyx-krater*, attributed to the Dokimasia Painter (ca. 470 BCE), The death of Agamemnon, Boston, Museum of Fine Arts, inv. 63.1246.

South Italian red-figure *calyx-krater* (late fourth century BCE), The death of Agamemnon, St Petersburg, The State Hermitage Museum.

EURYDICE

Neide, Emil (1870s), oil on canvas, *Orpheus and Eurydice*.

PHAEDRA

Red-figure *hydria* (fifth century BCE), showing Phaedra on a swing, Berlin, Antikensammlung.

MEDEA

Athenian black-figure *hydria* (ca. 510–500 BCE), attributed to the Leagros Group, Medea and the Rejuvenation of the Ram, London, British Museum, inv. 1843,1103.59.

Lucanian red-figure *calyx-krater* (ca. 400 BCE), near the Policoro Painter, Escape of Medea / Medea in a Chariot, Cleveland OH, Cleveland Museum of Art, inv. 1991.1.

Noble, Thomas Satterwhite (1867), oil on board, *Modern Medea*, Cincinnati, National Underground Railroad Freedom Center.

PENELOPE

Athenian red-figure *skyphos* (ca. 440 BCE), attributed to The Penelope Painter, Penelope and Telemachus at her loom, Chiusi, Museo Archeologico Nazionale, inv. 1831.

Cavelier, Jules (1842), marble, *Penelope* (or *Penelope Asleep*), Paris, Musée d'Orsay.

Ligare, David (1980), oil on canvas, *Penelope*, collection of the artist.

Athenian grave stele of Hegeso (late fifth century BCE), marble, Athens, National Archaeological Museum, inv. 3624.

Wheeler, Dora (1886), silk embroidered with silk thread, *Penelope Unraveling Her Work at Night*, New York, Metropolitan Museum, inv. 2002.230.

Maguire, Marian (2017), acrylic on wood, *Penelope weaves and waits*.